Chicken: Low Art, High Calorie

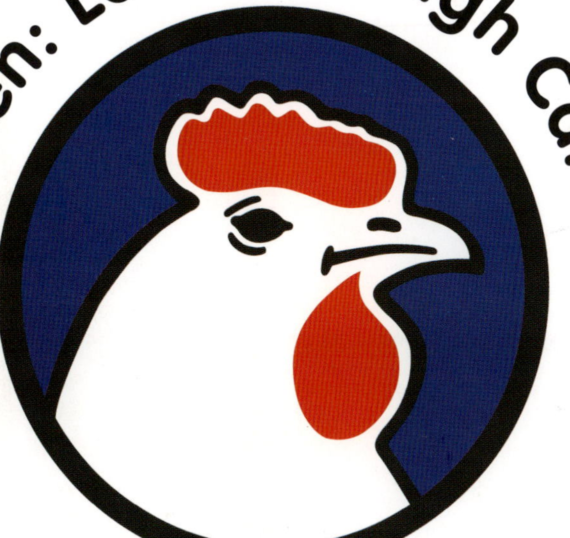

Siâron Hughes

Design: Siâron Hughes, www.su-ma.com.

Production Manager: Christopher D Salyers.
Editor: Buzz Poole.

This book is typeset in: Vag Rounded Light, Vag Rounded Bold and Amasis MT Regular. Headings typeset in: Cooper Black and Cooper Black Italic, ITC Franklin Gothic BT Medium, ITC Franklin Gothic BT Heavy, Franklin Gothic BT Roman, Franklin Gothic BT Condensed and Handel Gothic BT Regular.

Library of Congress Control Number: 2008929889

Printed and bound in China through Asia Pacific Offset.
Printed on 157 gsm Gold East white matt stock.

10 9 8 7 6 5 4 3 2 1 First Edition

Mark Batty Publisher, LLC
36 West 37th Street, Suite 409
New York, NY 10018, USA.
Phone: (347) 830-6271
Email: info@MarkBattyPublisher.com

www.markbattypublisher.com

ISBN: 978-0-9817805-2-8

Distributed outside North America by:

Thames & Hudson Ltd.
181A High Holburn
London WC1V 7QX
United Kingdom

Tel: 00 44 20 7845 5000
Fax: 00 44 20 7845 5055

www.thameshudson.co.uk

CONTENTS

Introduction

Not too long ago, a fast food flyer was stuck through my letterbox. In big, bright red and yellow letters a provocative order: "Dunk Your Dipper." I found this highly suggestive slogan quite amusing. At the time I could have never known that it would lead me down a path that has delivered me, and you, to this book!

I have been working as a graphic designer and illustrator for years, and have increasingly become interested in talking to people about their lives, resulting in me incorporating this dialogue into my design work. This book is the conclusion of one such endeavour, which has led me on a journey all over London taking photographs, trying to track down the various people responsible for the graphics, menus, neon-light signage and branding decorating fast food chicken shops. Everywhere I went, I was amusingly overwhelmed by the extravaganza of gaudy bright backgrounds ornamented with floating bits of fried chicken and burgers, chicken logos busy with numerous, incongruous fonts and a very evident American influence. These vernacular designs, mostly done by the untrained eyes of the shopkeepers, break every rule of typography but are ubiquitous.

At first sight, much of this signage appears the same, but there are differences, subtle as they may be. This is the real appeal of chicken shop signage. Most possess a homage to America, by employing a red, white and blue colour scheme. More than exuding American national colours, many of these shops include an American state or city in their names, not to mention variations of chicken images! The US states and place names I've come across so far include Hollywood, Dixy, Carolina, Orlando, Tennessee, Mississippi, Dallas, Kennedy and Texas.

Although there isn't an actual state called "Carolina" one very clever logo for Carolina Chicken mimics one of America's, and the world's, most famous brands: Coca Cola (see page 8). There are also tributes to John F. Kennedy, Stars and Stripes and the Statue of Liberty.

Abbreviations like CFC (City Fried Chicken), OFC (Orlando Fried Chicken), MFC (Mississippi Fried Chicken), FCKF (Fried Chicken Kebab Fish), HFC (Halal Fried Chicken) and PFC (Perfect Fried Chicken) all serve as a humorous nod to America's most famous fast food chicken: Kentucky Fried Chicken.

The chicken signage from New York City, on the other hand, surprisingly is a little more restrained, with no crazy gaudy collages in sight. These fast food façades seem to conform to a single aesthetic: a solid background colour and simple bold lettering advertising the establishment's name. Interestingly, they don't strike me as overtly American as the signage in London.

What's clear is that no hard and fast rules exist when it comes to these logos. The Perfect Fried Chicken shops all use the same chicken head, but some look as if they've been hand painted while others are left plain with no decoration. They also vary greatly in size, from being tiny to absolutely huge on the shop fronts. Same with the lettering and fonts used, some are lowercase, while others tower absurdly in 200-point uppercase. The chicken logos used in the Chicken Cottage shops seem to be fairly constant, but then again you also see variations of them popping up for the Orlando Fried Chicken chain. Other amusing names and puns are Chick Inn Village,

Chick King, ChickPizz (combination of chicken and pizza), Fri-Chicks (which makes you think you're getting a free chick with every meal!) and Lick'n Chick'n (presumably inspired by KFC's Finger Lickin' Good, as opposed to some gallinaceous fetish). More than conjuring chickens, several places go so far as to make it sound like you're the chicken and that it's time for you to enter the coop, using names like Cozy Chicken, Chicken Shack, Hen Cottage, Chicken Cottage, Chicken Hut, Chicken Land and Roosters! And then there's Funky Chicken, which makes you feel like you have to dance around with joy at having discovered this shop, so long as it doesn't taste funky!

The language used to persuade customers to buy all of this chicken also intrigued me. Hilarious strap lines such as "3-Piece Filler," "100% Whole Muscle," "Hot & Tasty," "Moist Dumplings," "Paradise Patties," "Taste Me," "Tasty Delights," to name but a few, made me think of all sorts of scenarios, most of which had nothing to do with fried chicken...

What has helped to make this book even more enjoyable, aside from all the innuendo, are the conversations and interviews I've had with the employees serving up all of this deep-fried goodness. I have been offered numerous jobs, as well as free food and beverages. And as I spoke with more and more people in the London eateries, I continually heard about a man nicknamed "Mr Chicken" as being the one responsible for most of London's fast food signage. I had to meet him. I did some detective work and tracked him down to an industrial estate in East London. He is a lovely man named Morris Cassanova, and I was lucky enough to have a chat with him about his career and thriving business in the fast food fried chicken industry (see page 75). He showed me the process they go through in producing these huge impressive neon signs and lettering, and shared some funny stories with me about his experiences. Morris has now since retired to Jamaica, enjoying the slower more relaxed pace of life, while his son Greg has taken over the family business.

What started as a curious quest instigated by my profession has grown into something more, something personal. More than dissecting the typographic and graphic design anomalies of fast food chicken signage, as if some technical case study, I have met the people who customise and adapt these unique and eye-catching visuals to suit their neighbourhoods. They are not so concerned with theories and practice so much as providing a service, which judging by the number of these establishments in London is a service in high demand! The workers I've met seem to genuinely love meeting and chatting with their customers. One man in particular sought to assist his customers with any life problems they might have, trying to make them happier or imparting advice before they left his shop.

My thanks and appreciation go out to all of these people, for they are the ones that welcome, and at times endure, the teenagers hankering for after-school snacks, the busy commuters looking for a quick meal and the late-night drunken revellers. Their work has not gone unnoticed, whether it is something seen or eaten.

Anyone hungry for chicken?

SHOP FRONTS
[NAMES AND BRANDING]

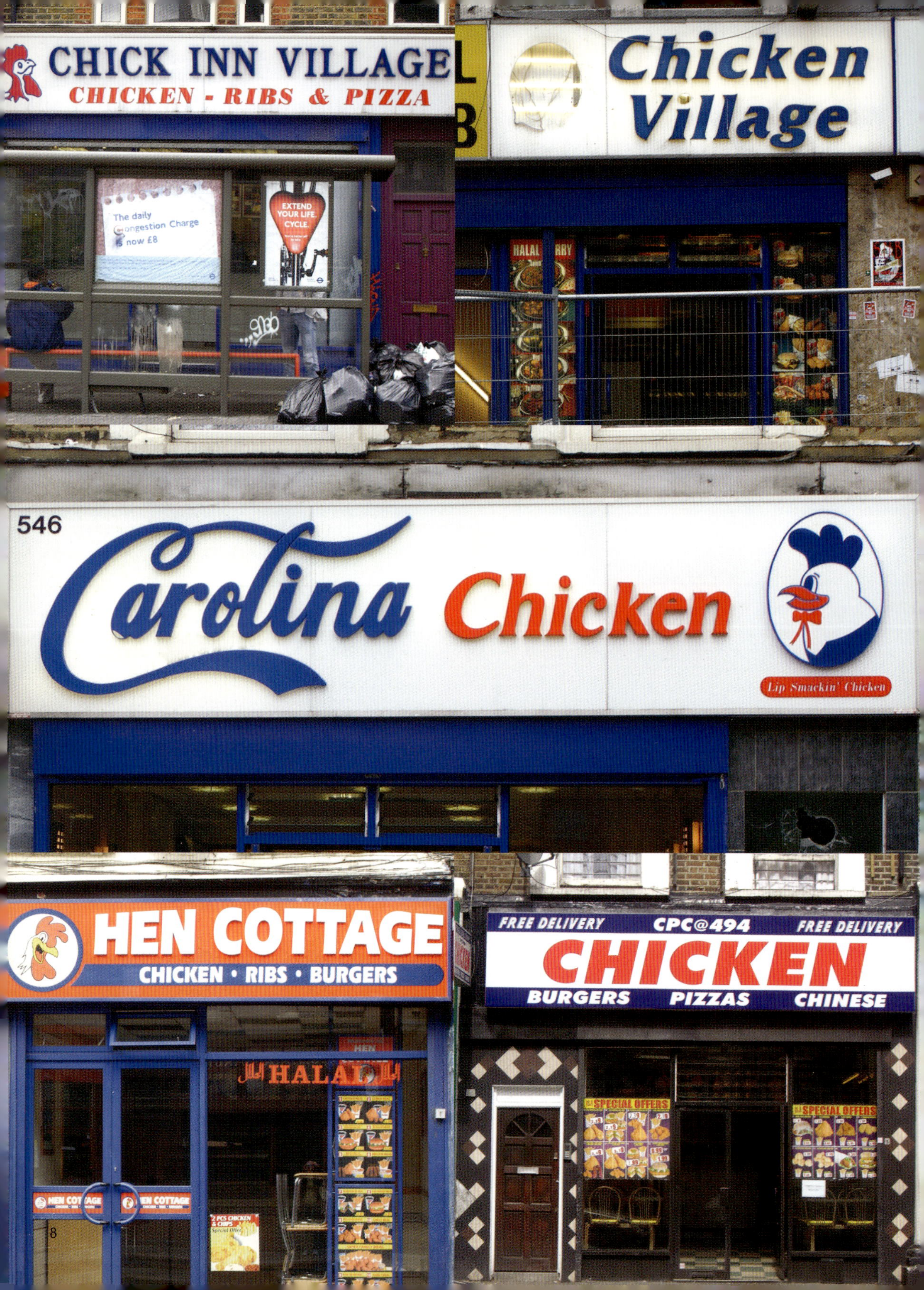
CHICK INN VILLAGE
CHICKEN - RIBS & PIZZA
Chicken Village
EXTEND YOUR LIFE. CYCLE.
546
Carolina Chicken
Lip Smackin' Chicken
HEN COTTAGE
CHICKEN • RIBS • BURGERS
HALAL
FREE DELIVERY CPC@494 FREE DELIVERY
CHICKEN
BURGERS PIZZAS CHINESE
SPECIAL OFFERS

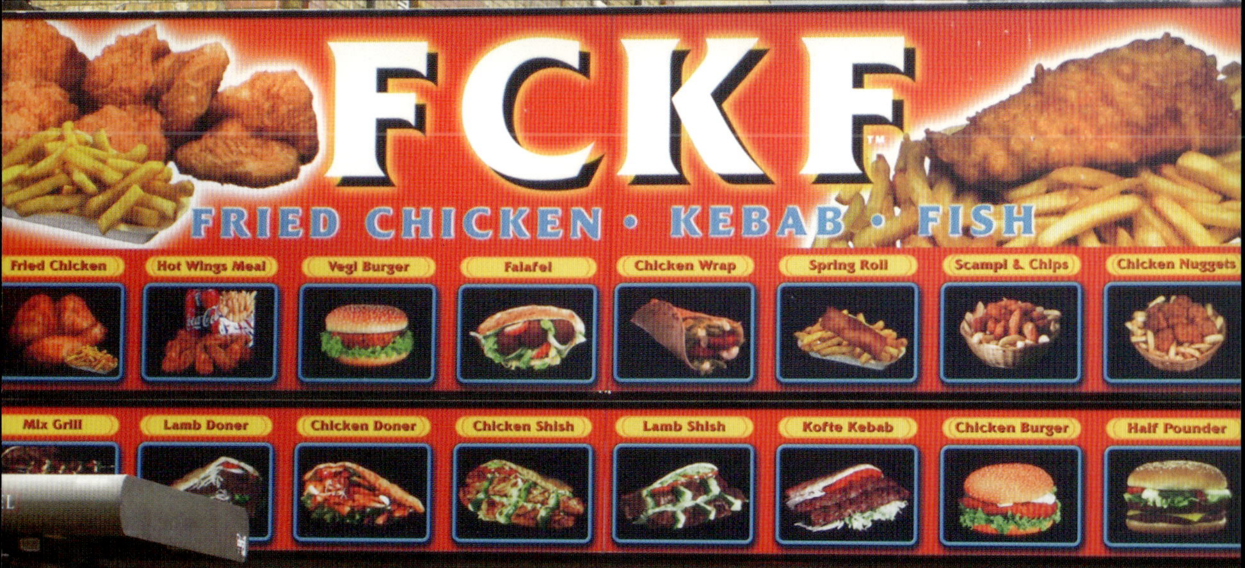
FCKF
TM
FRIED CHICKEN • KEBAB • FISH
Fried Chicken
Hot Wings Meal
Vegi Burger
Falafel
Chicken Wrap
Spring Roll
Scampi & Chips
Chicken Nuggets
Mix Grill
Lamb Doner
Chicken Doner
Chicken Shish
Lamb Shish
Kofte Kebab
Chicken Burger
Half Pounder

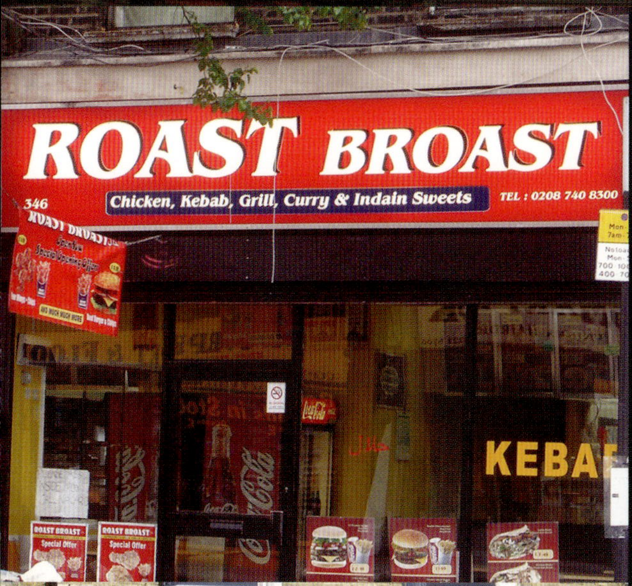
ROAST BROAST
346
Chicken, Kebab, Grill, Curry & Indain Sweets
TEL : 0208 740 8300
KEBAB

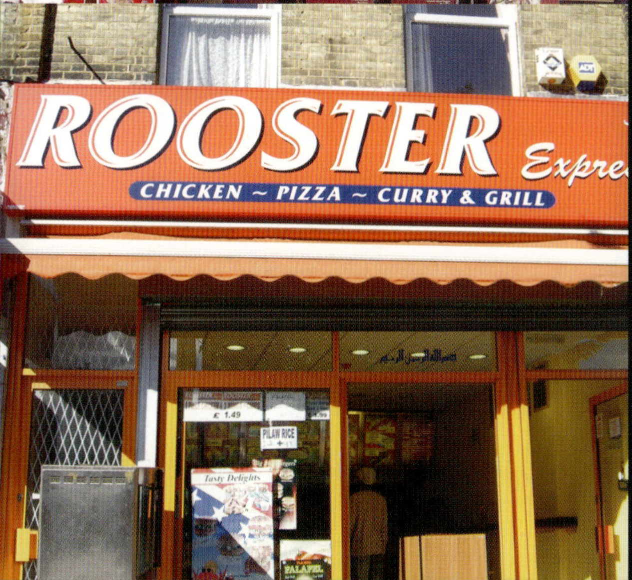
ROOSTER
Expre
CHICKEN ~ PIZZA ~ CURRY & GRILL
PILAW RICE
Tasty Delights
FALAFEL

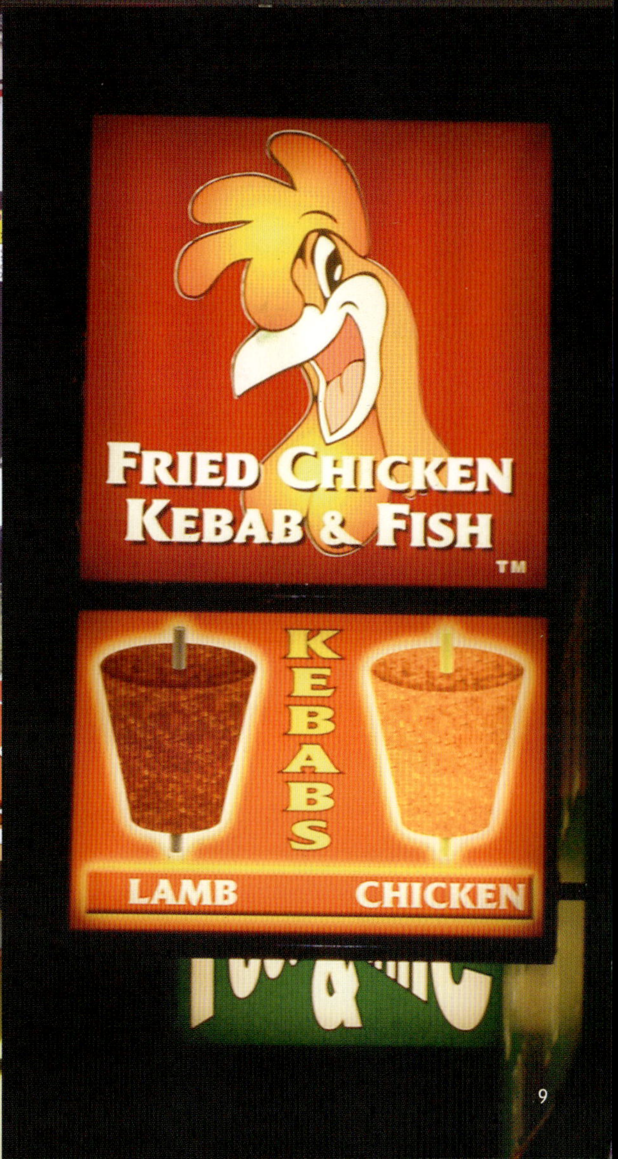
FRIED CHICKEN
KEBAB & FISH
TM
KEBABS
LAMB
CHICKEN

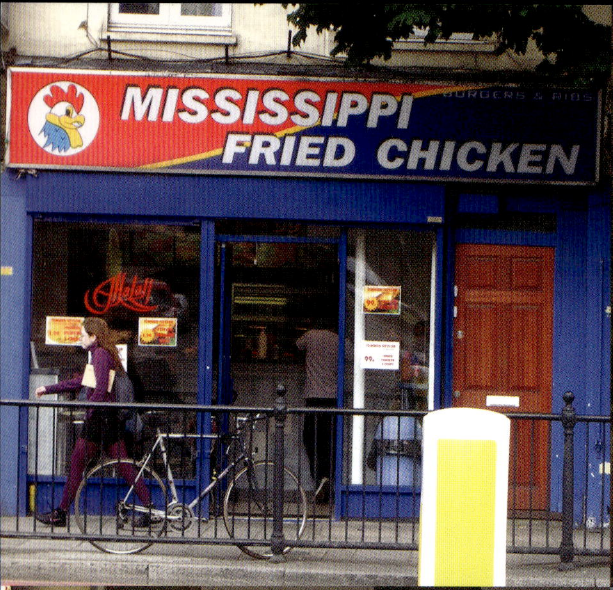
MISSISSIPPI
FRIED CHICKEN
BURGERS & RIBS

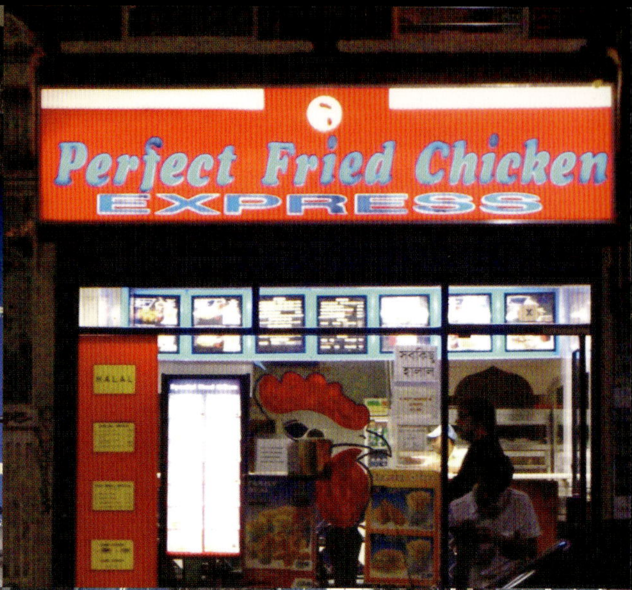
Perfect Fried Chicken
EXPRESS

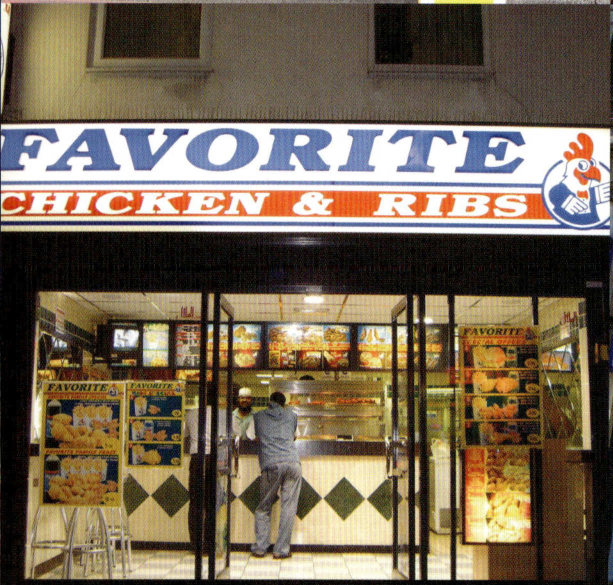
FAVORITE
CHICKEN & RIBS

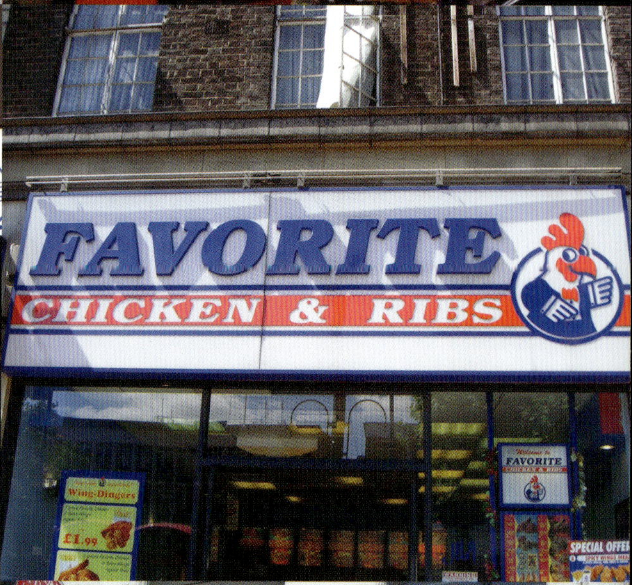
FAVORITE
CHICKEN & RIBS
Wing-Dingers
£1.99
SPECIAL OFFER

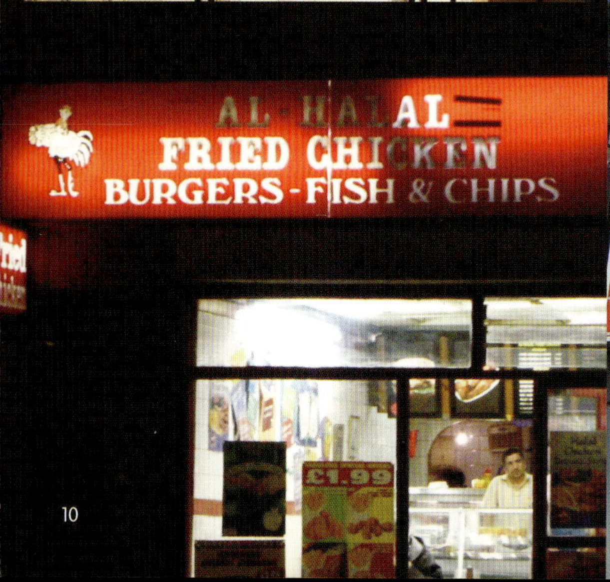
AL HALAL
FRIED CHICKEN
BURGERS-FISH & CHIPS
£1.99

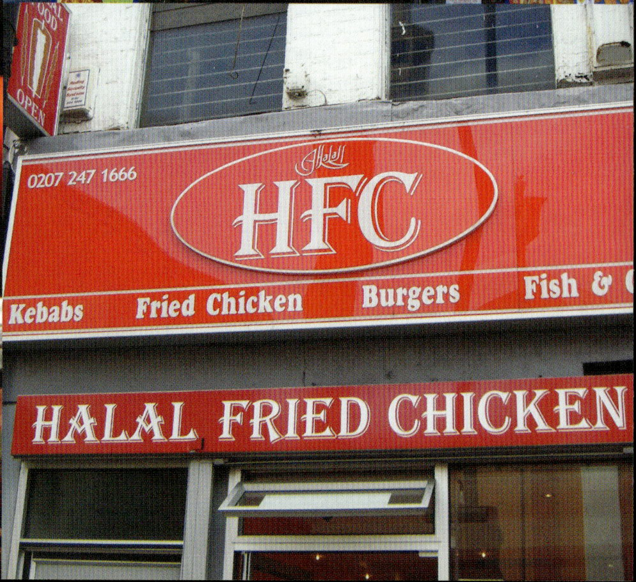
0207 247 1666
HFC
Kebabs
Fried Chicken
Burgers
HALAL FRIED CHICKEN

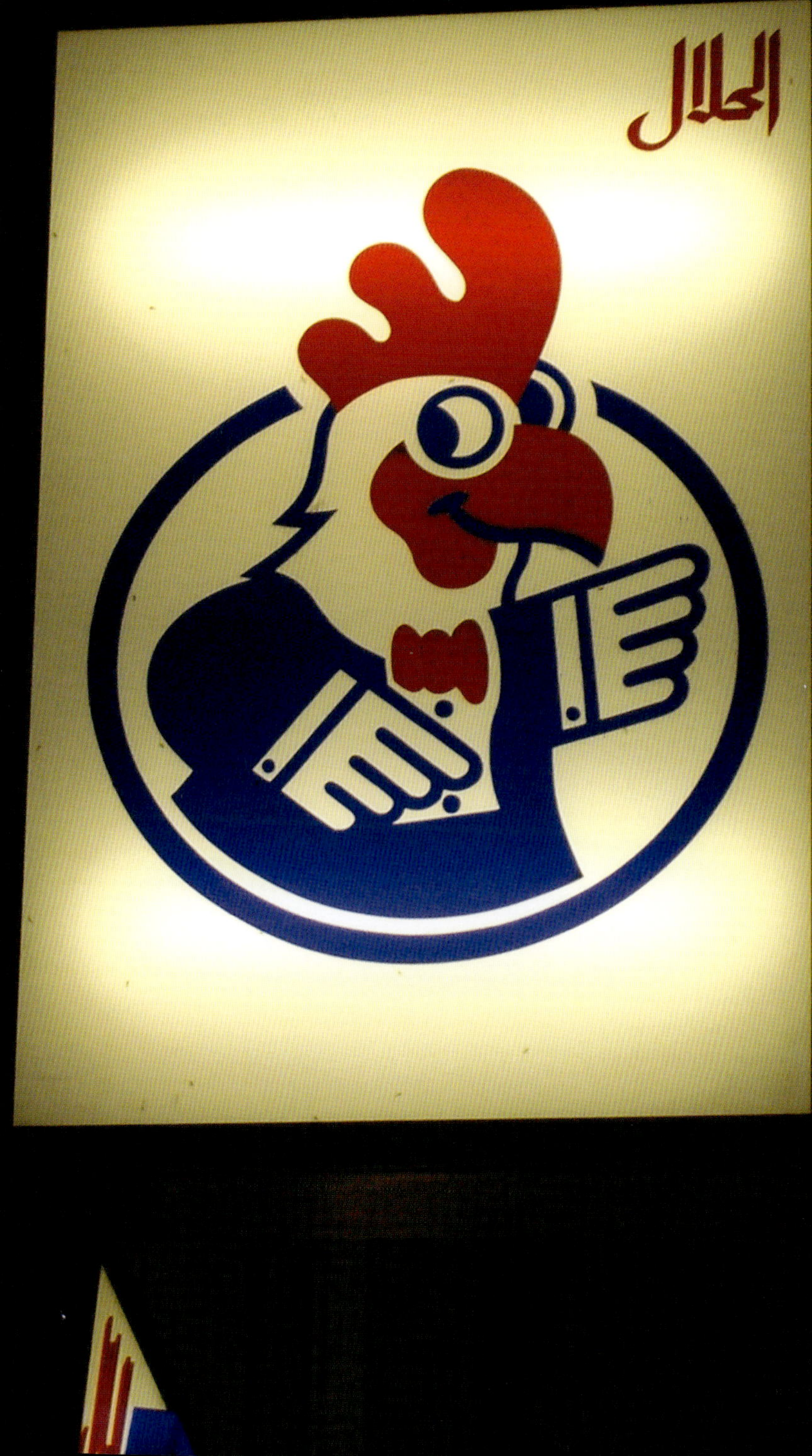
الحلال

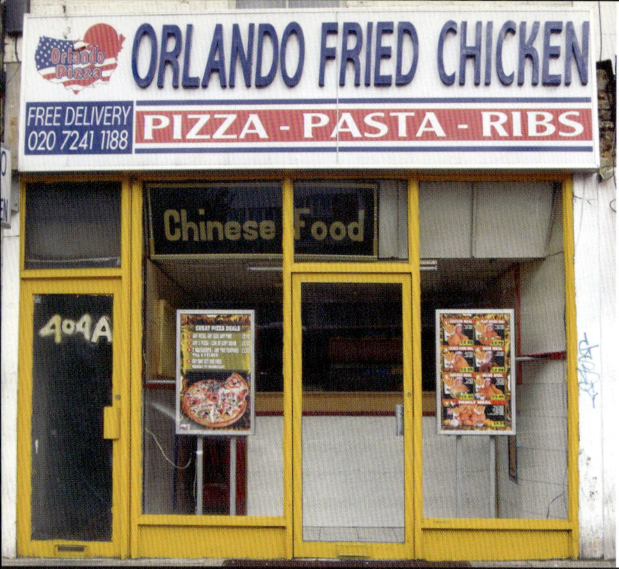
ORLANDO FRIED CHICKEN
Orlando Pizza
FREE DELIVERY
020 7241 1188
PIZZA - PASTA - RIBS
Chinese Food
404A

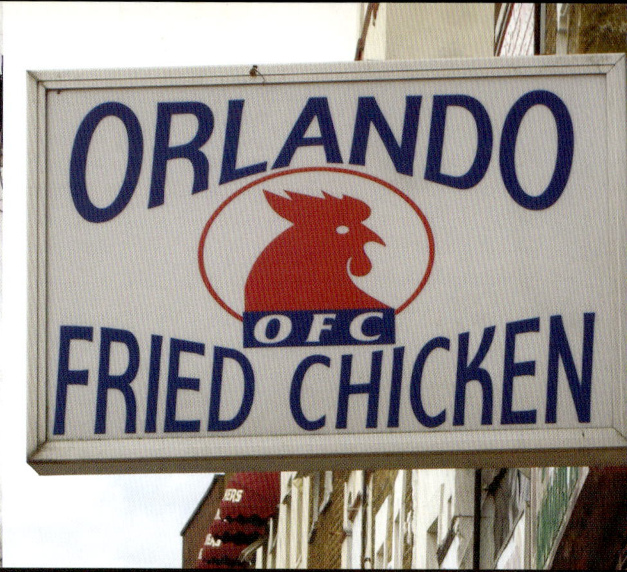
ORLANDO
OFC
FRIED CHICKEN

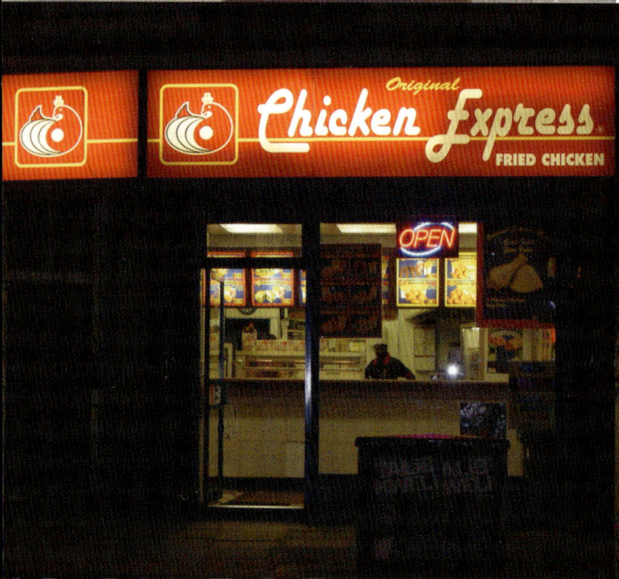
Original
Chicken Express
FRIED CHICKEN
OPEN

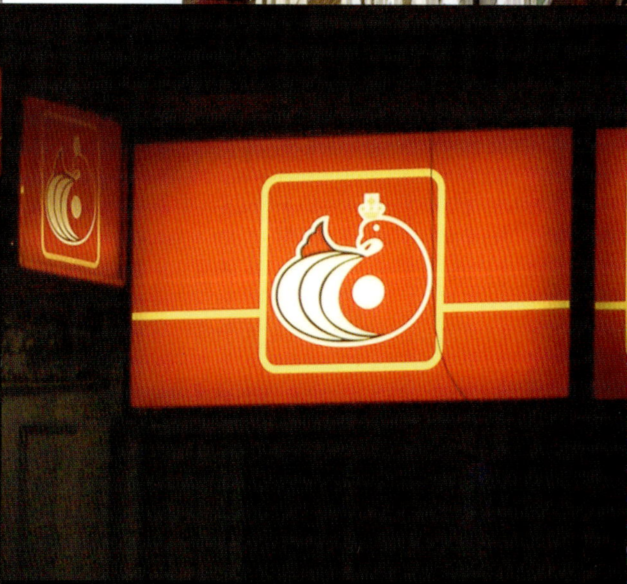

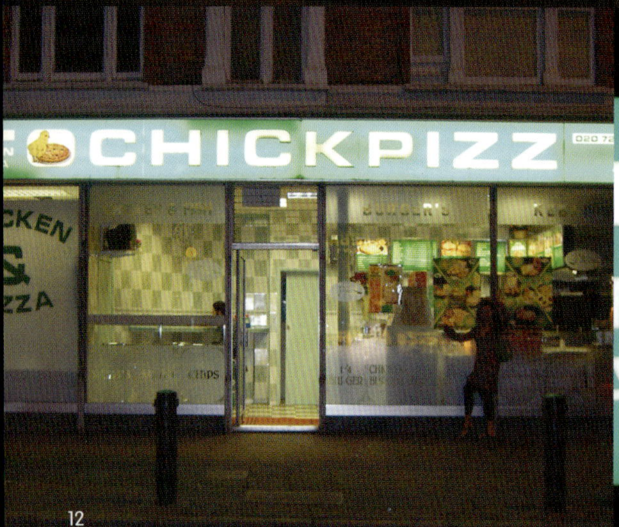
CHICKPIZZ

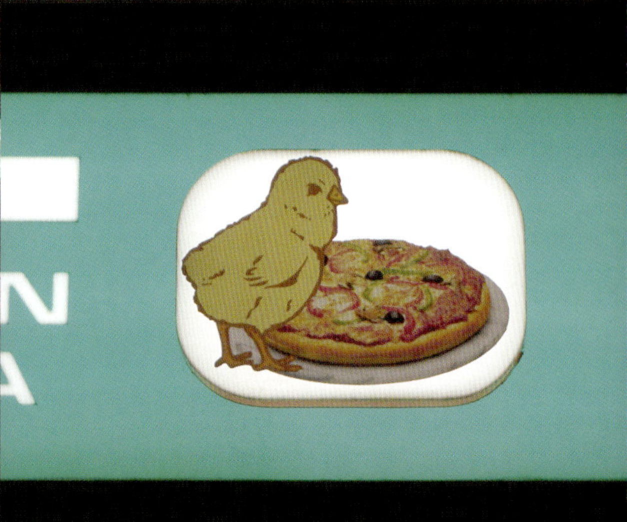

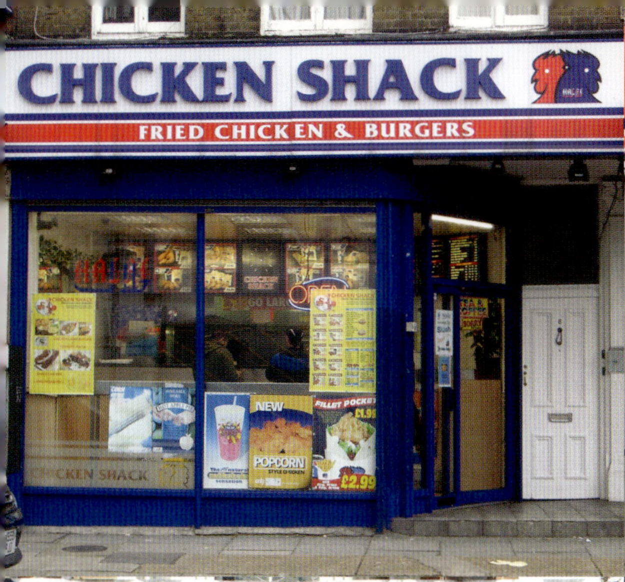
CHICKEN SHACK
FRIED CHICKEN & BURGERS

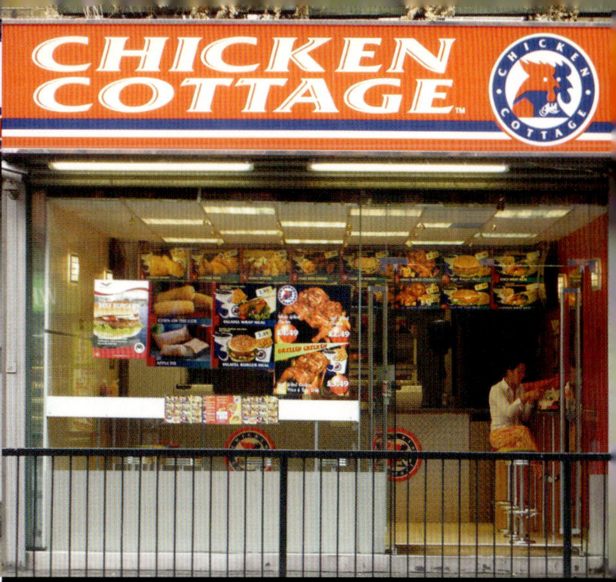
CHICKEN COTTAGE

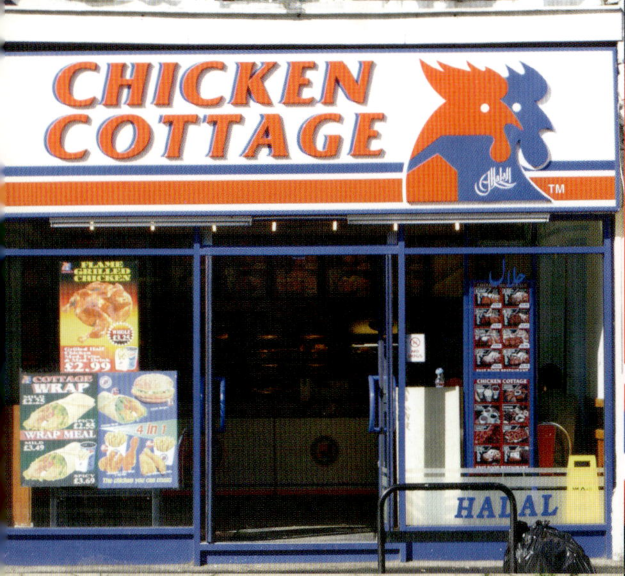
CHICKEN COTTAGE
HALAL

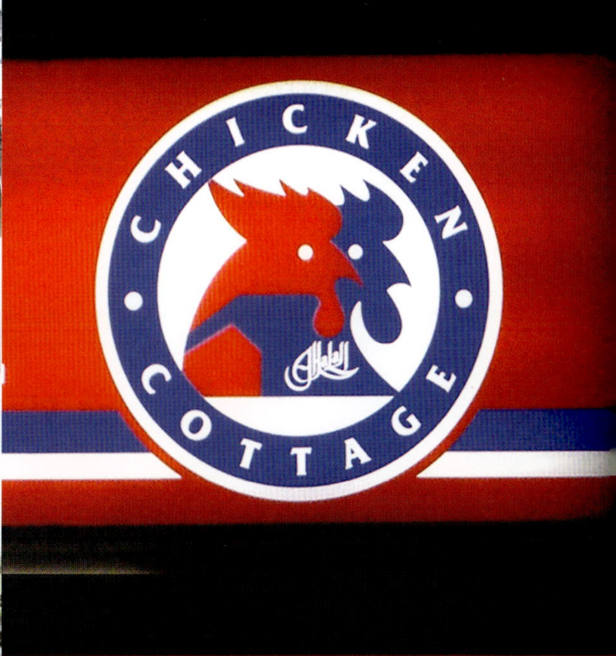
CHICKEN COTTAGE

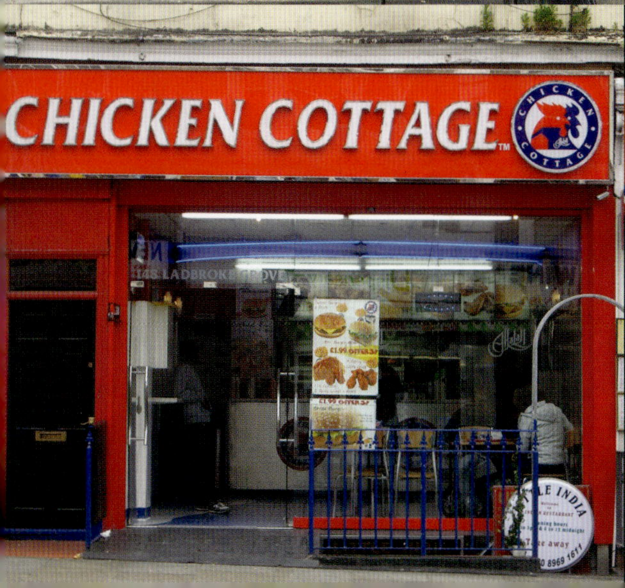
CHICKEN COTTAGE

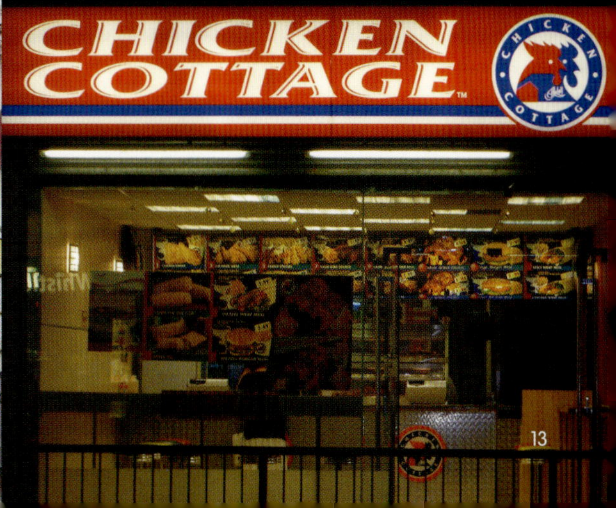
CHICKEN COTTAGE

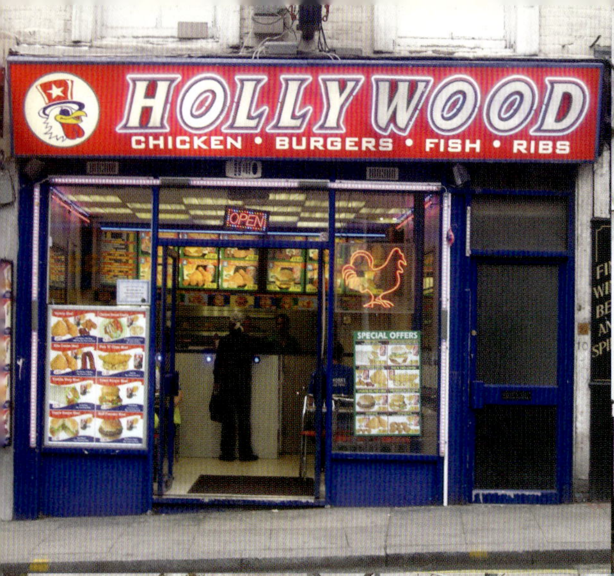
HOLLYWOOD
CHICKEN • BURGERS • FISH • RIBS
OPEN
SPECIAL OFFERS

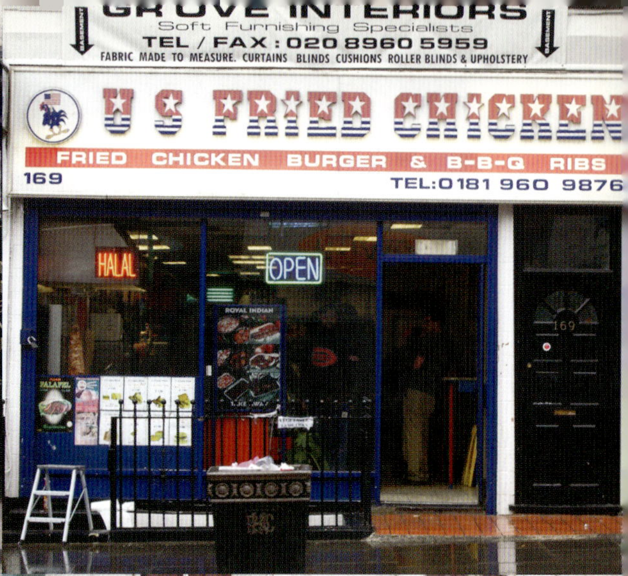
GROVE INTERIORS
Soft Furnishing Specialists
TEL / FAX : 020 8960 5959
FABRIC MADE TO MEASURE. CURTAINS BLINDS CUSHIONS ROLLER BLINDS & UPHOLSTERY
U S FRIED CHICKEN
FRIED CHICKEN BURGER & B-B-Q RIBS
169
TEL:0181 960 9876
HALAL
OPEN

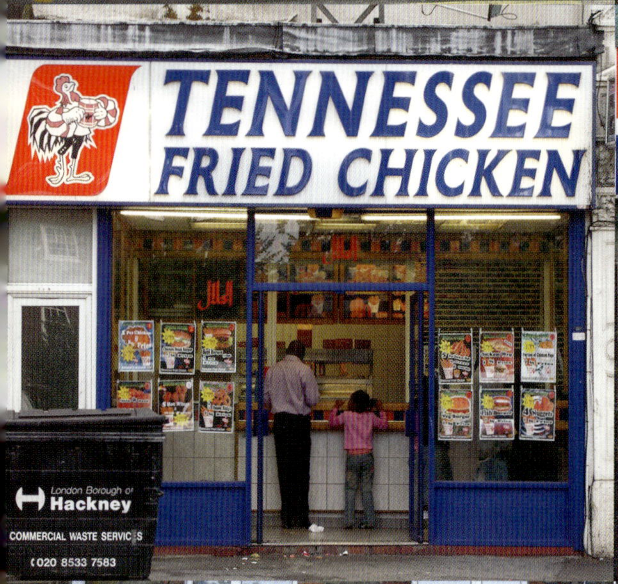
TENNESSEE
FRIED CHICKEN
London Borough of
Hackney
COMMERCIAL WASTE SERVICES
020 8533 7583

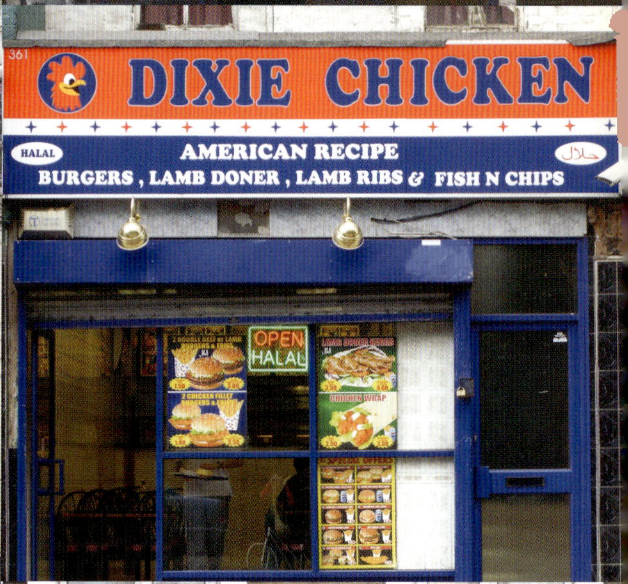
DIXIE CHICKEN
HALAL
AMERICAN RECIPE
حلال
BURGERS , LAMB DONER , LAMB RIBS & FISH N CHIPS
OPEN
HALAL

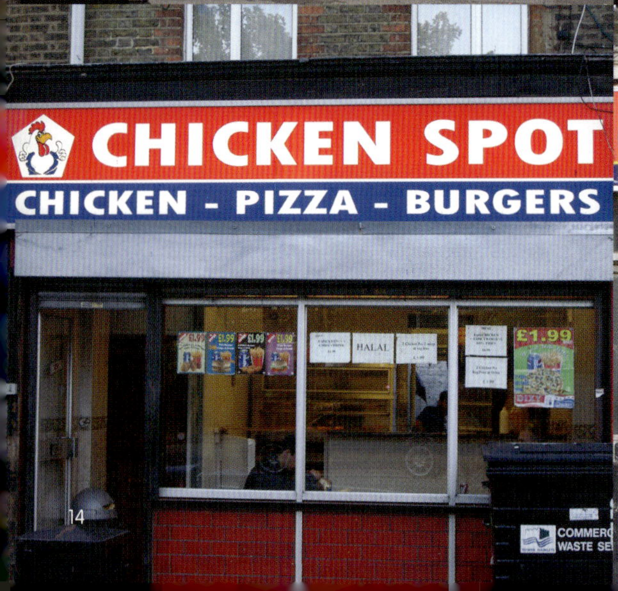
CHICKEN SPOT
CHICKEN - PIZZA - BURGERS
HALAL
£1.99

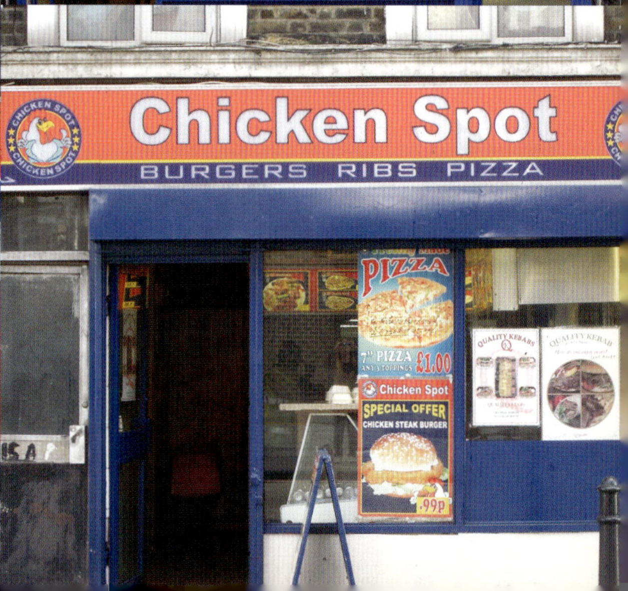
Chicken Spot
BURGERS RIBS PIZZA
PIZZA
£1.00
Chicken Spot
SPECIAL OFFER
CHICKEN STEAK BURGER
.99p

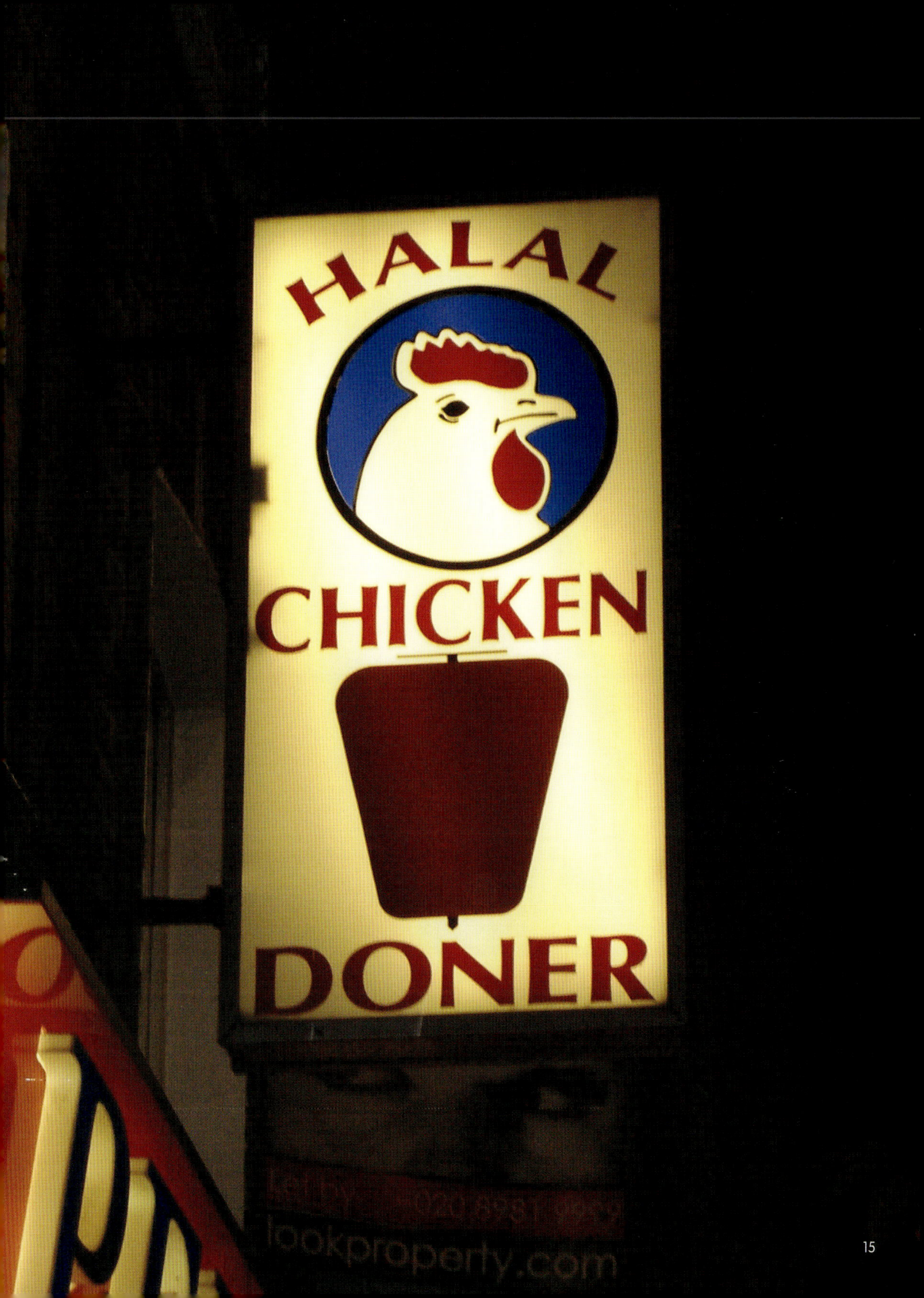
HALAL
CHICKEN
DONER
lookproperty.com

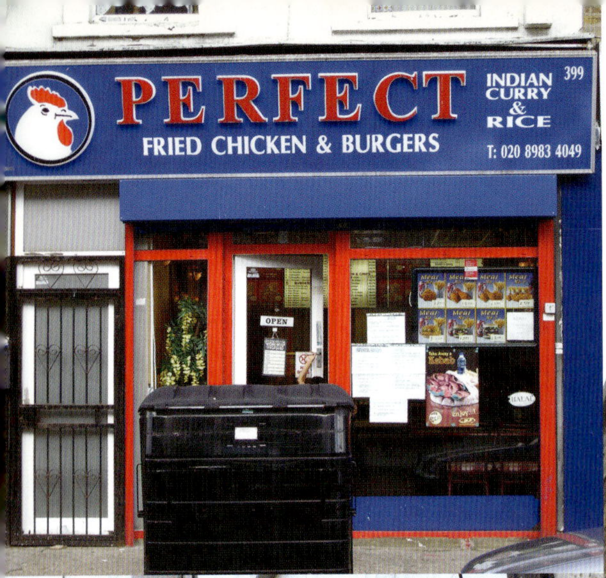
PERFECT
FRIED CHICKEN & BURGERS
INDIAN CURRY & RICE
399
T: 020 8983 4049
OPEN

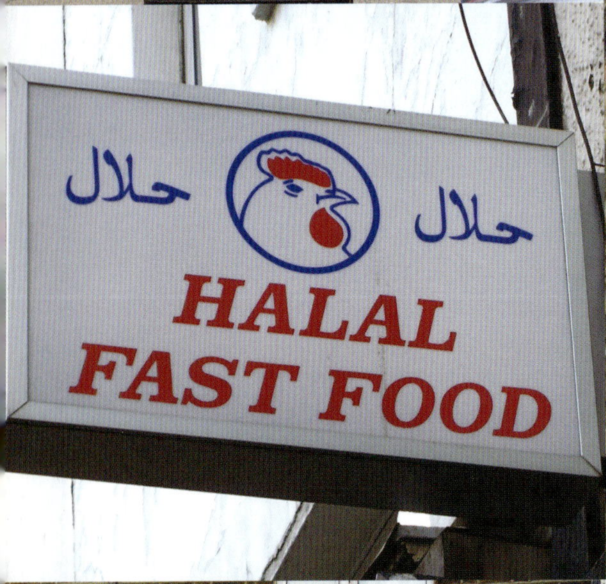
حلال
حلال
HALAL
FAST FOOD

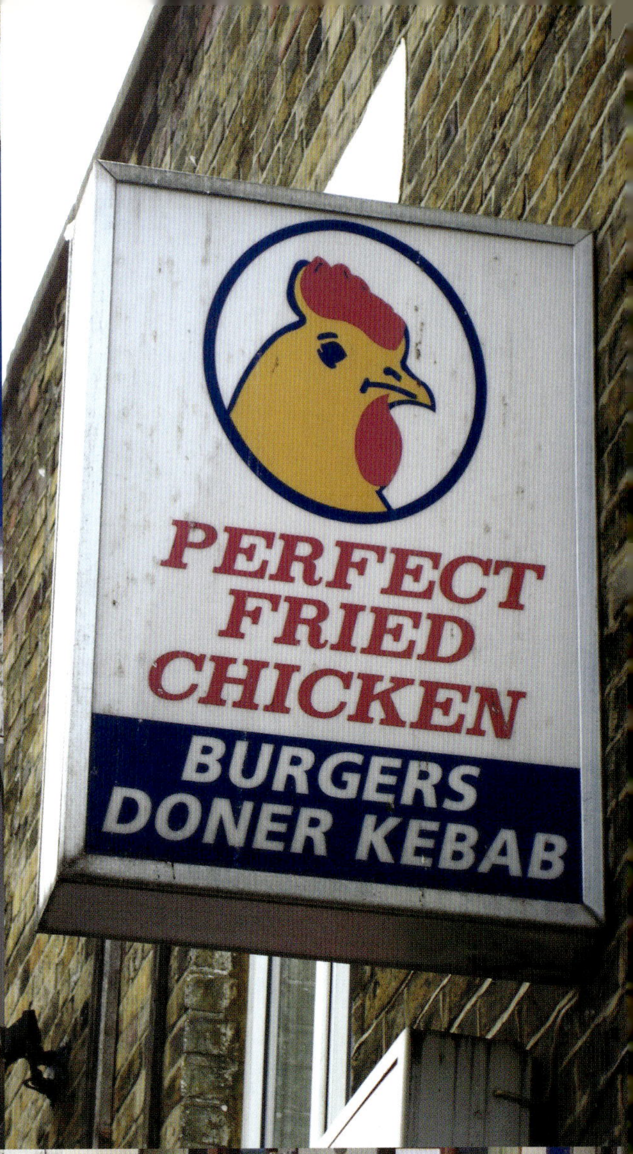
PERFECT
FRIED
CHICKEN
BURGERS
DONER KEBAB

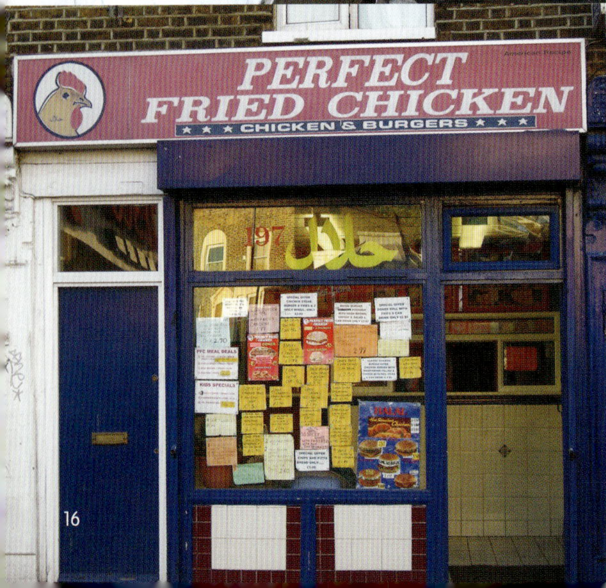
PERFECT
FRIED CHICKEN
CHICKEN & BURGERS
197
حلال

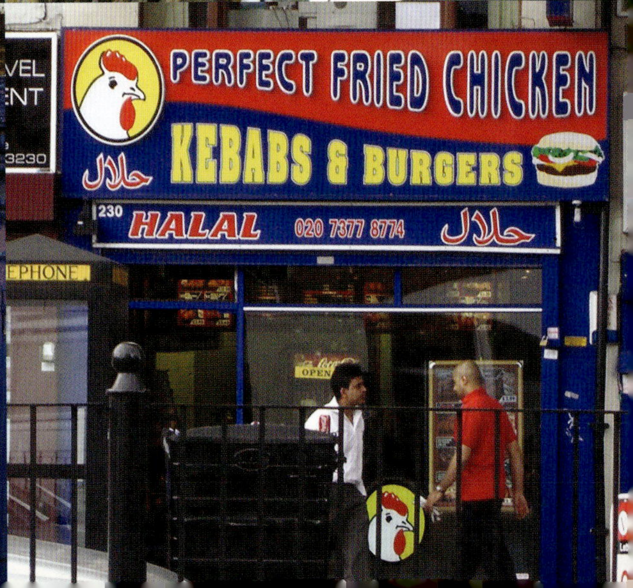
PERFECT FRIED CHICKEN
KEBABS & BURGERS
حلال
230
HALAL
020 7377 8774
حلال

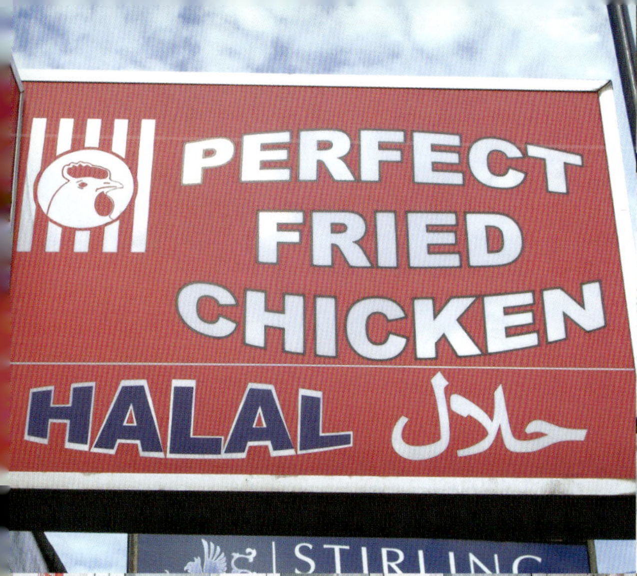
PERFECT
FRIED
CHICKEN
HALAL حلال
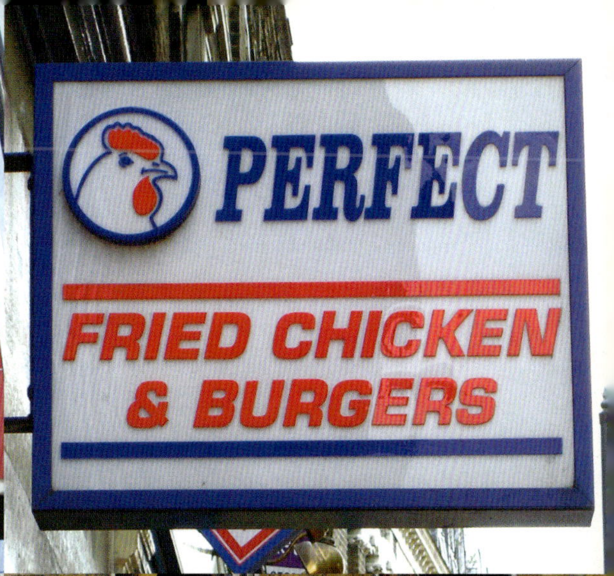
PERFECT
FRIED CHICKEN
& BURGERS
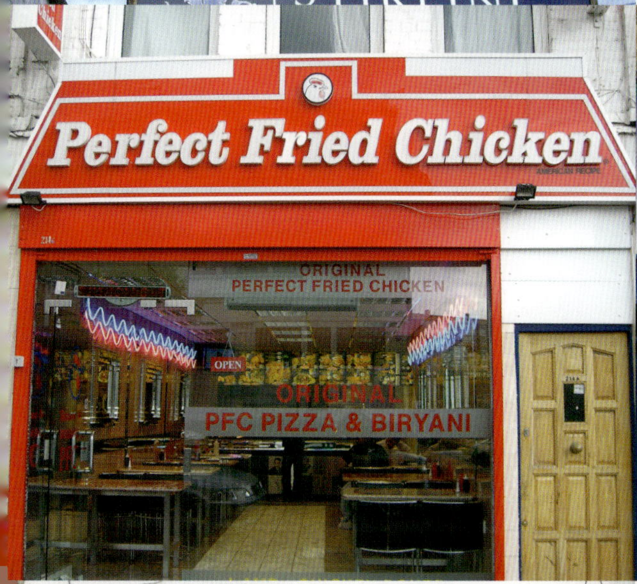
Perfect Fried Chicken
ORIGINAL
PERFECT FRIED CHICKEN
OPEN
ORIGINAL
PFC PIZZA & BIRYANI
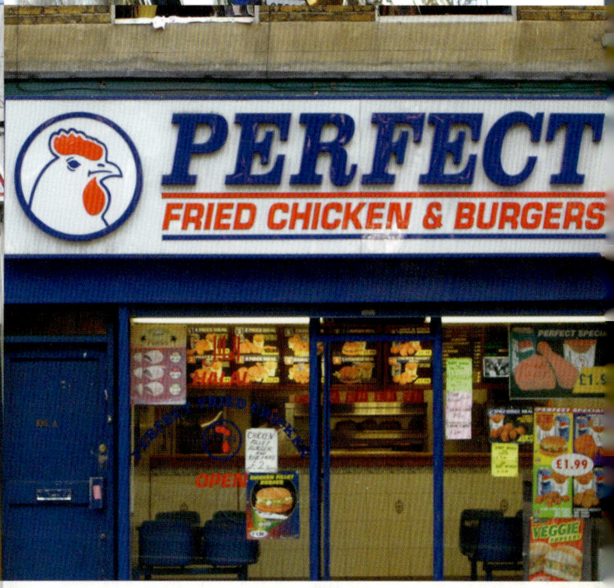
PERFECT
FRIED CHICKEN & BURGERS
HALAL
OPEN
£1.99
VEGGIE
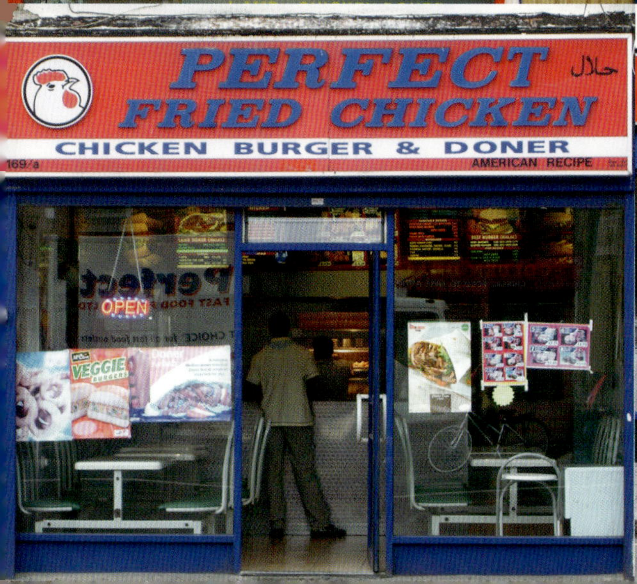
PERFECT
FRIED CHICKEN
حلال
CHICKEN BURGER & DONER
AMERICAN RECIPE
OPEN
VEGGIE
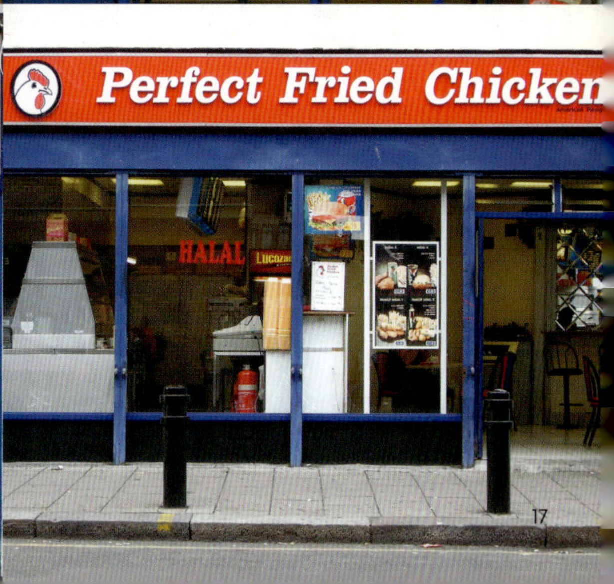
Perfect Fried Chicken
HALAL

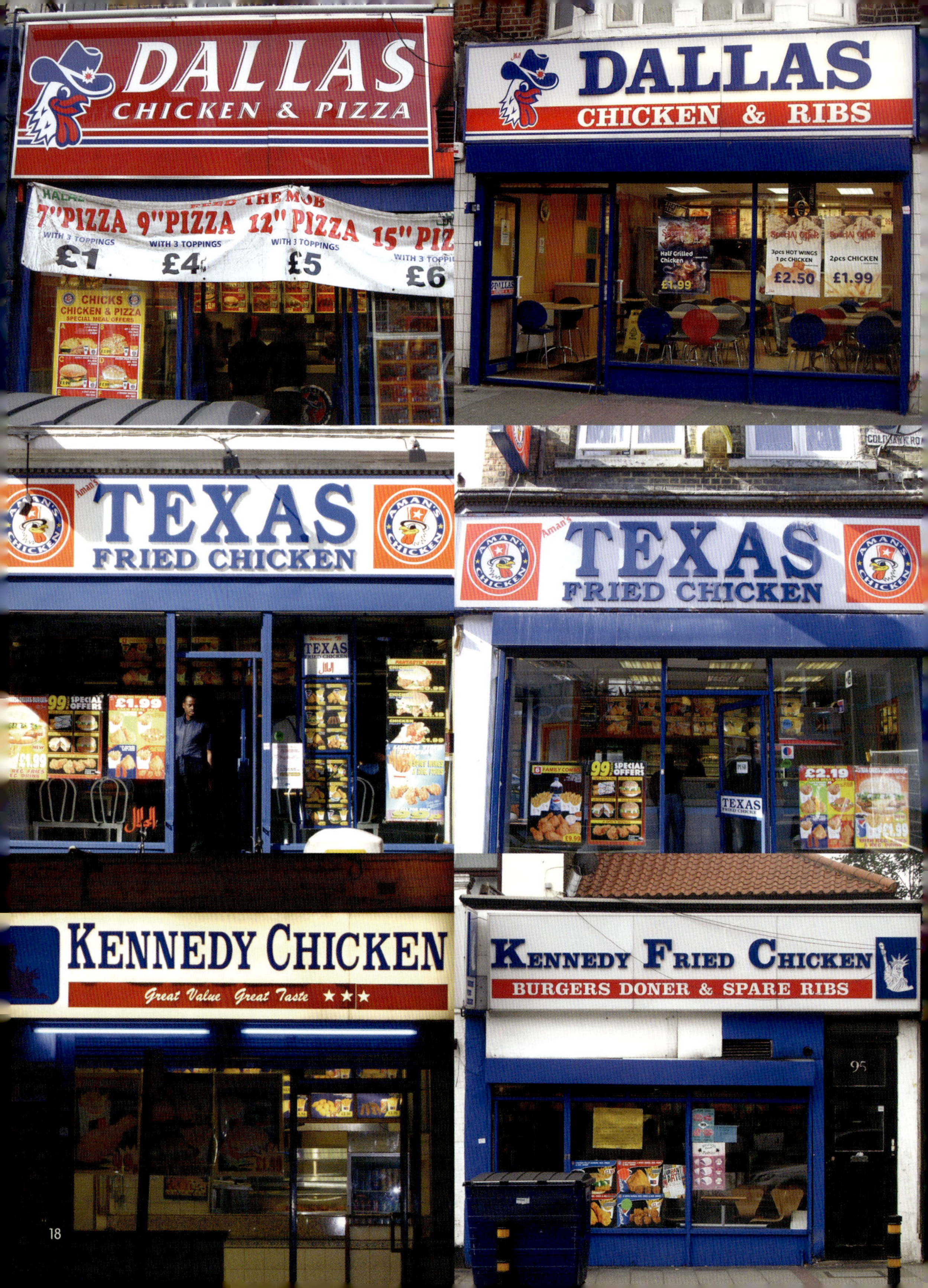
DALLAS
CHICKEN & PIZZA
7"PIZZA 9"PIZZA 12"PIZZA
WITH 3 TOPPINGS
£1 £4 £5 £6
DALLAS
CHICKEN & RIBS
TEXAS
FRIED CHICKEN
TEXAS
FRIED CHICKEN
KENNEDY CHICKEN
Great Value Great Taste ★★★
KENNEDY FRIED CHICKEN
BURGERS DONER & SPARE RIBS

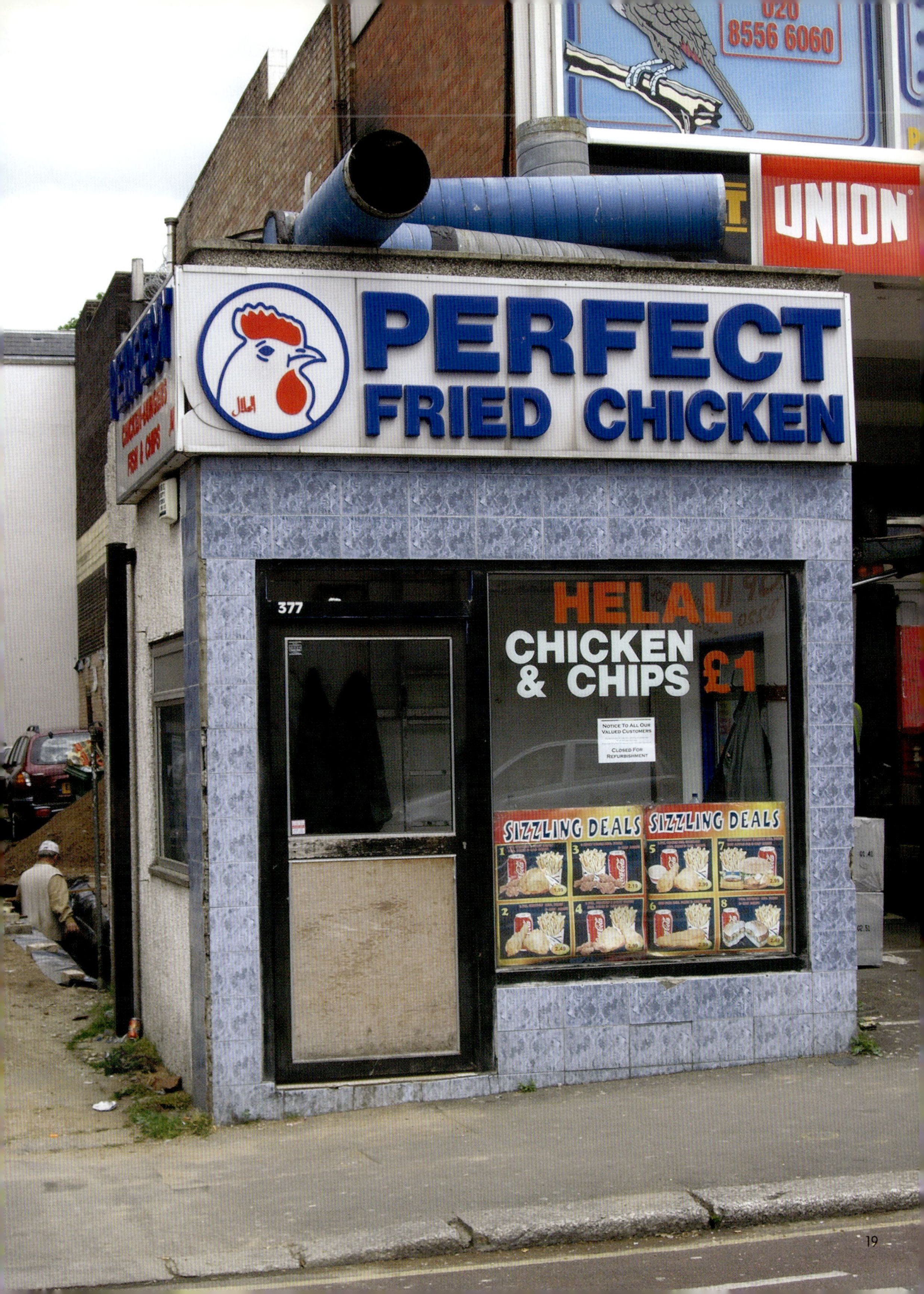
020
8556 6060
UNION
PERFECT
FRIED CHICKEN
377
HELAL
CHICKEN
& CHIPS
£1
SIZZLING DEALS
SIZZLING DEALS

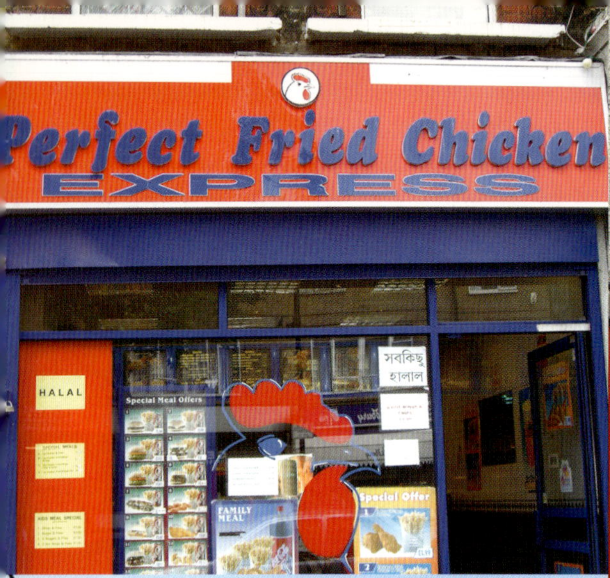
Perfect Fried Chicken
EXPRESS
HALAL
সবকিছু হালাল
Special Meal Offers
Special Offer
FAMILY MEAL

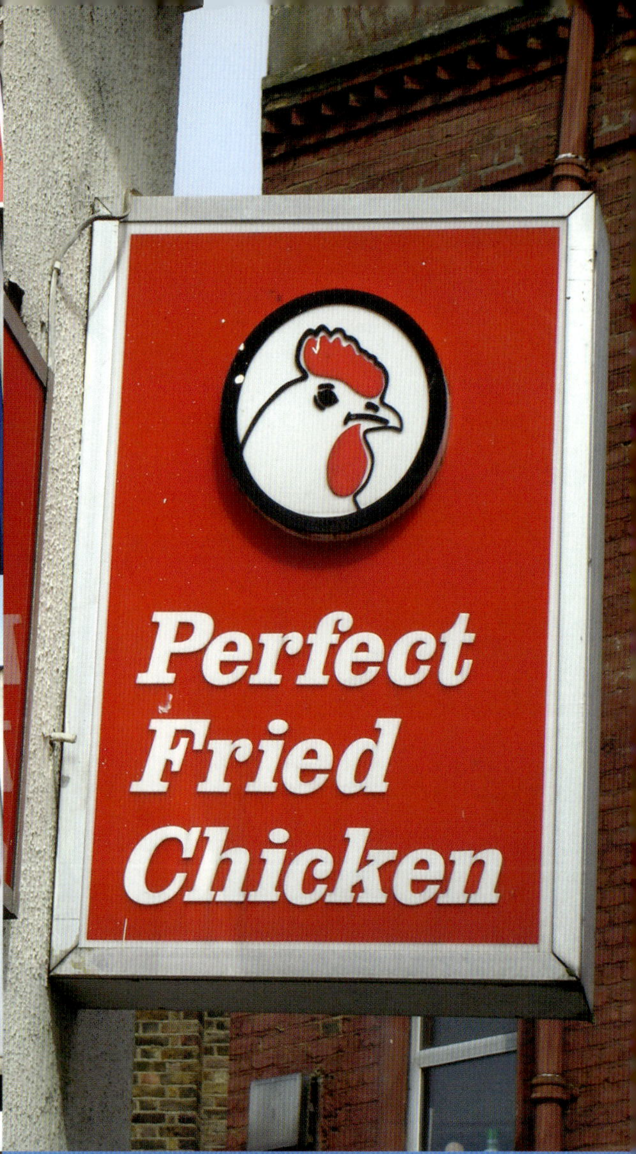
Perfect
Fried
Chicken

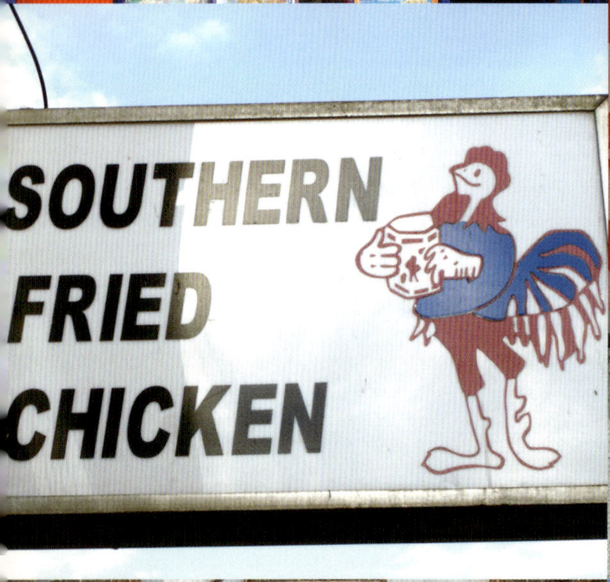
SOUTHERN
FRIED
CHICKEN

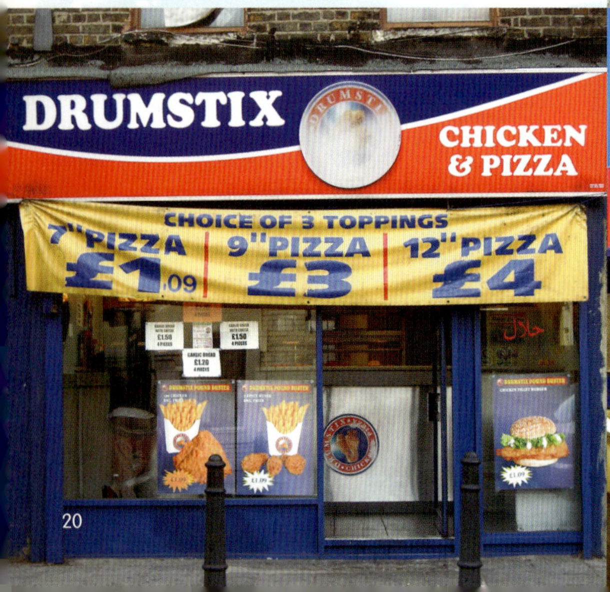
DRUMSTIX
CHICKEN
& PIZZA
CHOICE OF 3 TOPPINGS
7" PIZZA £1.09
9" PIZZA £3
12" PIZZA £4
حلال

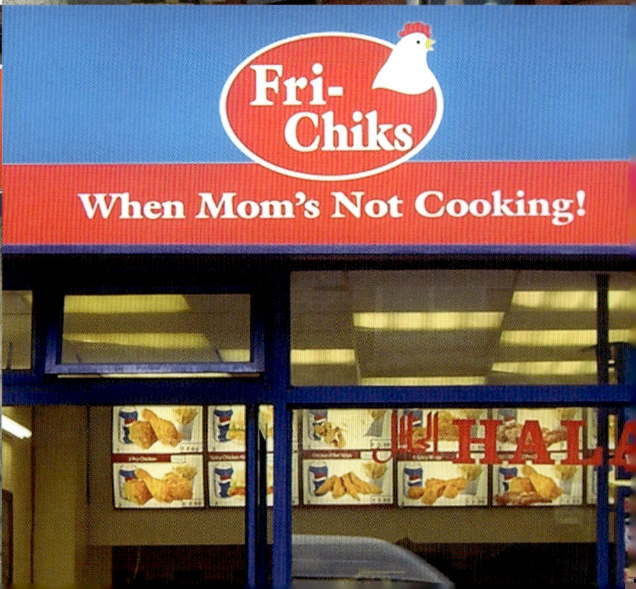
Fri-
Chiks
When Mom's Not Cooking!
حلال

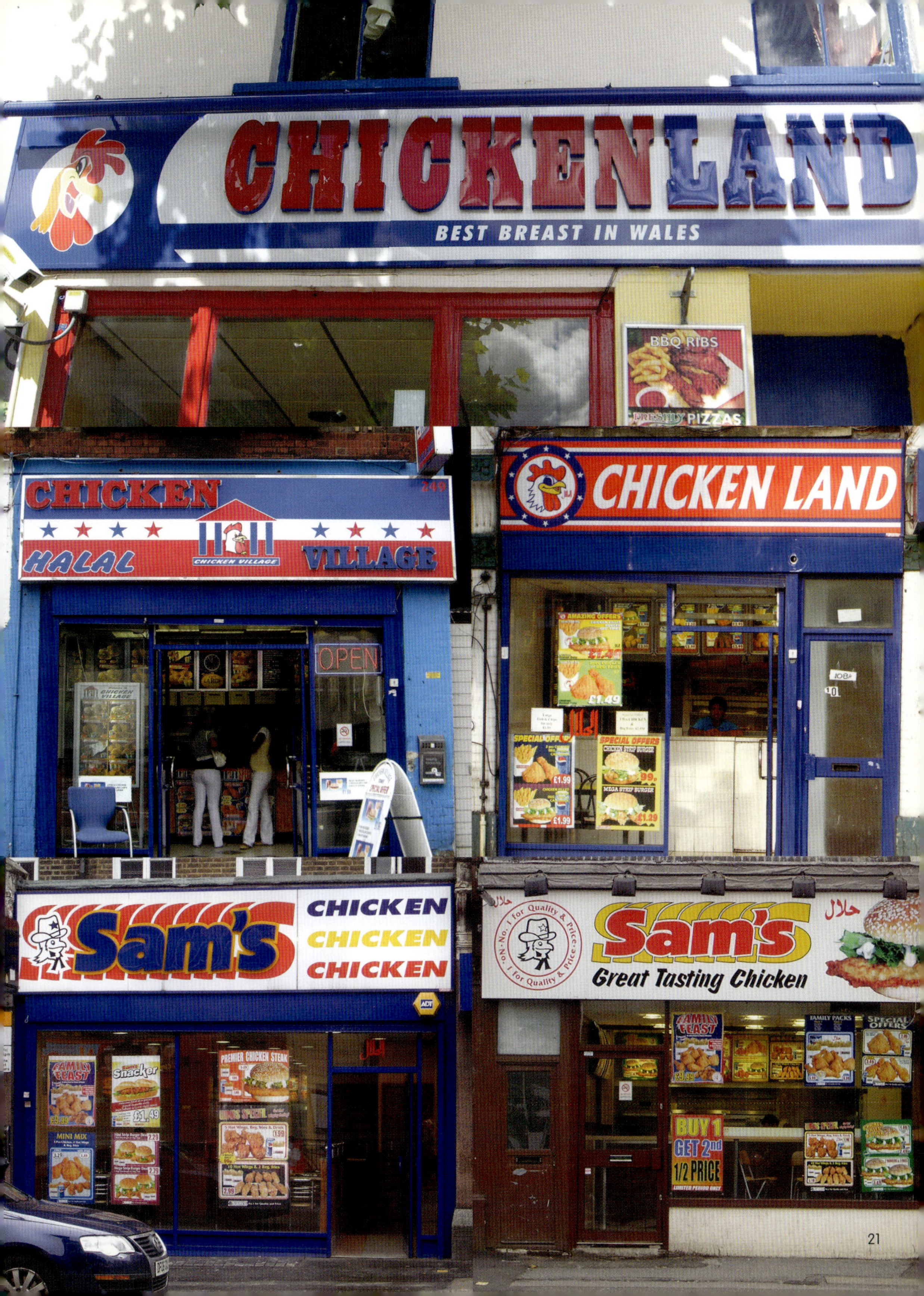
CHICKENLAND
BEST BREAST IN WALES
BBQ RIBS
FRESHLY PIZZAS
CHICKEN
HALAL
CHICKEN VILLAGE
VILLAGE
249
OPEN
CHICKEN LAND
£1.49
£1.99
£1.29
Sam's
CHICKEN
CHICKEN
CHICKEN
Snacker
£1.49
MINI MIX
PREMIER CHICKEN STEAK
No. 1 for Quality & Price
Sam's
Great Tasting Chicken
حلال
FAMILY PACKS
SPECIAL OFFERS
BUY 1
GET 2nd
1/2 PRICE
LIMITED PERIOD ONLY

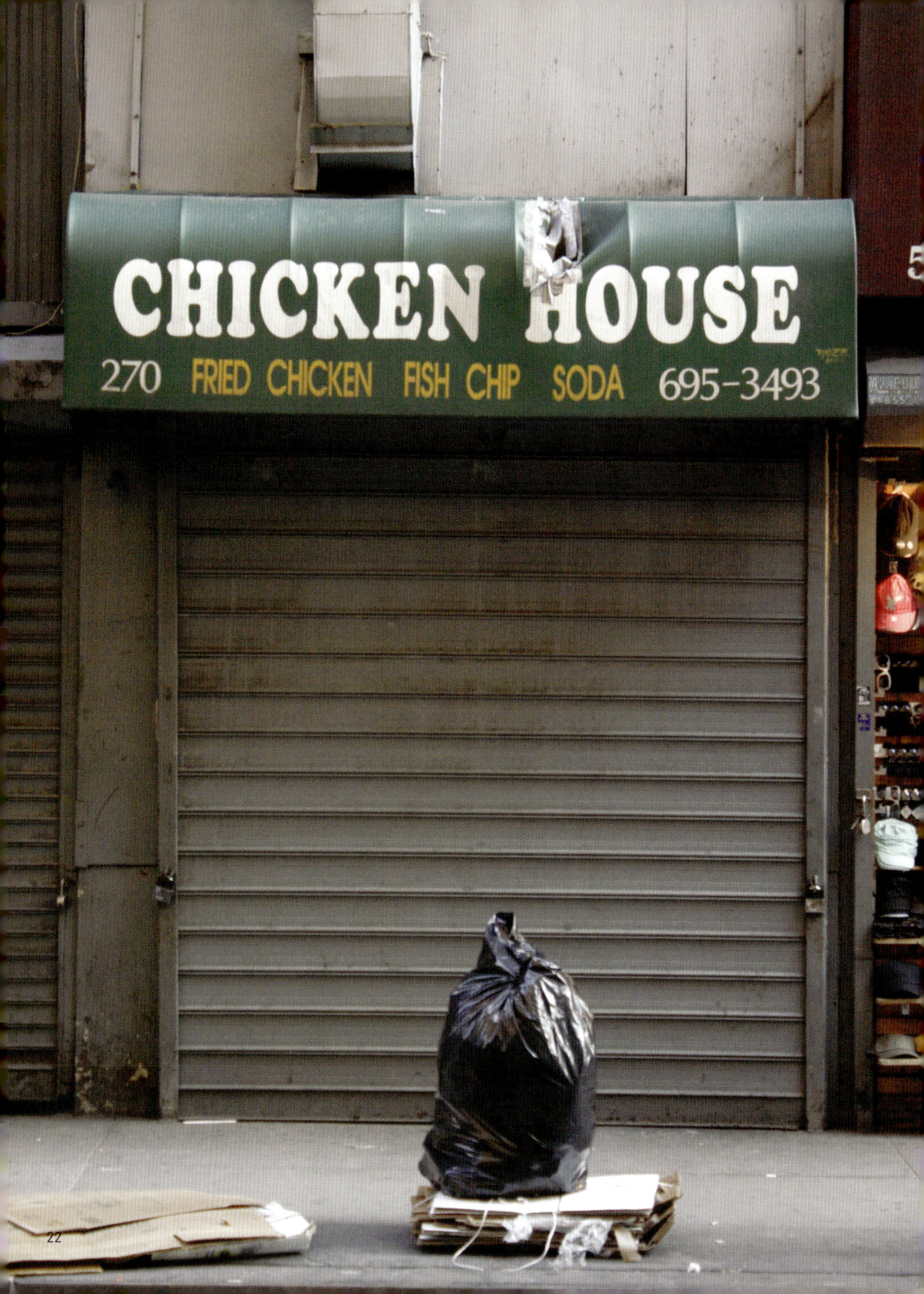
CHICKEN HOUSE
270 FRIED CHICKEN FISH CHIP SODA 695-3493

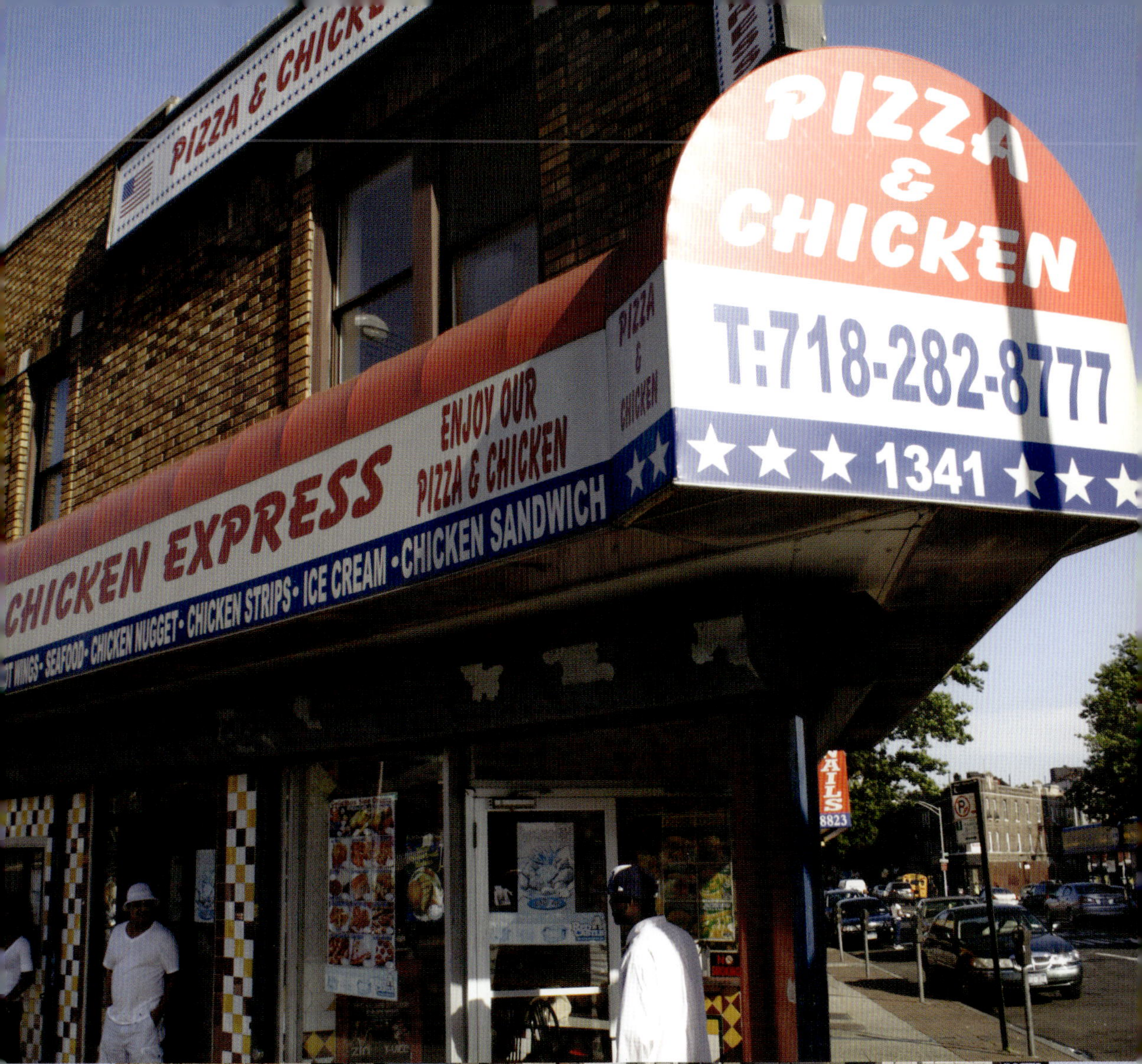
PIZZA & CHICKEN
T:718-282-8777
1341
PIZZA & CHICKEN
CHICKEN EXPRESS
ENJOY OUR PIZZA & CHICKEN
WINGS • SEAFOOD • CHICKEN NUGGET • CHICKEN STRIPS • ICE CREAM • CHICKEN SANDWICH

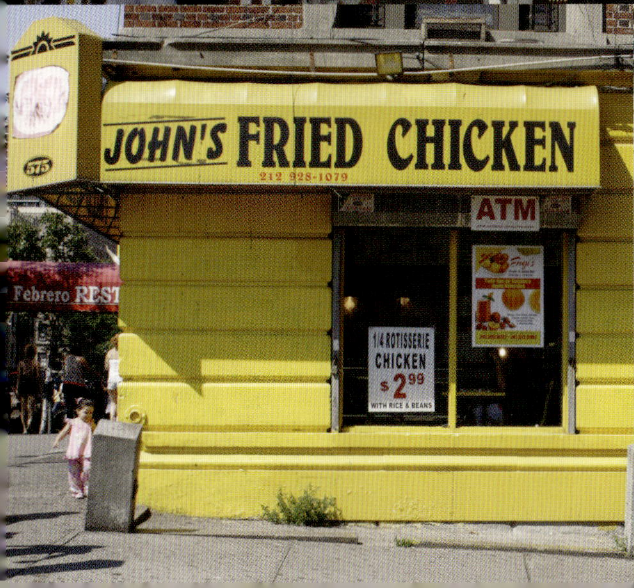
575
JOHN'S FRIED CHICKEN
212 928-1079
ATM
1/4 ROTISSERIE CHICKEN $2.99
WITH RICE & BEANS

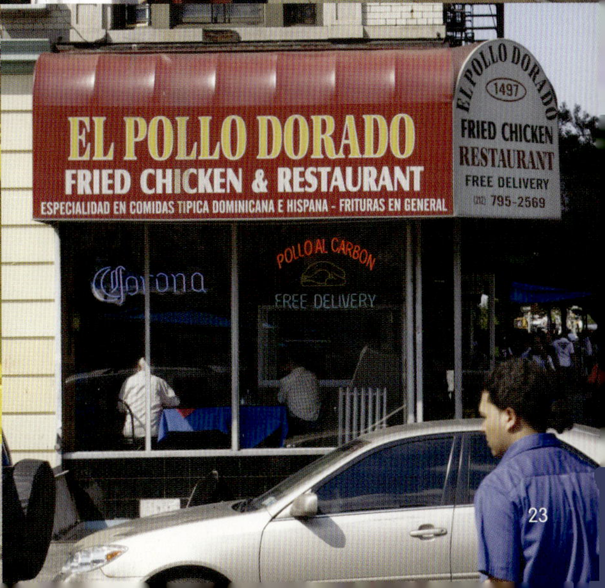
EL POLLO DORADO
FRIED CHICKEN & RESTAURANT
ESPECIALIDAD EN COMIDAS TIPICA DOMINICANA E HISPANA - FRITURAS EN GENERAL
EL POLLO DORADO
1497
FRIED CHICKEN
RESTAURANT
FREE DELIVERY
(212) 795-2569
Corona
POLLO AL CARBON
FREE DELIVERY

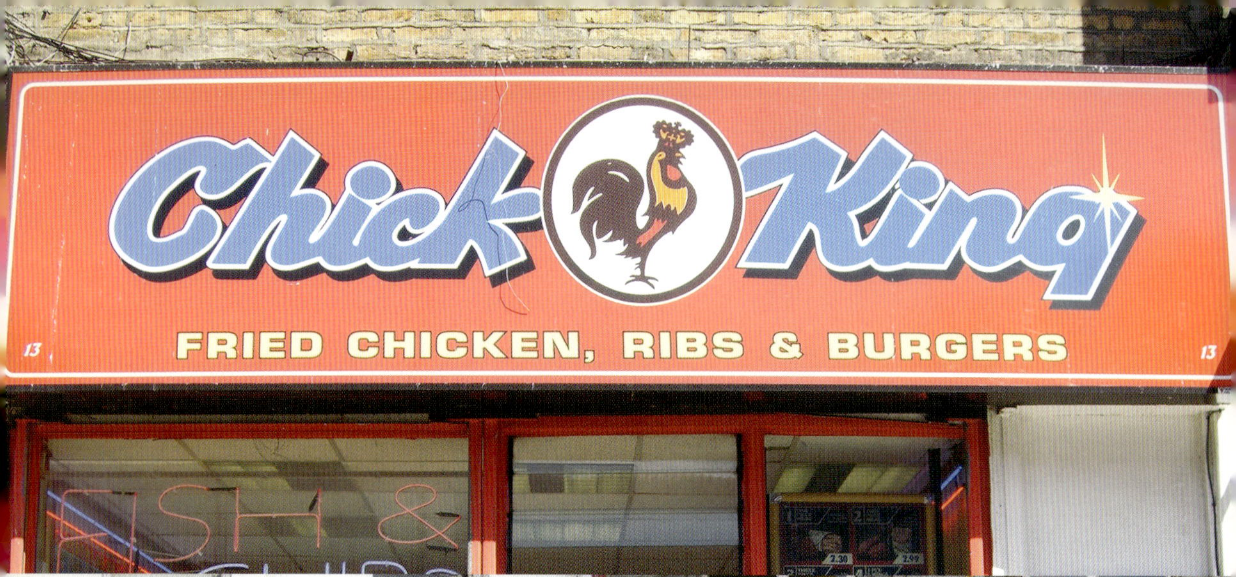
13
Chick King
13
FRIED CHICKEN, RIBS & BURGERS
13

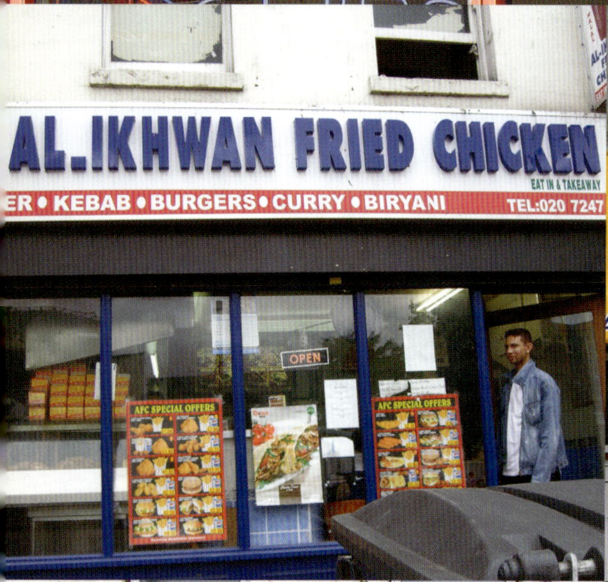
AL.IKHWAN FRIED CHICKEN
EAT IN & TAKEAWAY
ER • KEBAB • BURGERS • CURRY • BIRYANI
TEL:020 7247
OPEN
AFC SPECIAL OFFERS
AFC SPECIAL OFFERS

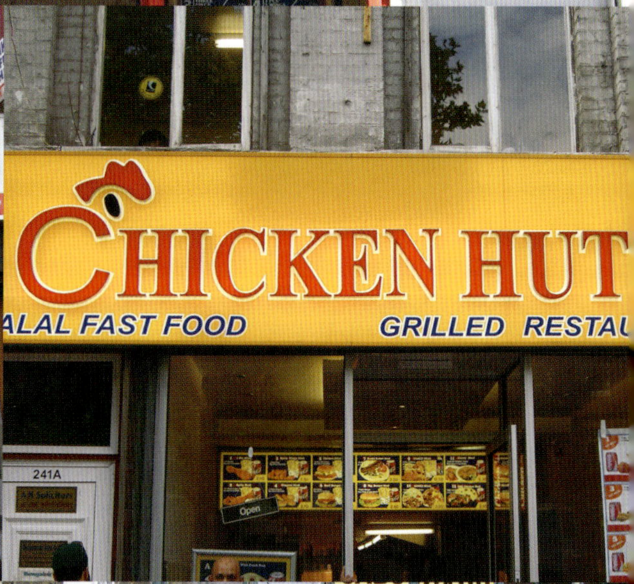
CHICKEN HUT
ALAL FAST FOOD
GRILLED RESTAU
241A
Open

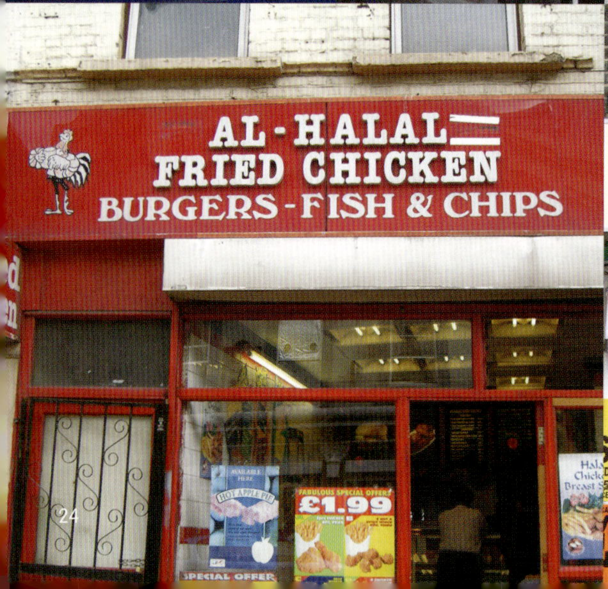
AL-HALAL
FRIED CHICKEN
BURGERS-FISH & CHIPS
£1.99

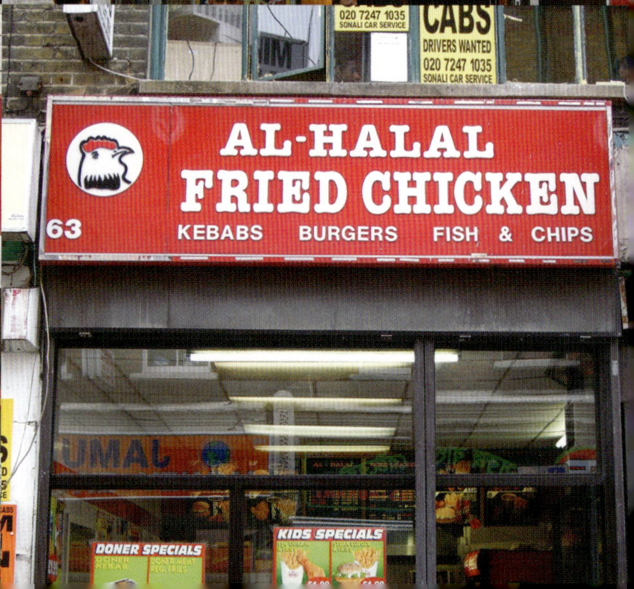
020 7247 1035
SONALI CAR SERVICE
CABS
DRIVERS WANTED
020 7247 1035
SONALI CAR SERVICE
AL-HALAL
FRIED CHICKEN
63
KEBABS BURGERS FISH & CHIPS
DONER SPECIALS
KIDS SPECIALS

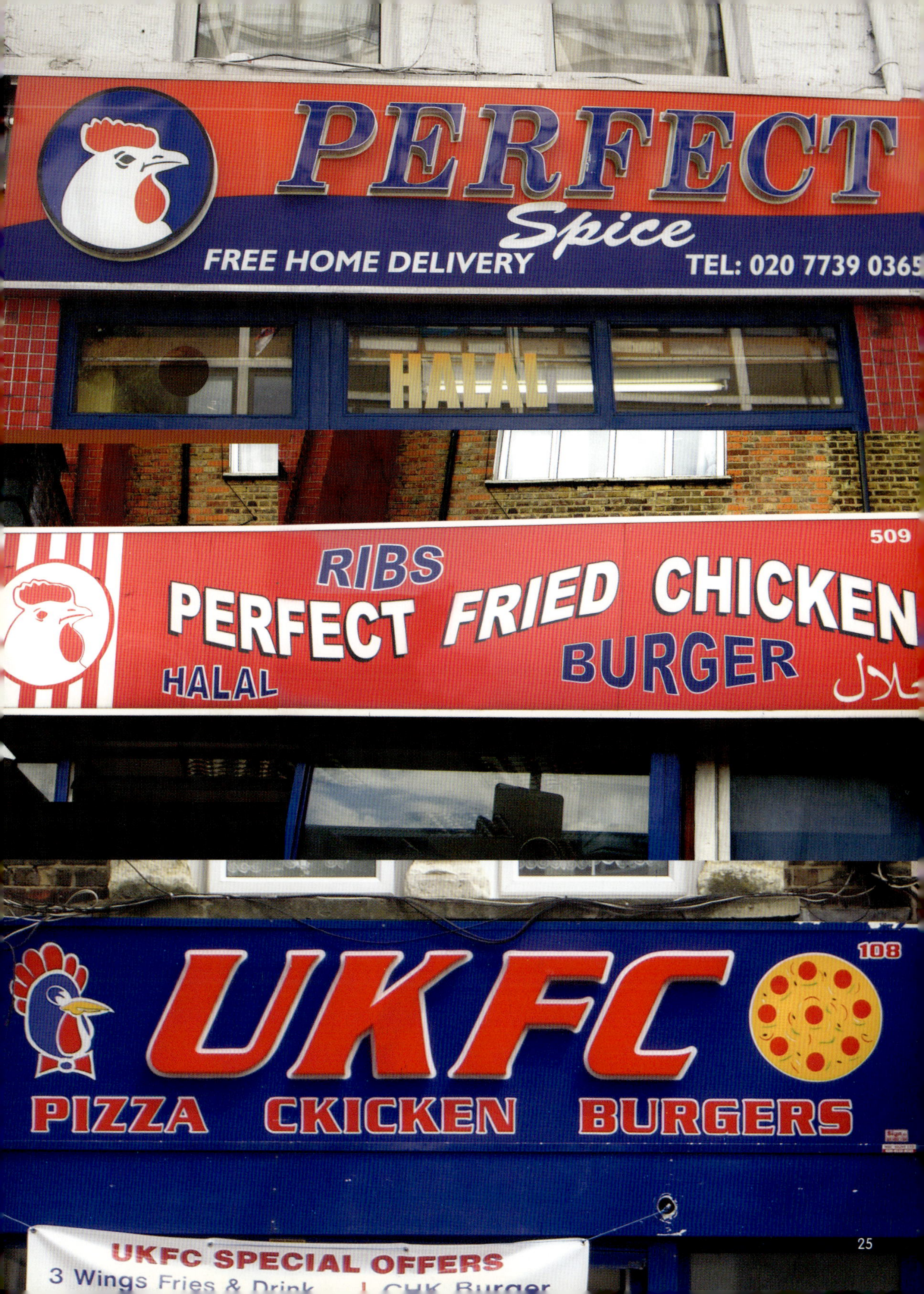
PERFECT
Spice
FREE HOME DELIVERY
TEL: 020 7739 0365
HALAL
509
RIBS
PERFECT FRIED CHICKEN
HALAL
BURGER
108
UKFC
PIZZA CKICKEN BURGERS
UKFC SPECIAL OFFERS

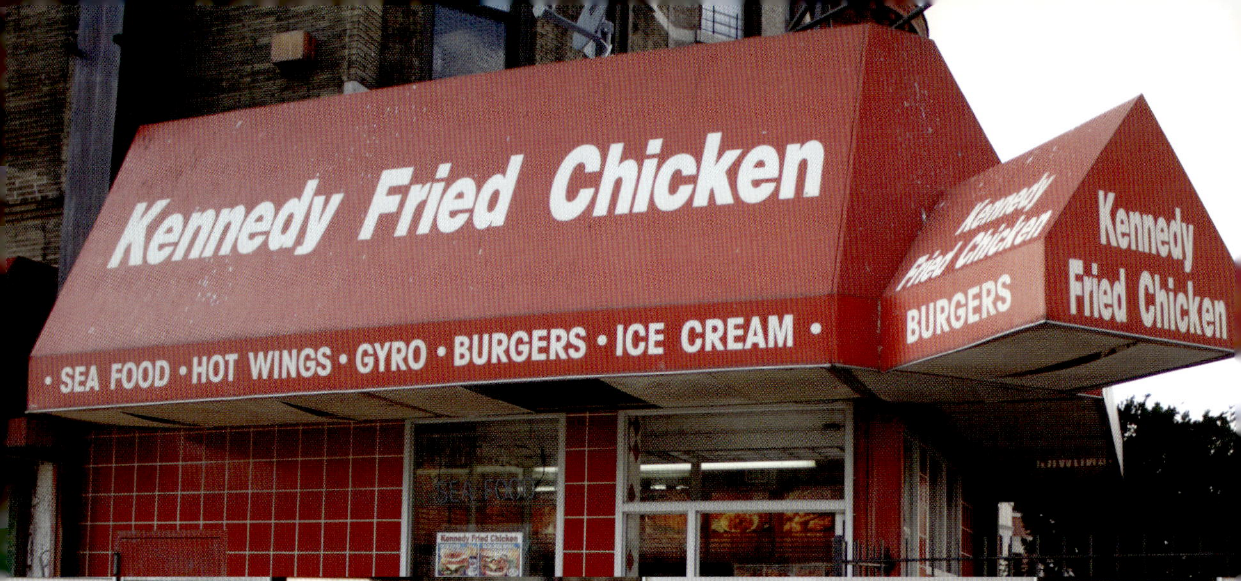
Kennedy Fried Chicken
• SEA FOOD • HOT WINGS • GYRO • BURGERS • ICE CREAM •
Kennedy Fried Chicken
BURGERS
Kennedy Fried Chicken

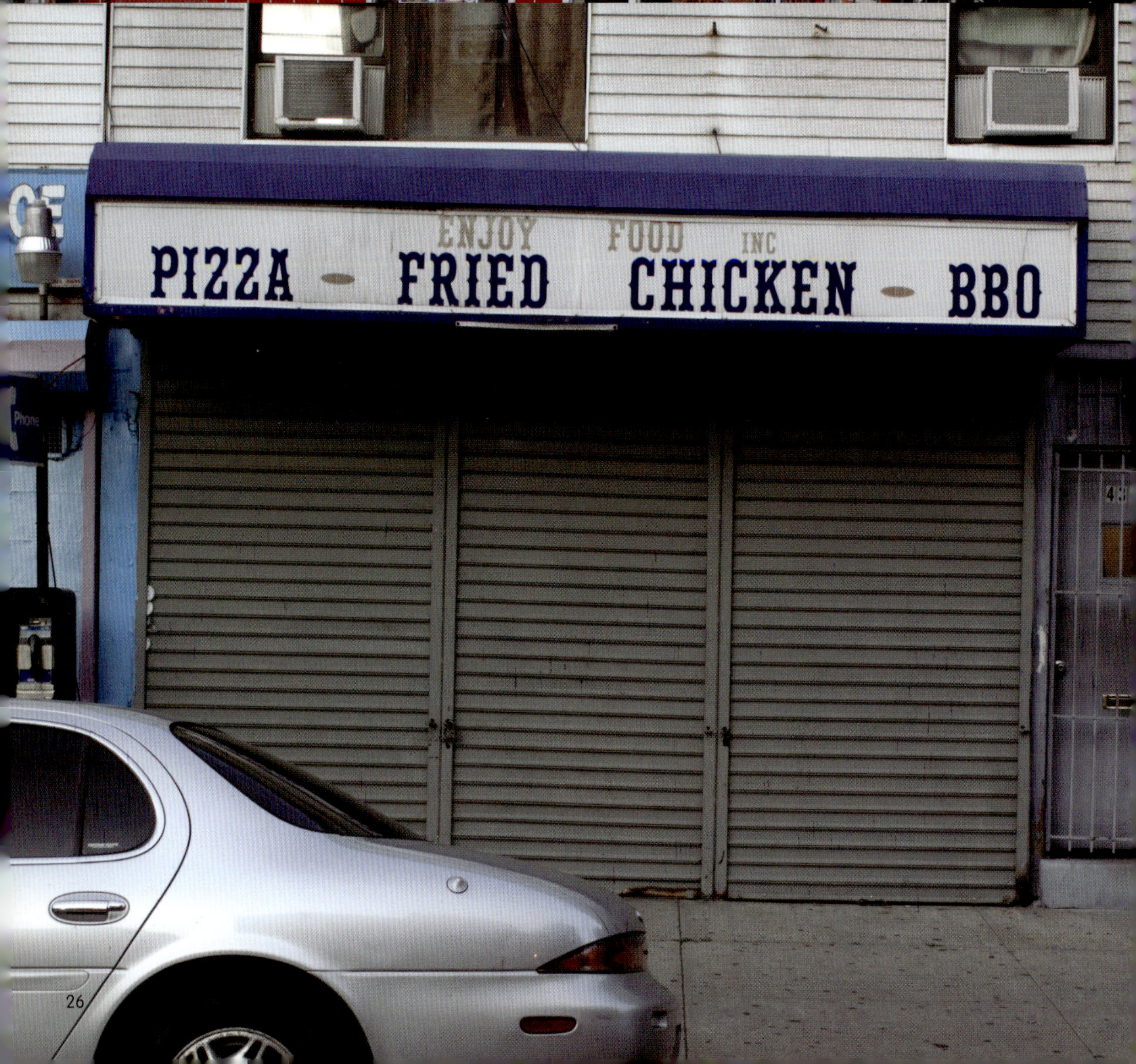
ENJOY FOOD INC
PIZZA FRIED CHICKEN BBQ

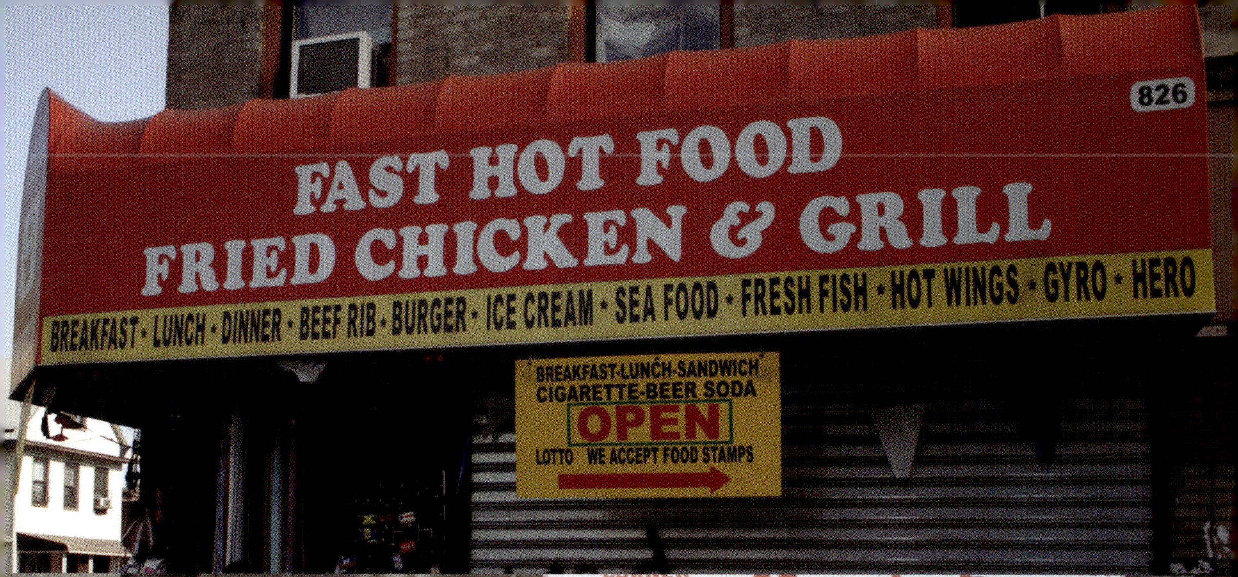
826
FAST HOT FOOD
FRIED CHICKEN & GRILL
BREAKFAST • LUNCH • DINNER • BEEF RIB • BURGER • ICE CREAM • SEA FOOD • FRESH FISH • HOT WINGS • GYRO • HERO
BREAKFAST-LUNCH-SANDWICH
CIGARETTE-BEER SODA
OPEN
LOTTO WE ACCEPT FOOD STAMPS

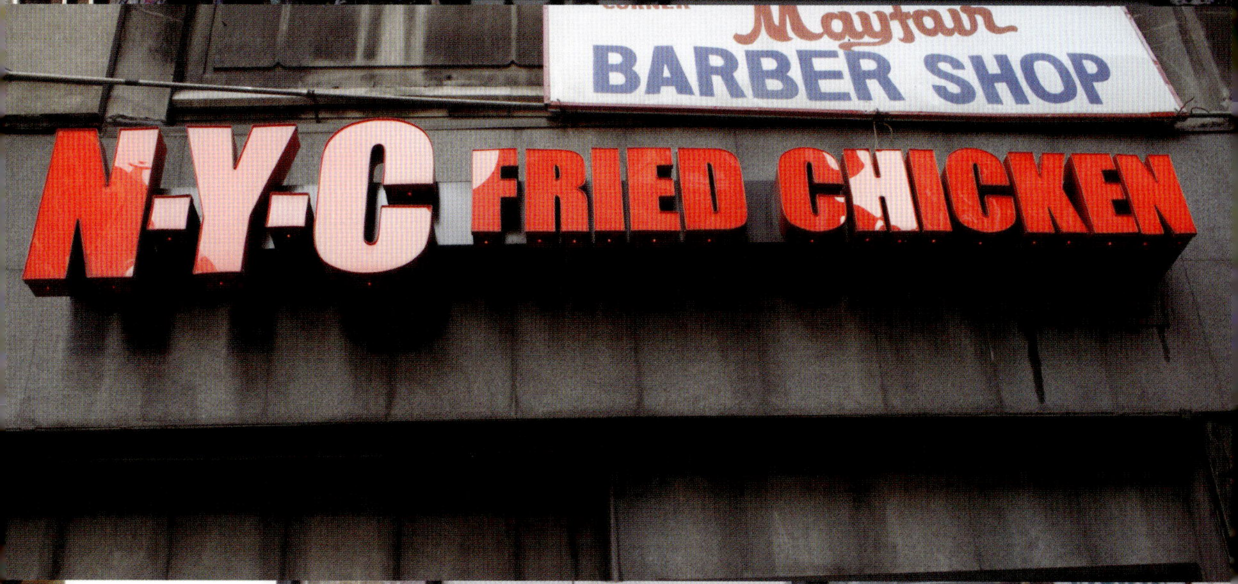
Mayfair
BARBER SHOP
N-Y-C FRIED CHICKEN

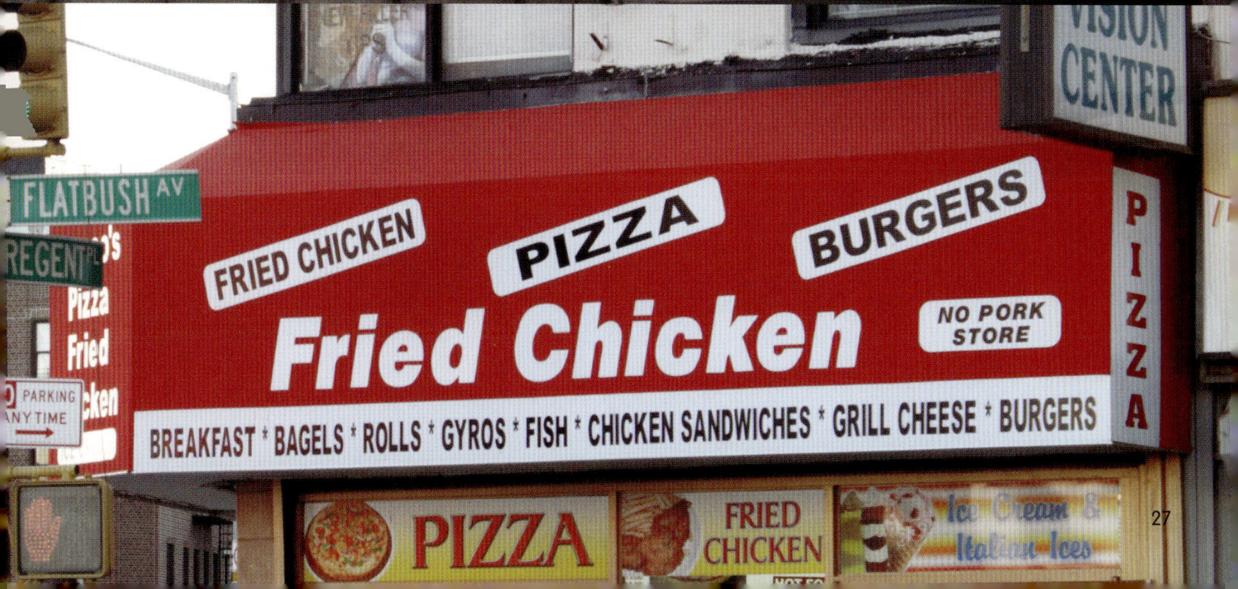
CENTER
FLATBUSH AV
FRIED CHICKEN
PIZZA
BURGERS
Fried Chicken
NO PORK STORE
PIZZA
BREAKFAST * BAGELS * ROLLS * GYROS * FISH * CHICKEN SANDWICHES * GRILL CHEESE * BURGERS
Pizza
Fried
PIZZA
FRIED CHICKEN
Ice Cream &
Italian Ices

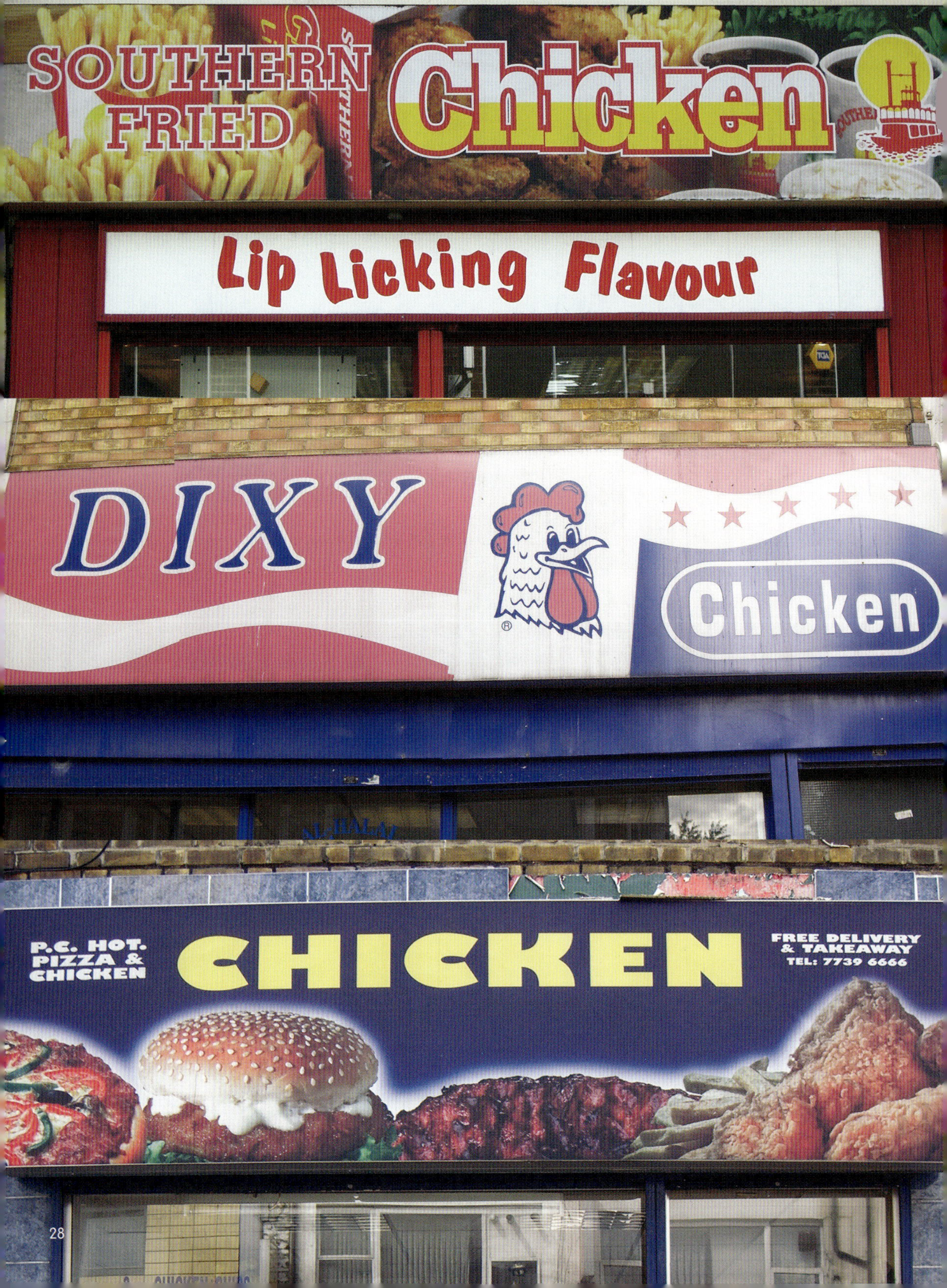
SOUTHERN FRIED
Chicken
Lip Licking Flavour
DIXY
Chicken
P.C. HOT. PIZZA & CHICKEN
CHICKEN
FREE DELIVERY & TAKEAWAY
TEL: 7739 6666

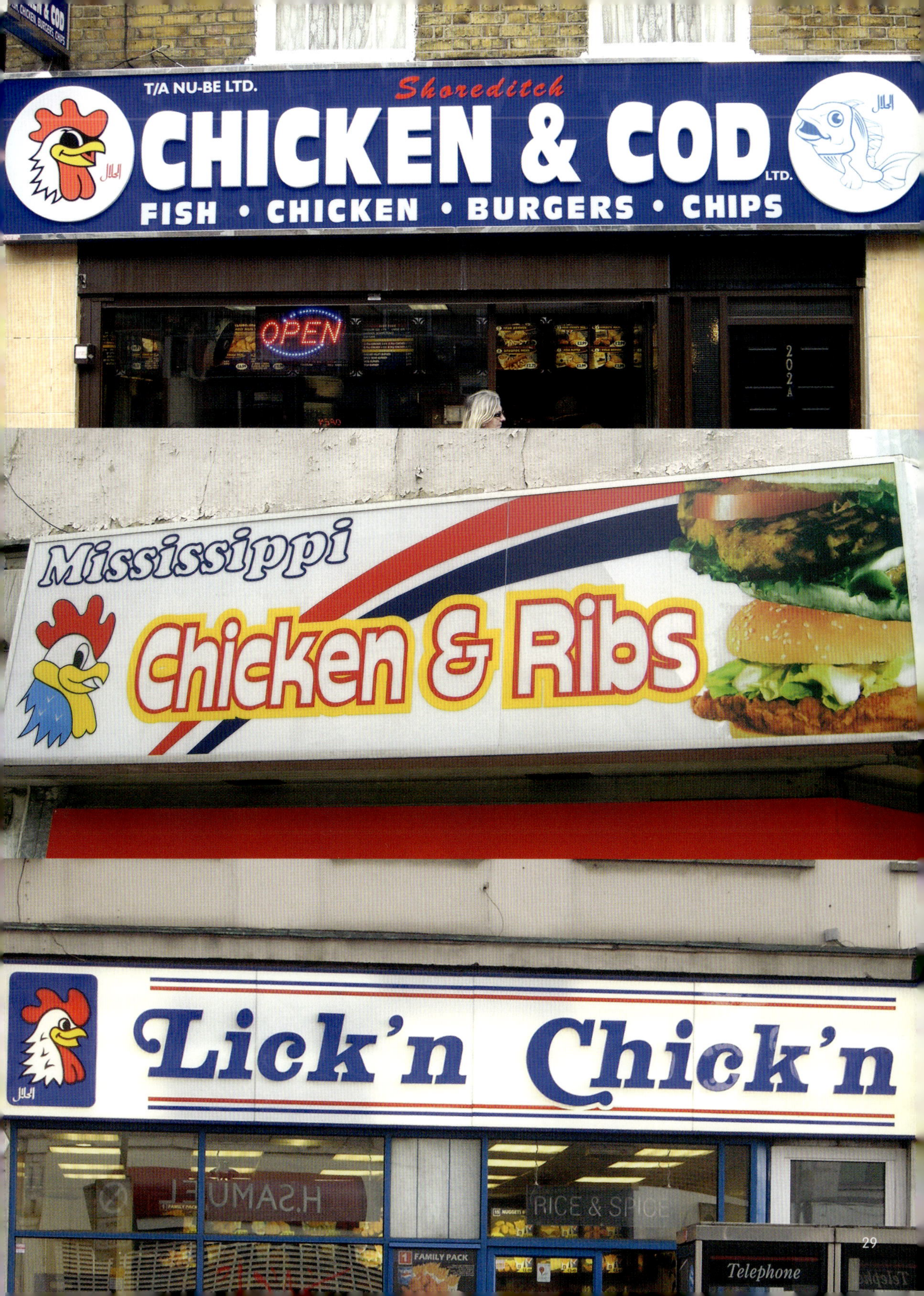
T/A NU-BE LTD.
Shoreditch
CHICKEN & COD
LTD.
FISH • CHICKEN • BURGERS • CHIPS
OPEN
202A
Mississippi
Chicken & Ribs
Lick'n Chick'n
FAMILY PACK
RICE & SPICE
H.SAMUEL
Telephone

MENU GRAPHICS AND DISPLAY

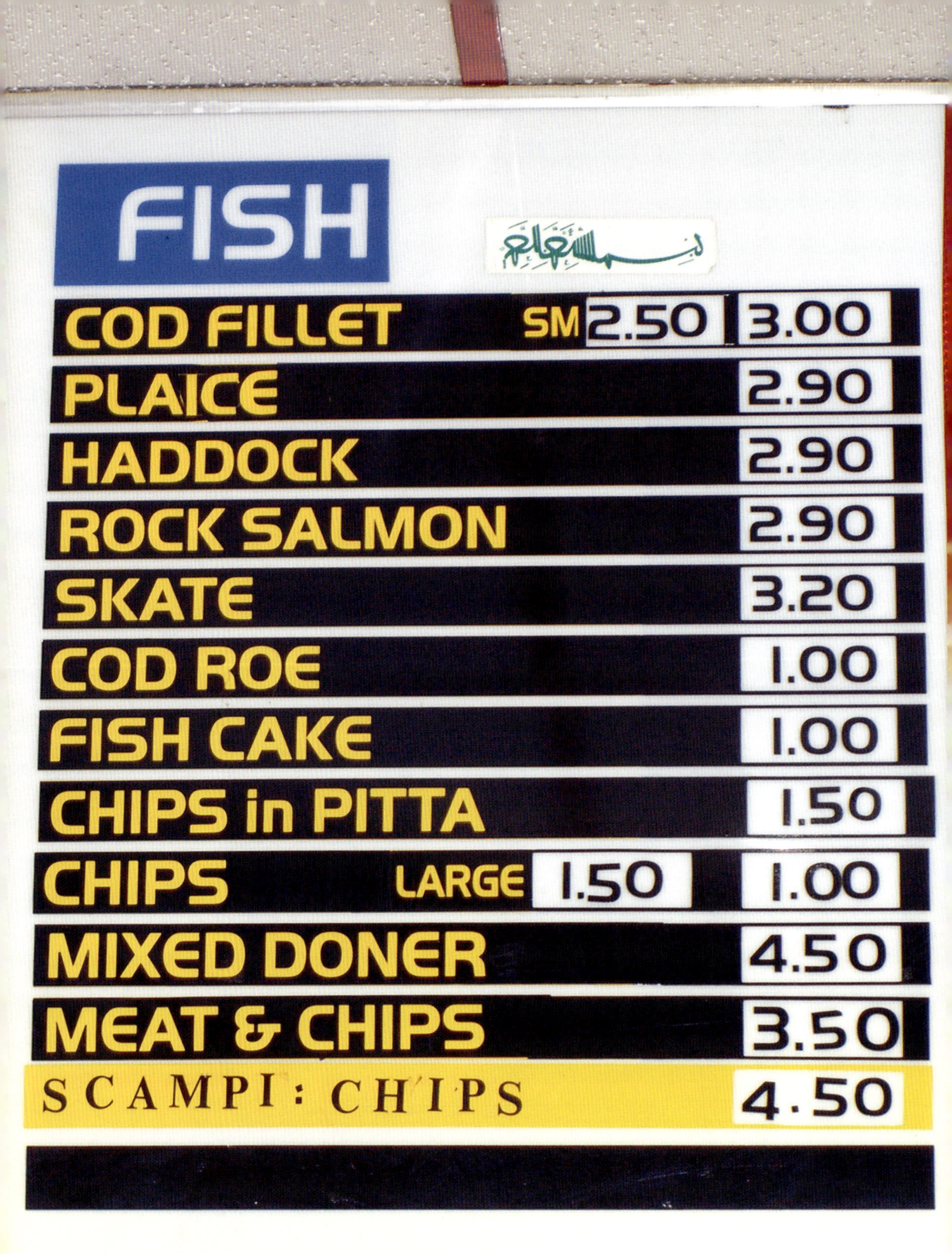

FISH
COD FILLET SM 2.50 3.00
PLAICE 2.90
HADDOCK 2.90
ROCK SALMON 2.90
SKATE 3.20
COD ROE 1.00
FISH CAKE 1.00
CHIPS in PITTA 1.50
CHIPS LARGE 1.50 1.00
MIXED DONER 4.50
MEAT & CHIPS 3.50
SCAMPI : CHIPS 4.50

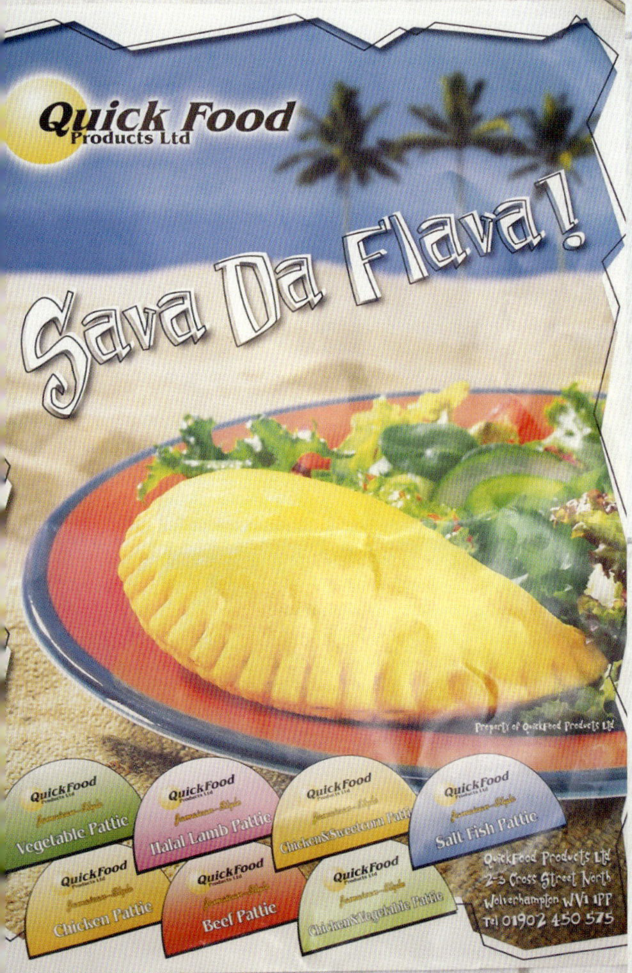
Quick Food
Products Ltd
Sava Da Flava!
Property of QuickFood Products Ltd
Vegetable Pattie
Halal Lamb Pattie
Chicken&Sweetcorn Pattie
Salt Fish Pattie
Chicken Pattie
Beef Pattie
Chicken&Vegetable Pattie
QuickFood Products Ltd
2-3 Cross Street North
Wolverhampton WV1 1PP
Tel 01902 450 575

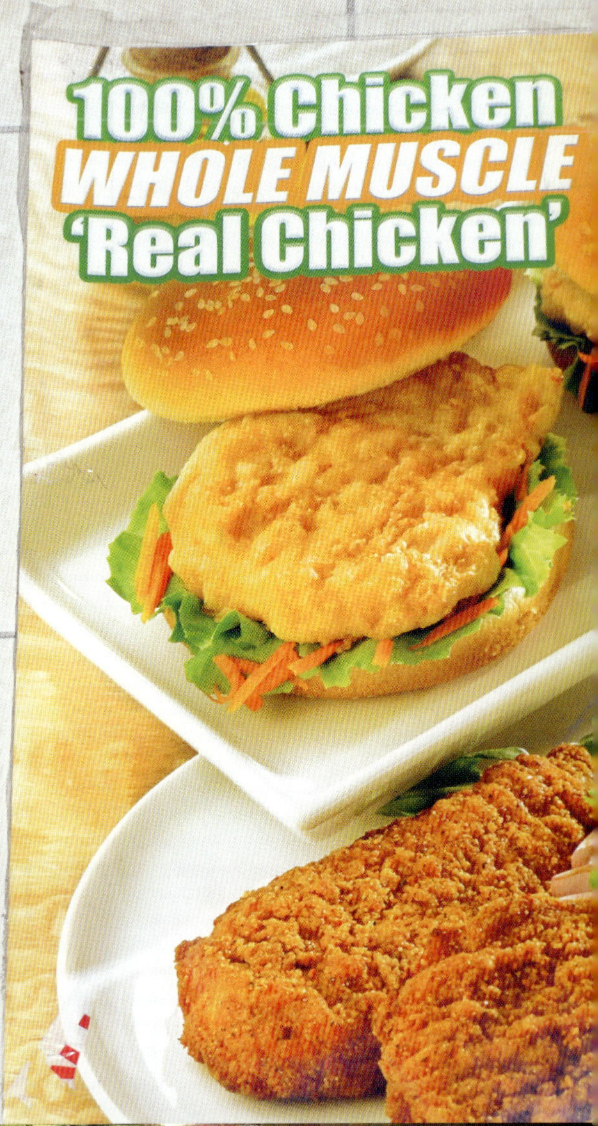
100% Chicken
WHOLE MUSCLE
'Real Chicken'

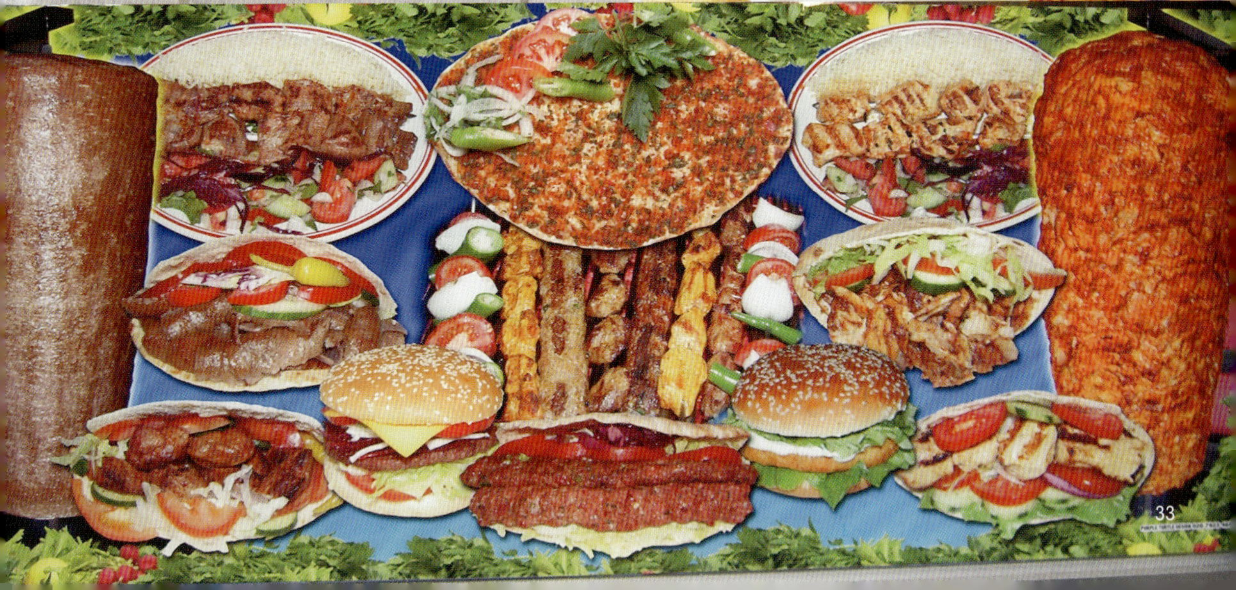

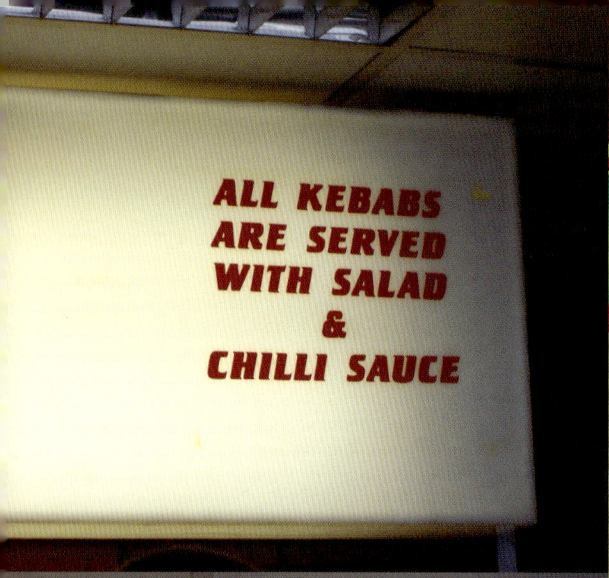

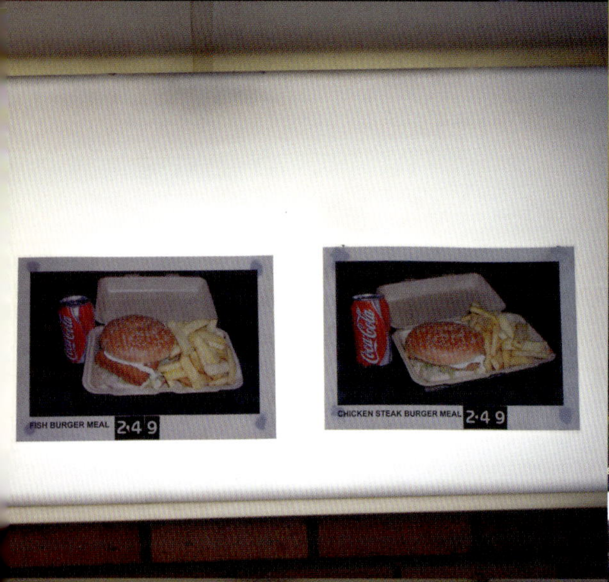

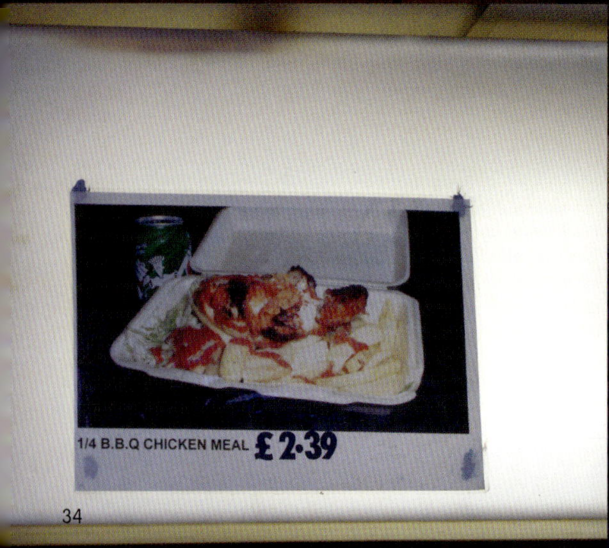

Ewelina Swierczek:

It's very funny, tourists make me laugh. They love the name Hollywood Chicken, especially the Chinese. They take pictures of the outside, and of the plates of food! I think they don't have fried chicken in China!

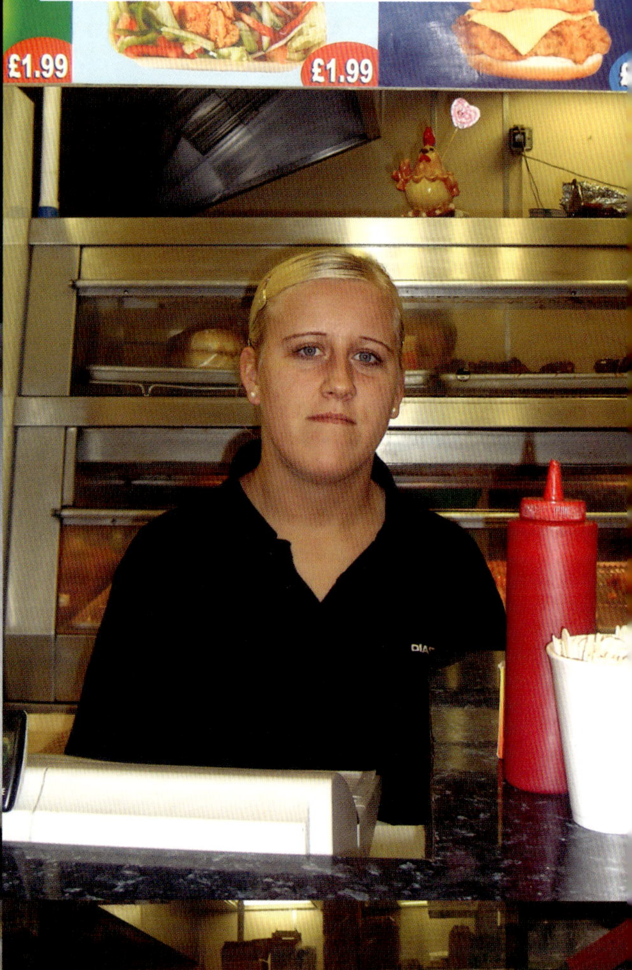

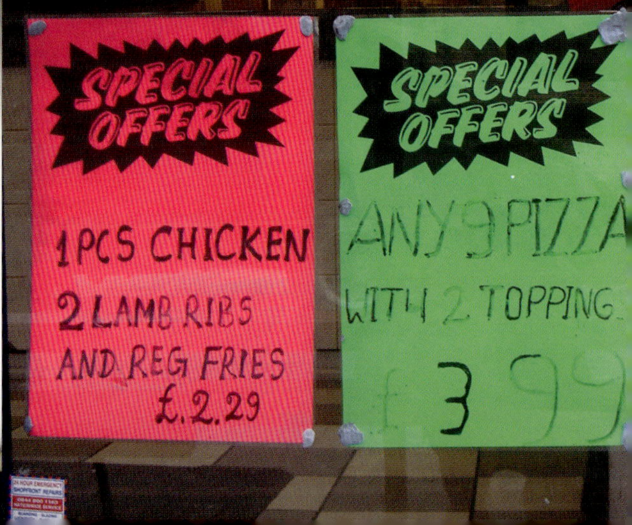

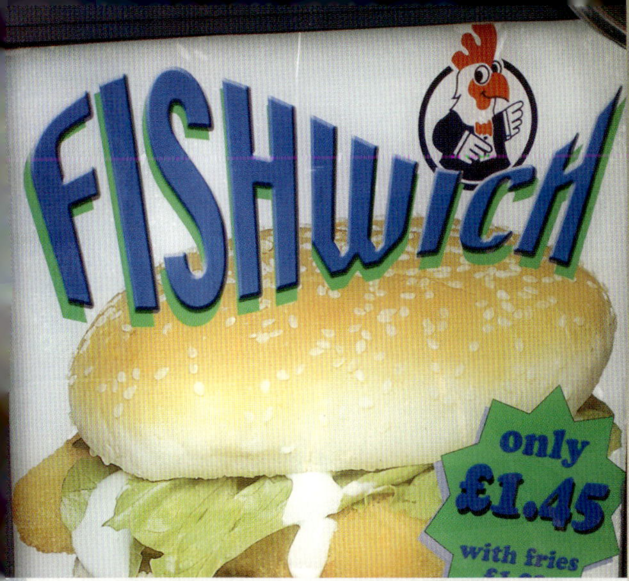
FISHWICH
only
£1.45
with fries

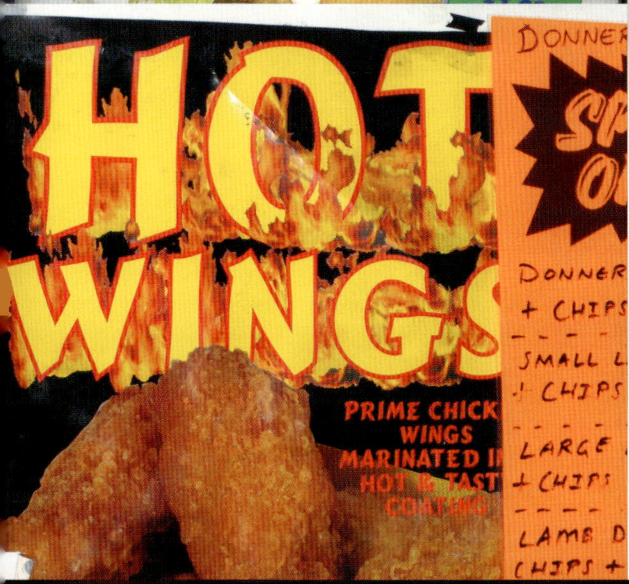
HOT
WINGS
PRIME CHICK
WINGS
MARINATED I
HOT & TAST
COATING
DONNER
DONNER
+ CHIPS
SMALL
+ CHIPS
LARGE
+ CHIPS
LAMB D
CHIPS +

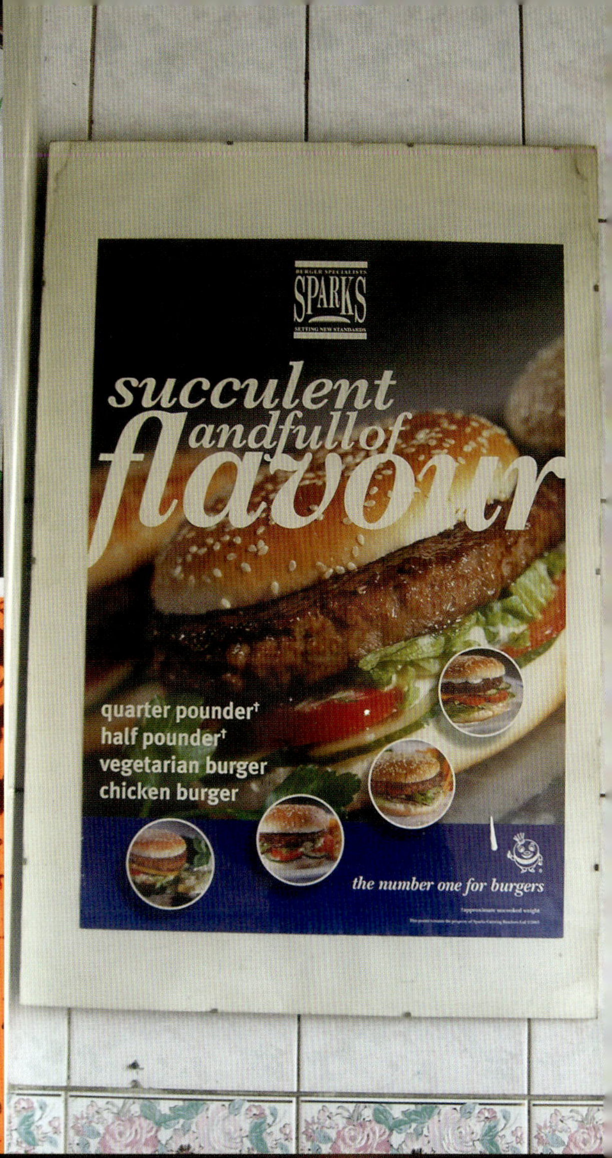
BURGER SPECIALISTS
SPARKS
SETTING NEW STANDARDS
succulent
and full of
flavour
quarter pounder†
half pounder†
vegetarian burger
chicken burger
the number one for burgers

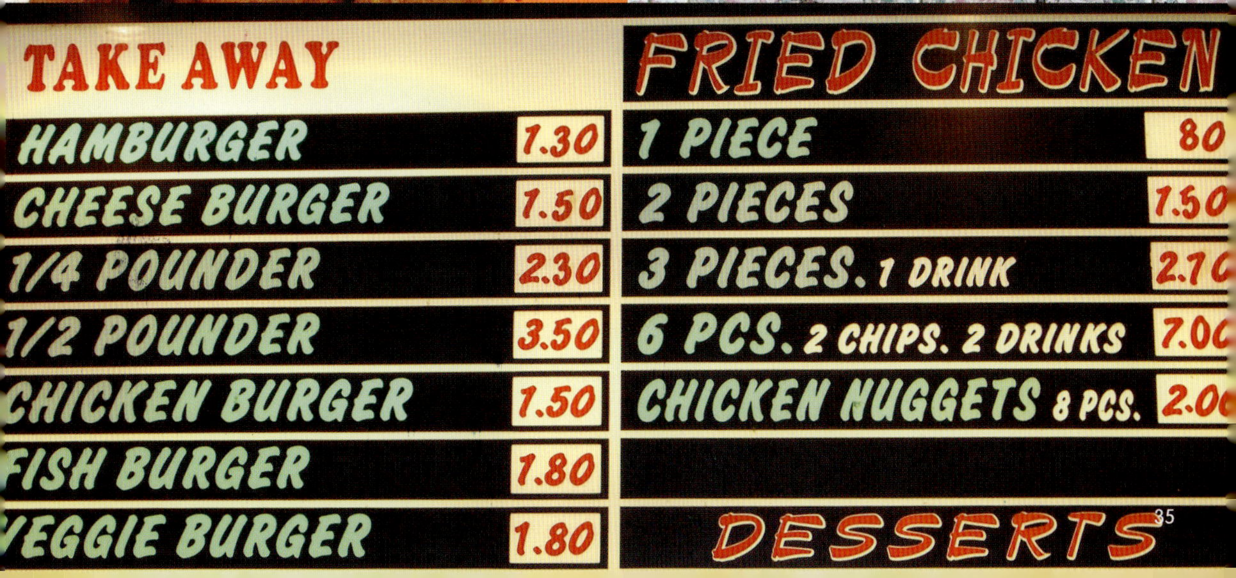
TAKE AWAY
HAMBURGER 1.30
CHEESE BURGER 1.50
1/4 POUNDER 2.30
1/2 POUNDER 3.50
CHICKEN BURGER 1.50
FISH BURGER 1.80
VEGGIE BURGER 1.80
FRIED CHICKEN
1 PIECE 80
2 PIECES 1.50
3 PIECES. 1 DRINK
6 PCS. 2 CHIPS. 2 DRINKS
CHICKEN NUGGETS 8 PCS.
DESSERTS

Ian Milsolm:

We have so many moments in here, but you just don't seem to remember them. We did a wake last week, because it was the old boy's favourite place to eat. Bit of a strange request, we've done parties but never wakes!

There's this guy that comes in for breakfast every day, and he tells me how happy he is that we are here. He loves fried bread, six rashes of bacon and tinned tomatoes. If we haven't done it before, we'll give it a go! (laughs) From deep-fried Mars Bars to anything, I'm easy.

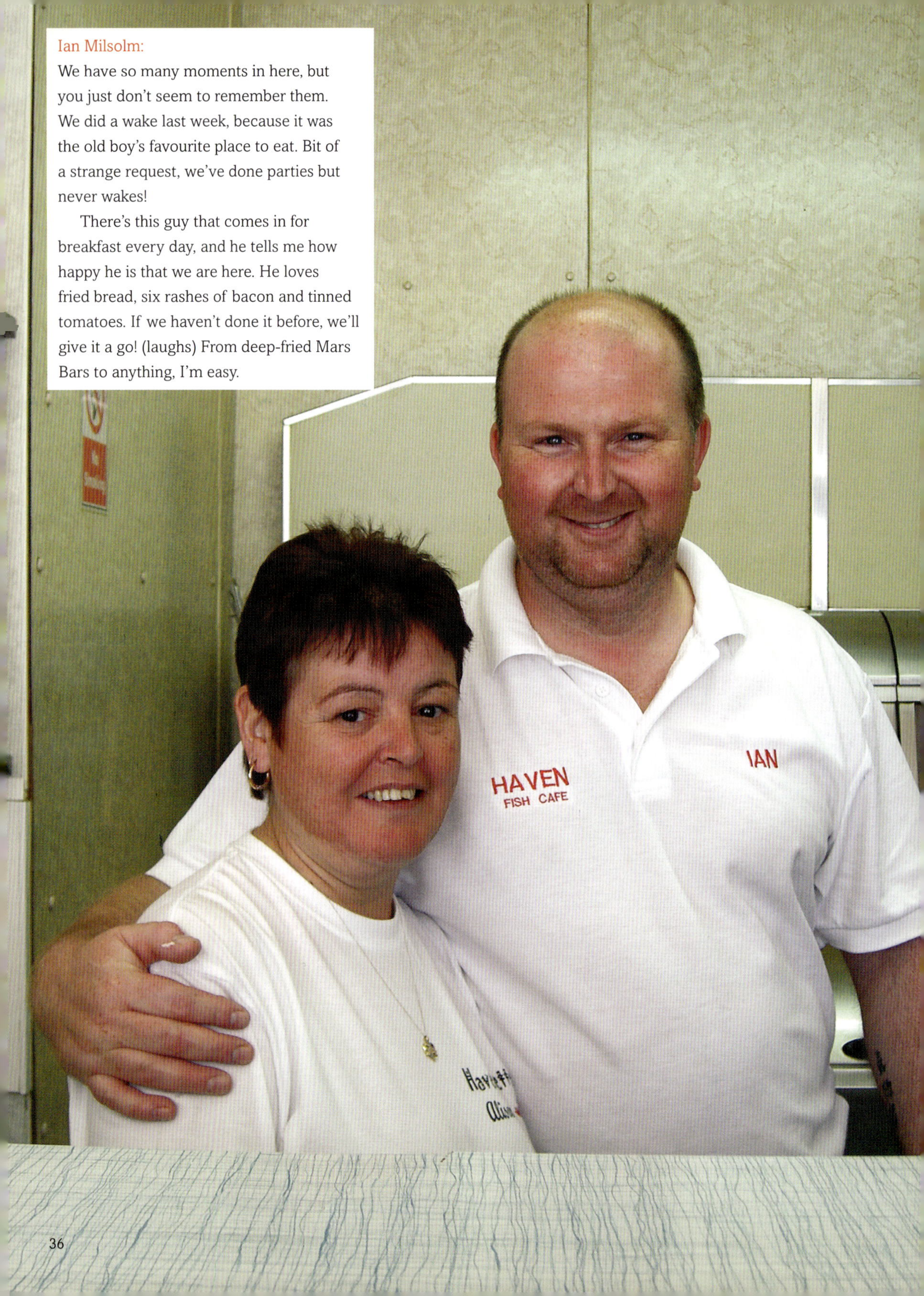

Hussein Ahmet:

The memories I have...Before I used to work 16 hours a day, from 12pm till 4am and it was hard. Can't socialise with the kids and wife. Some people think it's easy to do business but it's not. Sundays I have a rest, with family. If you don't have life with your family it's no good.

Once or twice a year you get the odd hiccup, you have a few incidents people get shot. Nothing much else goes on...

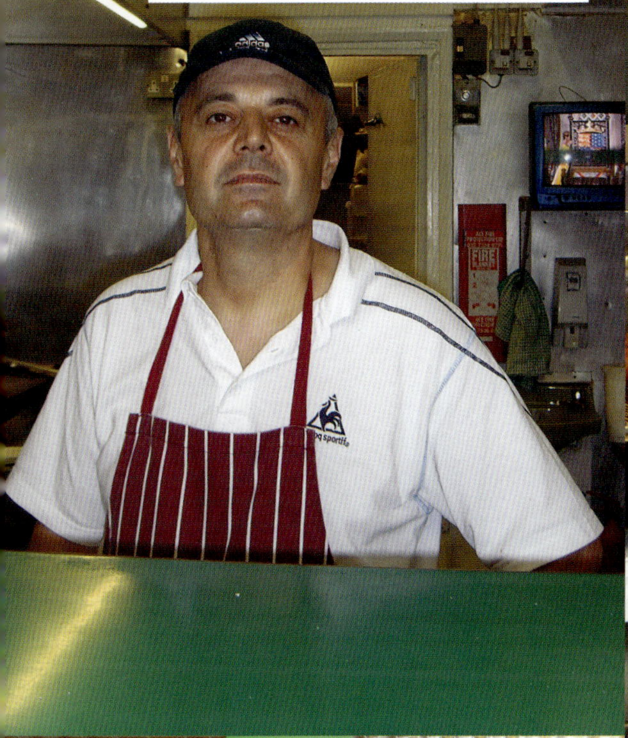

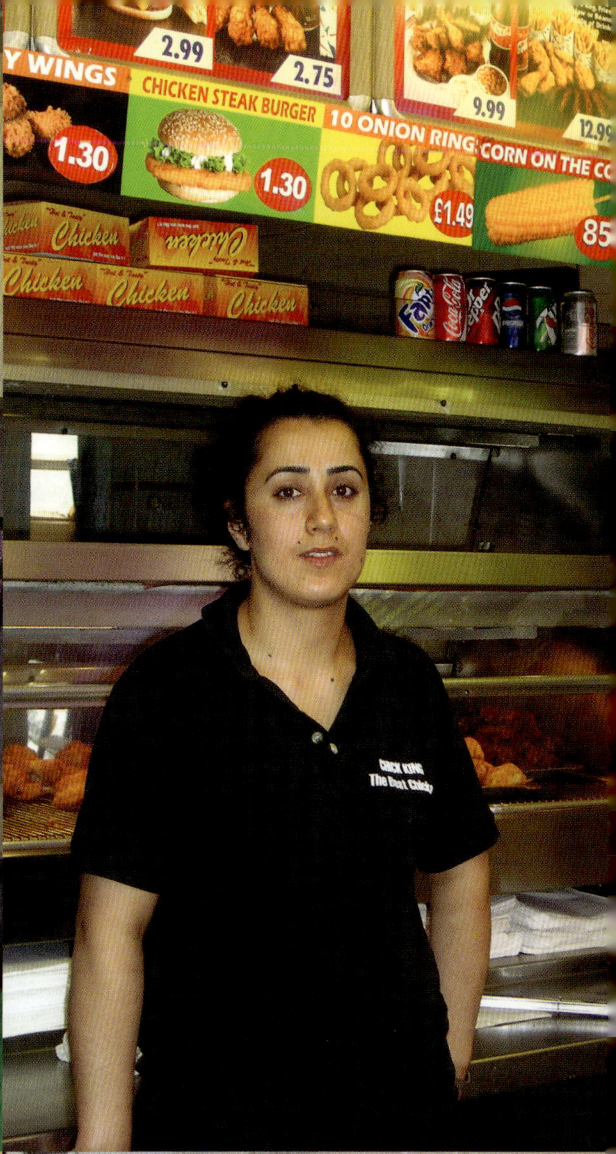

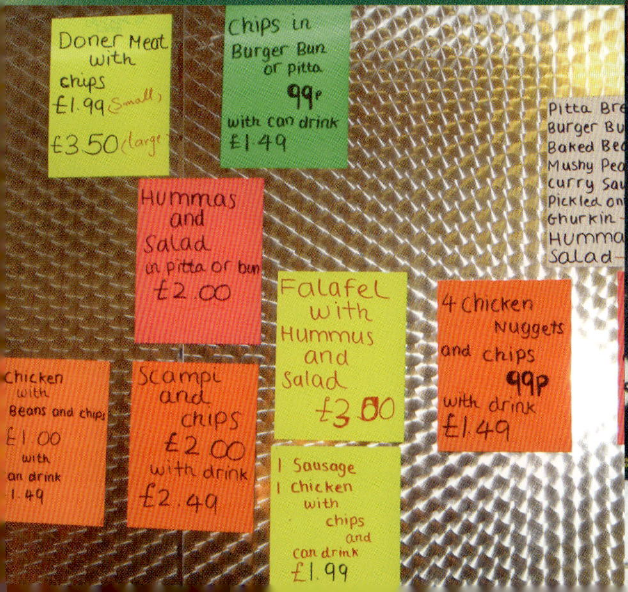

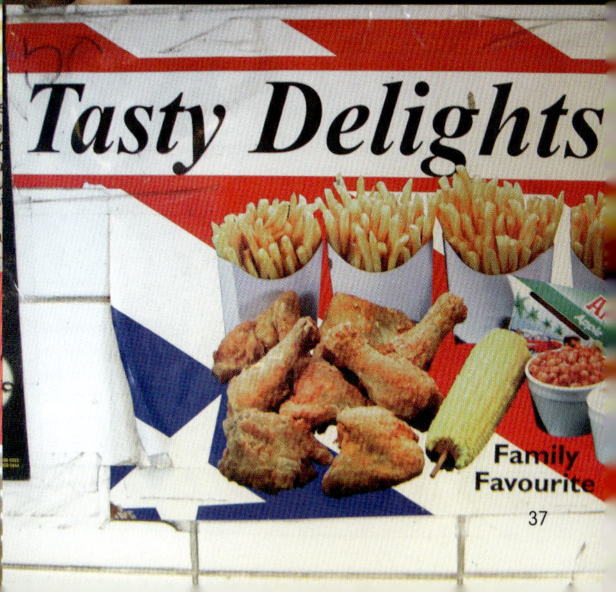

Mohammad Khalil Khan:

I always try my best....sometimes the customers come in in a bad mood and they leave smiling, and I feel very good when I can make someone happy. I don't know in which mood they are going to come to us, we don't expect everyone to come in happy.

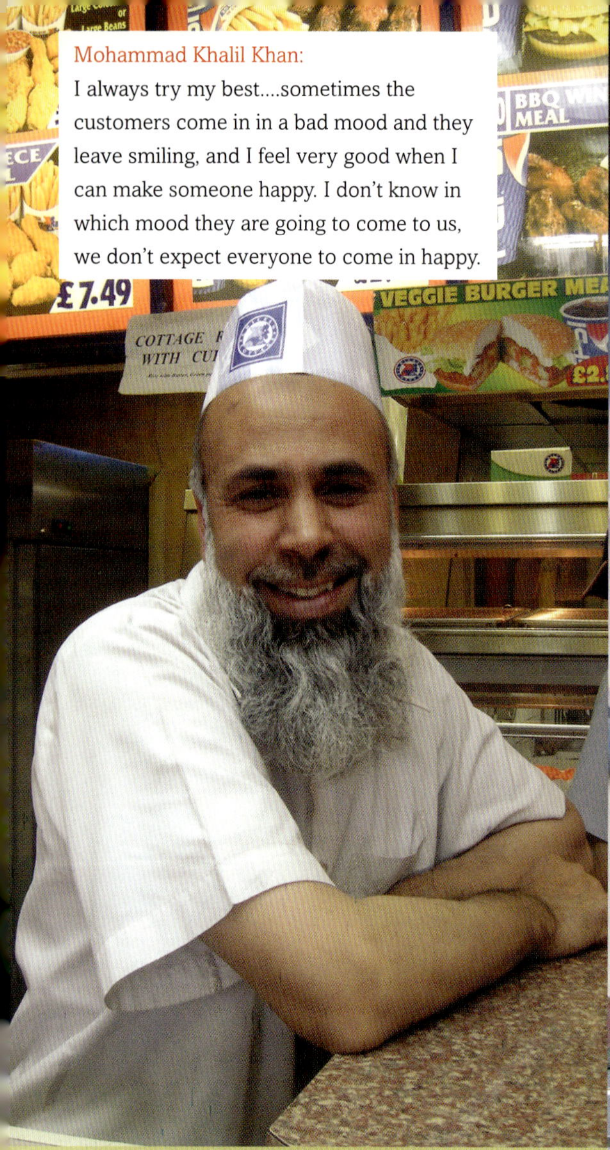

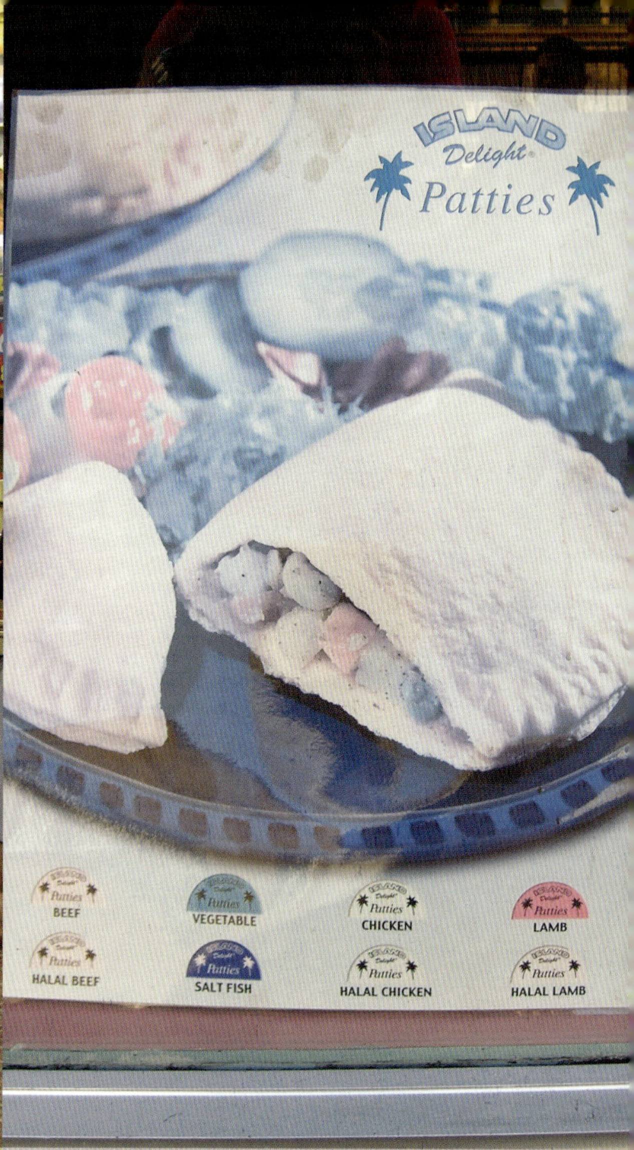

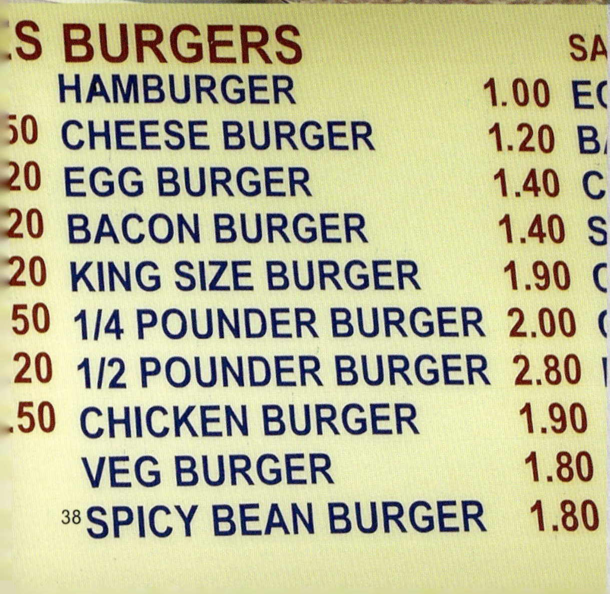

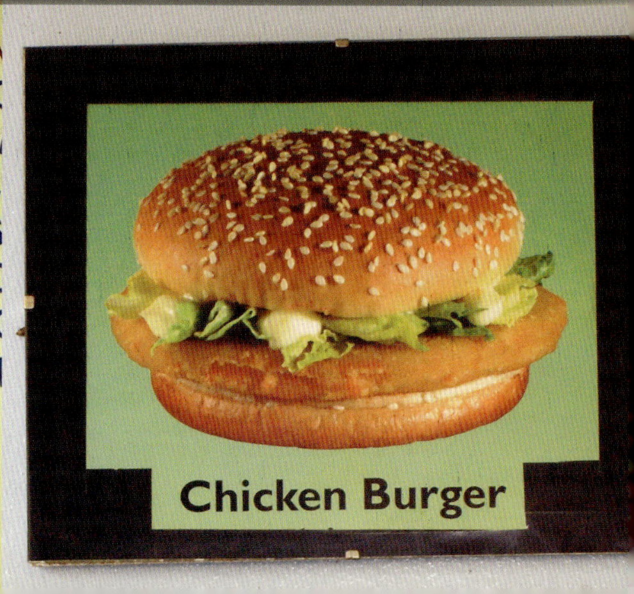

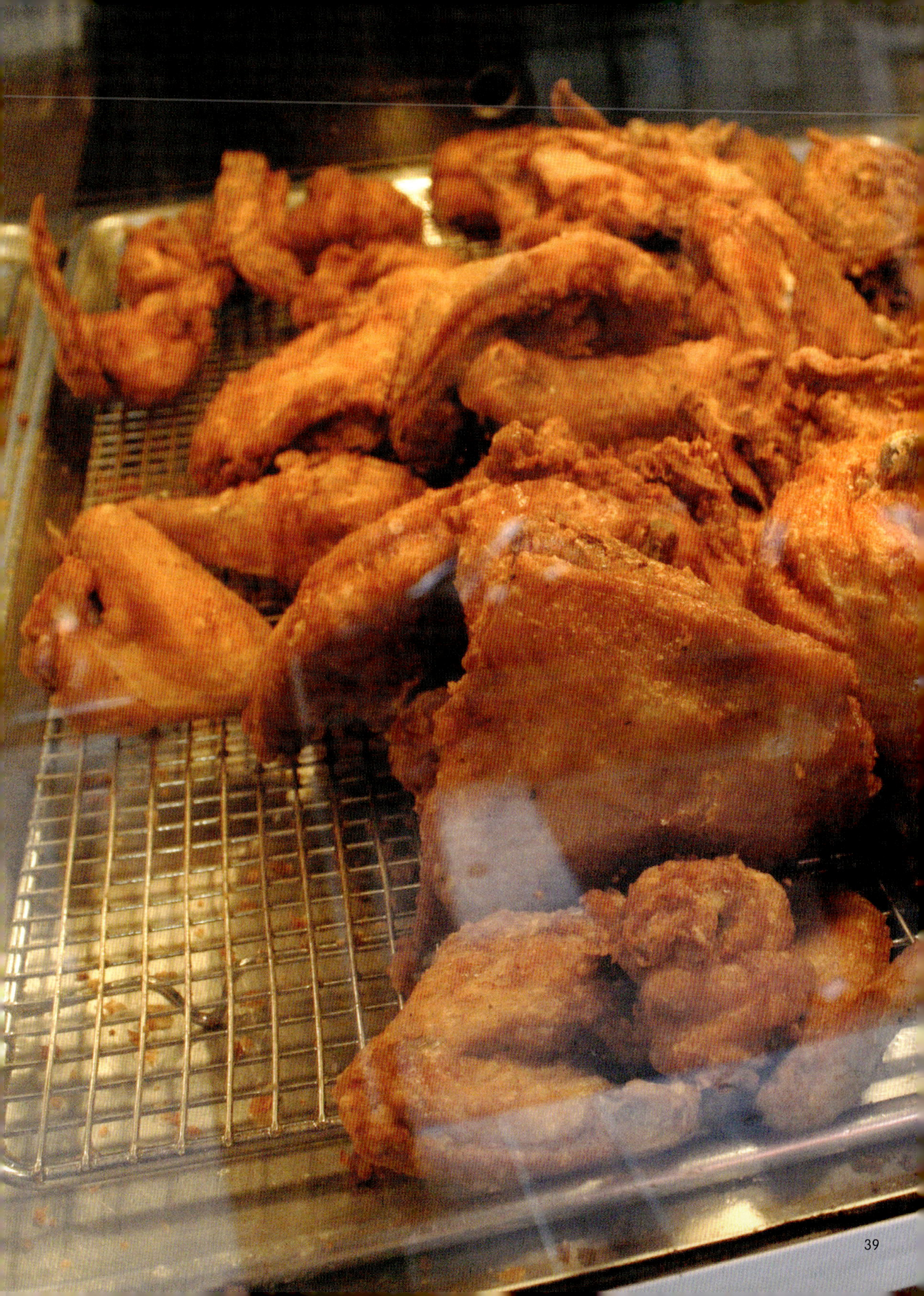

Mr Ferdousah:

If I can't eat it, I don't give to customer. When customers come in who can't speak English they just point to something, so we have fun with them. They say, "Chicken, chicken...." My future plan is business, do something nice, biggish business. Would you like something to eat or drink?

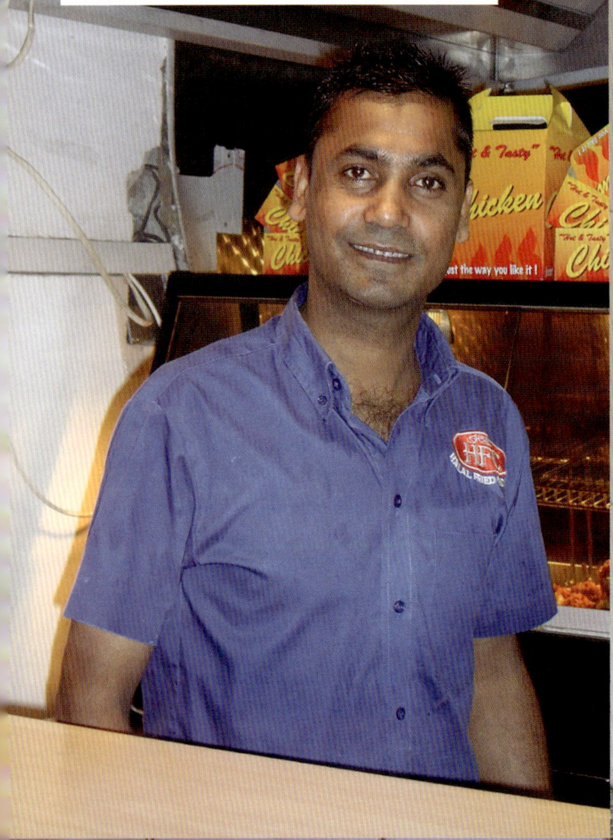

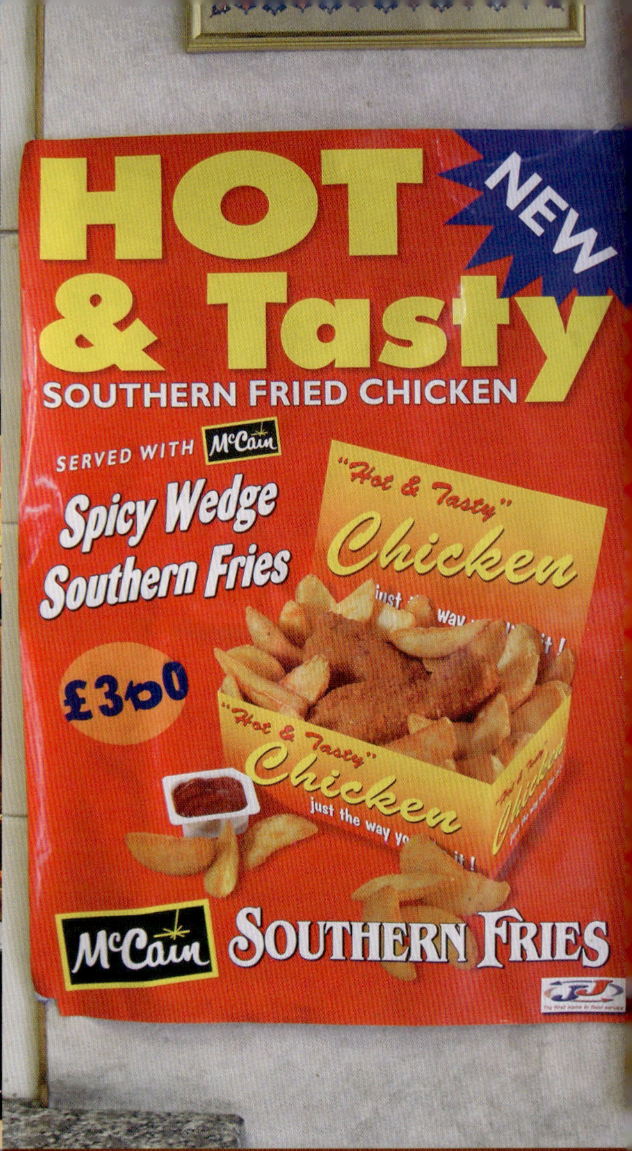

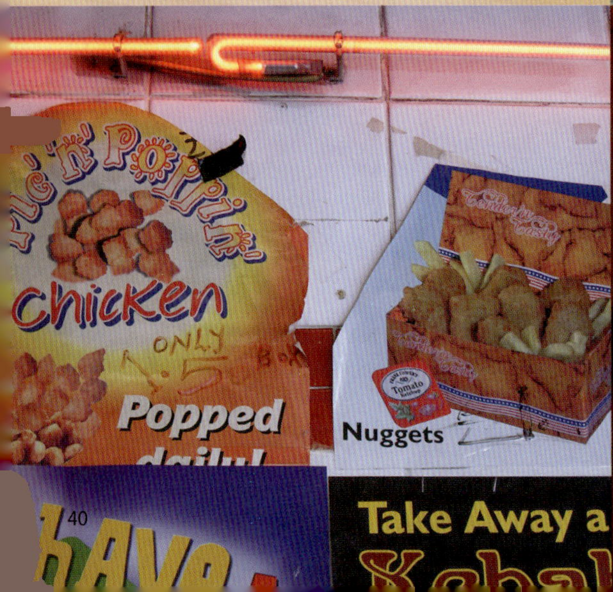

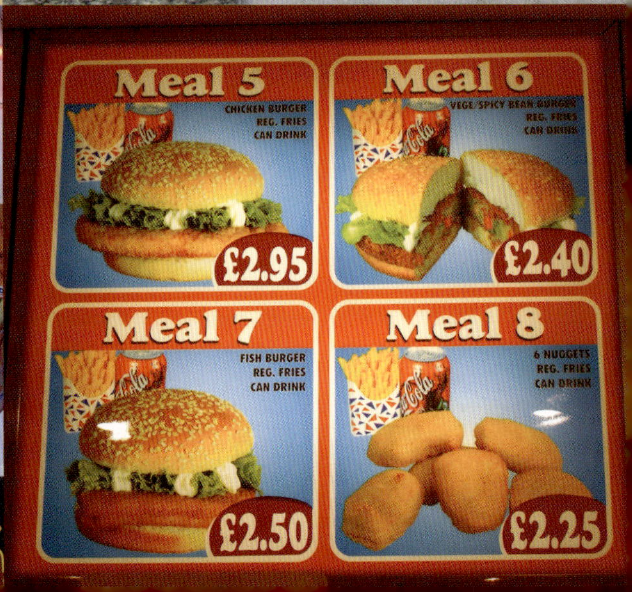

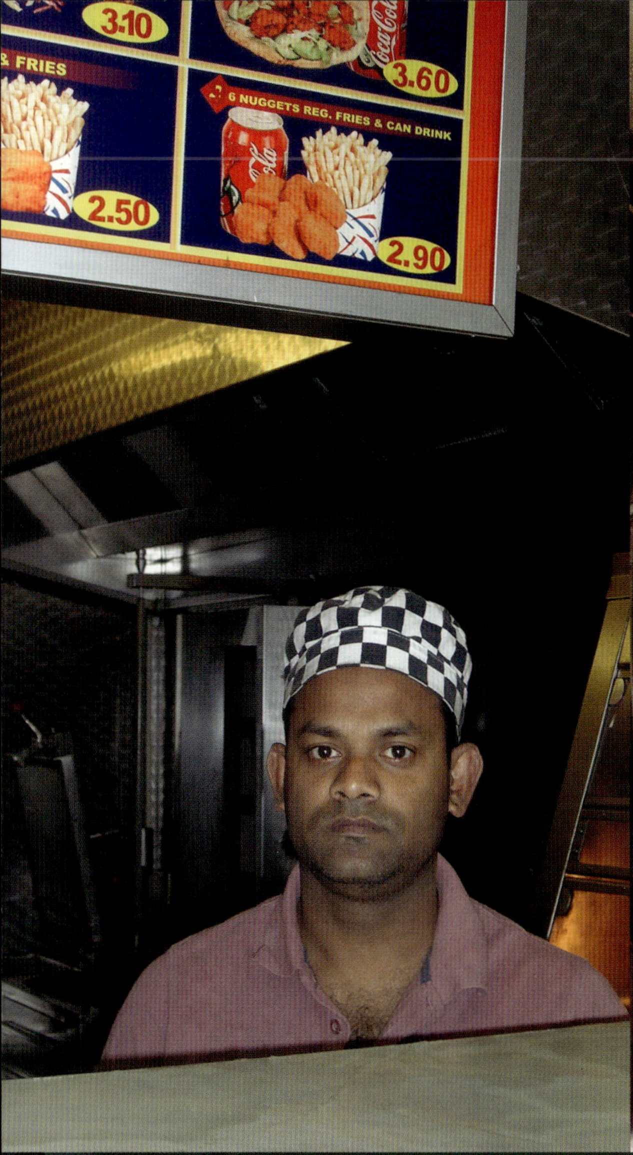
3.10
& FRIES
3.60
2.50
6 NUGGETS REG. FRIES & CAN DRINK
2.90

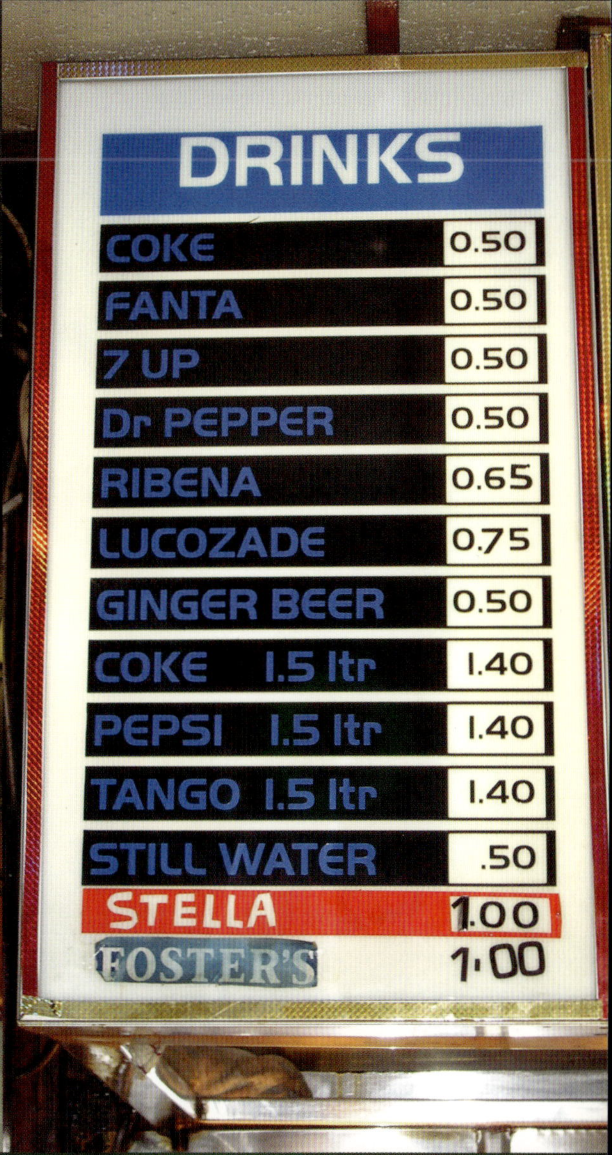
DRINKS
COKE 0.50
FANTA 0.50
7 UP 0.50
Dr PEPPER 0.50
RIBENA 0.65
LUCOZADE 0.75
GINGER BEER 0.50
COKE 1.5 ltr 1.40
PEPSI 1.5 ltr 1.40
TANGO 1.5 ltr 1.40
STILL WATER .50
STELLA 1.00
FOSTER'S 1.00

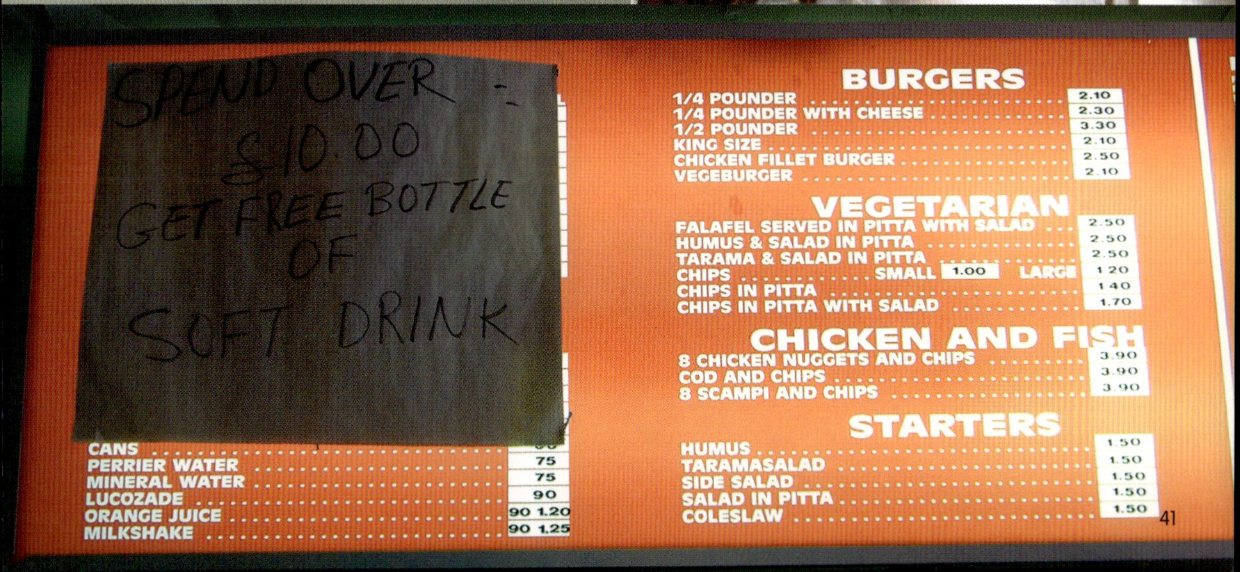
SPEND OVER £10.00 GET FREE BOTTLE OF SOFT DRINK
CANS
PERRIER WATER 75
MINERAL WATER 75
LUCOZADE 90
ORANGE JUICE 90 1.20
MILKSHAKE 90 1.25
BURGERS
1/4 POUNDER 2.10
1/4 POUNDER WITH CHEESE 2.30
1/2 POUNDER 3.30
KING SIZE 2.10
CHICKEN FILLET BURGER 2.50
VEGEBURGER 2.10
VEGETARIAN
FALAFEL SERVED IN PITTA WITH SALAD 2.50
HUMUS & SALAD IN PITTA 2.50
TARAMA & SALAD IN PITTA 2.50
CHIPS SMALL 1.00 LARGE 1.20
CHIPS IN PITTA 1.40
CHIPS IN PITTA WITH SALAD 1.70
CHICKEN AND FISH
8 CHICKEN NUGGETS AND CHIPS 3.90
COD AND CHIPS 3.90
8 SCAMPI AND CHIPS 3.90
STARTERS
HUMUS 1.50
TARAMASALAD 1.50
SIDE SALAD 1.50
SALAD IN PITTA 1.50
COLESLAW 1.50

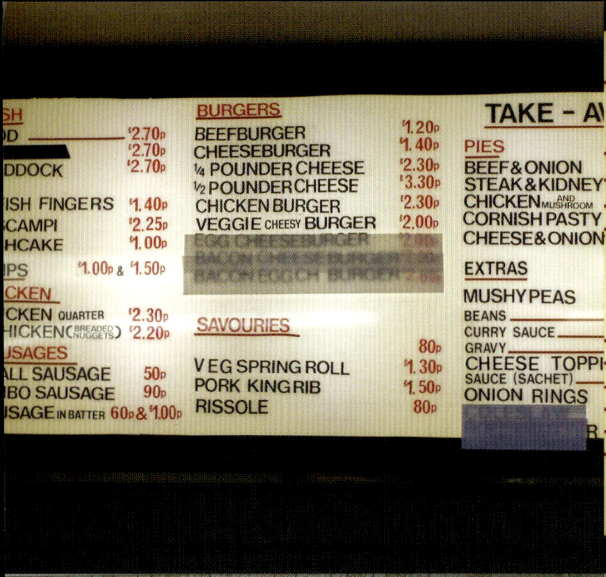
BURGERS
BEEFBURGER £1.20p
CHEESEBURGER £1.40p
¼ POUNDER CHEESE £2.30p
½ POUNDER CHEESE £3.30p
CHICKEN BURGER £2.30p
VEGGIE CHEESY BURGER £2.00p
SAVOURIES
VEG SPRING ROLL 80p
PORK KING RIB £1.30p
RISSOLE £1.50p
80p
TAKE - A
PIES
BEEF & ONION
STEAK & KIDNEY
CHICKEN AND MUSHROOM
CORNISH PASTY
CHEESE & ONION
EXTRAS
MUSHY PEAS
BEANS
CURRY SAUCE
GRAVY
CHEESE TOPPI
SAUCE (SACHET)
ONION RINGS

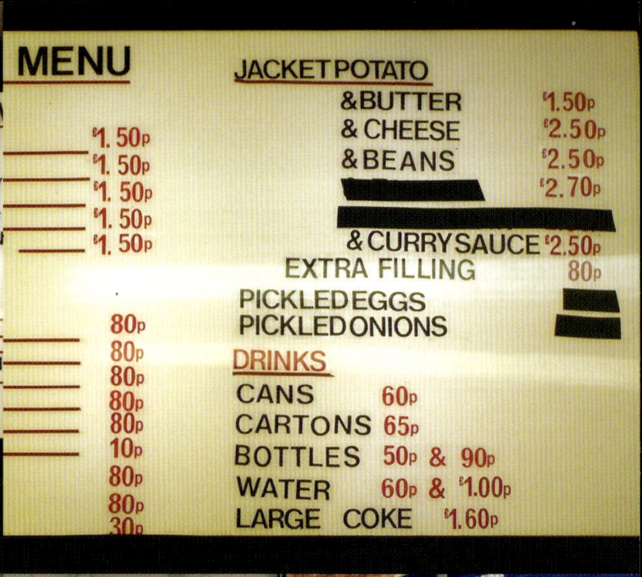
MENU
£1. 50p
£1. 50p
£1. 50p
£1. 50p
£1. 50p
JACKET POTATO
& BUTTER £1.50p
& CHEESE £2.50p
& BEANS £2.50p
£2.70p
& CURRY SAUCE £2.50p
EXTRA FILLING 80p
PICKLED EGGS
PICKLED ONIONS
DRINKS
CANS 60p
CARTONS 65p
BOTTLES 50p & 90p
WATER 60p & £1.00p
LARGE COKE £1.60p

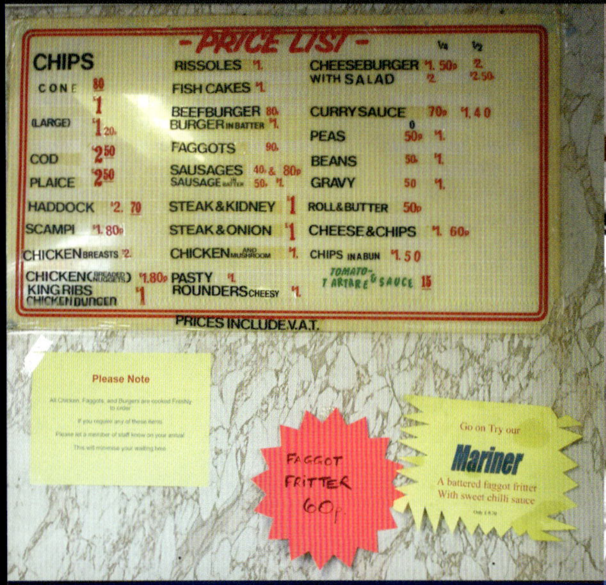
- PRICE LIST -
CHIPS
RISSOLES
FISH CAKES
BEEFBURGER
BURGER IN BATTER
FAGGOTS
SAUSAGES
COD
PLAICE
HADDOCK
SCAMPI
STEAK & KIDNEY
STEAK & ONION
CHICKEN
PASTY
ROUNDERS CHEESY
CHEESEBURGER WITH SALAD
CURRY SAUCE
PEAS
BEANS
GRAVY
ROLL & BUTTER
CHEESE & CHIPS
CHIPS IN A BUN
TOMATO-TARTARE SAUCE
PRICES INCLUDE V.A.T.
Please Note
FAGGOT FRITTER 60p
Go on Try our
Mariner
A battered faggot fritter
With sweet chilli sauce

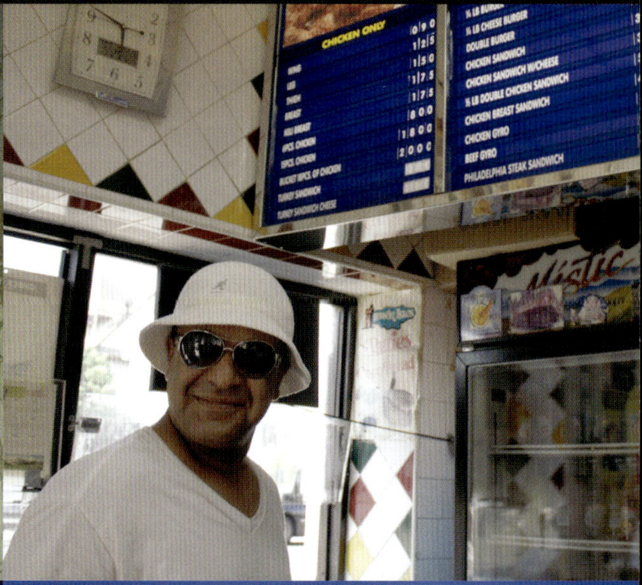

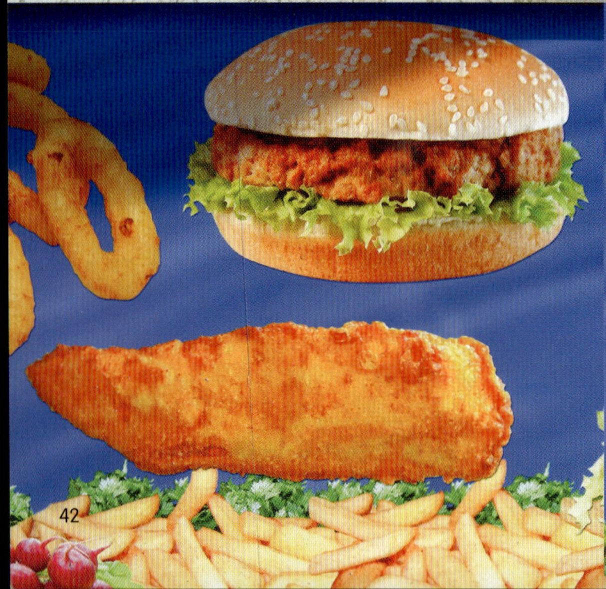

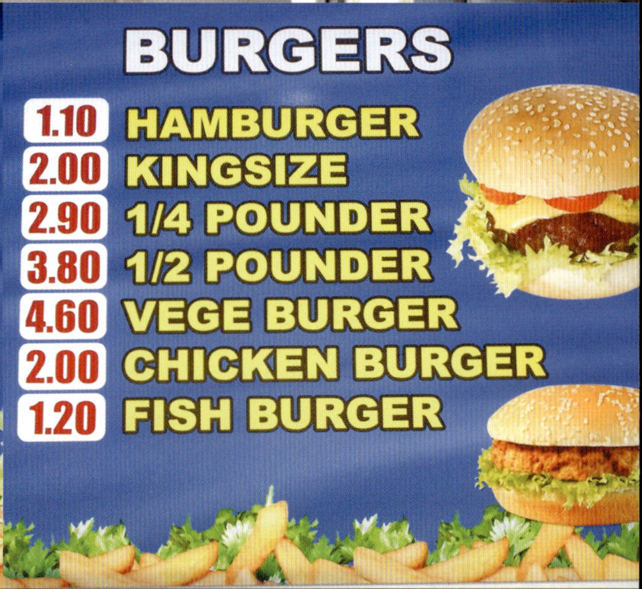
BURGERS
1.10 HAMBURGER
2.00 KINGSIZE
2.90 1/4 POUNDER
3.80 1/2 POUNDER
4.60 VEGE BURGER
2.00 CHICKEN BURGER
1.20 FISH BURGER

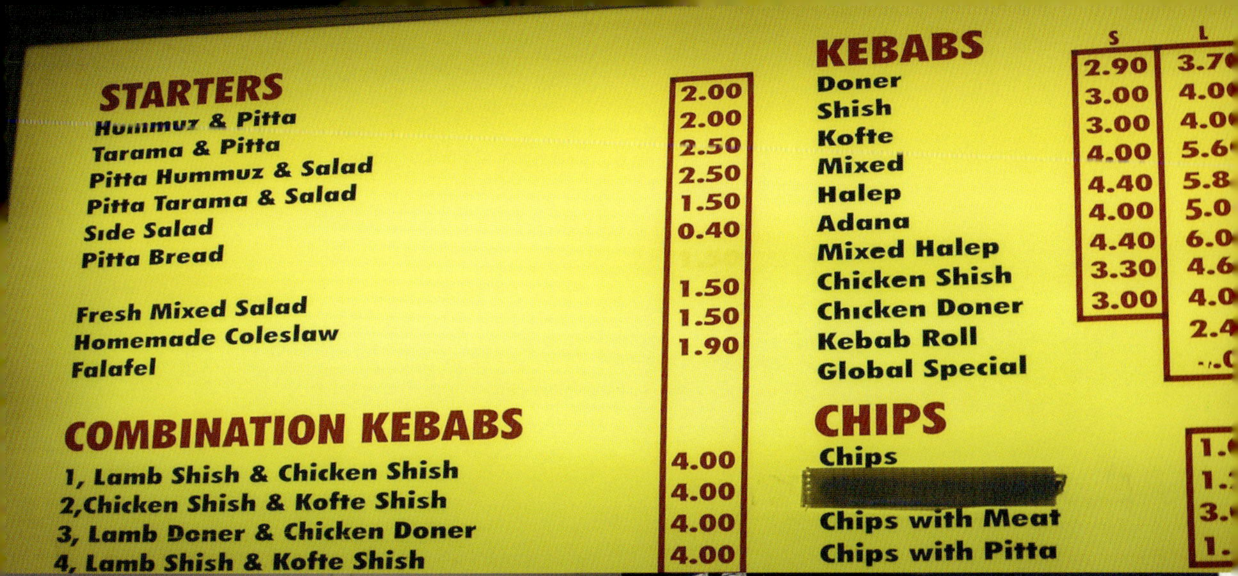
STARTERS
Hummuz & Pitta 2.00
Tarama & Pitta 2.00
Pitta Hummuz & Salad 2.50
Pitta Tarama & Salad 2.50
Side Salad 1.50
Pitta Bread 0.40
Fresh Mixed Salad 1.50
Homemade Coleslaw 1.50
Falafel 1.90
COMBINATION KEBABS
1, Lamb Shish & Chicken Shish 4.00
2,Chicken Shish & Kofte Shish 4.00
3, Lamb Doner & Chicken Doner 4.00
4, Lamb Shish & Kofte Shish 4.00
KEBABS
S L
Doner 2.90
Shish 3.00
Kofte 3.00
Mixed 4.00
Halep 4.40
Adana 4.00
Mixed Halep 4.40
Chicken Shish 3.30
Chicken Doner 3.00
Kebab Roll
Global Special
CHIPS
Chips
Chips with Meat
Chips with Pitta
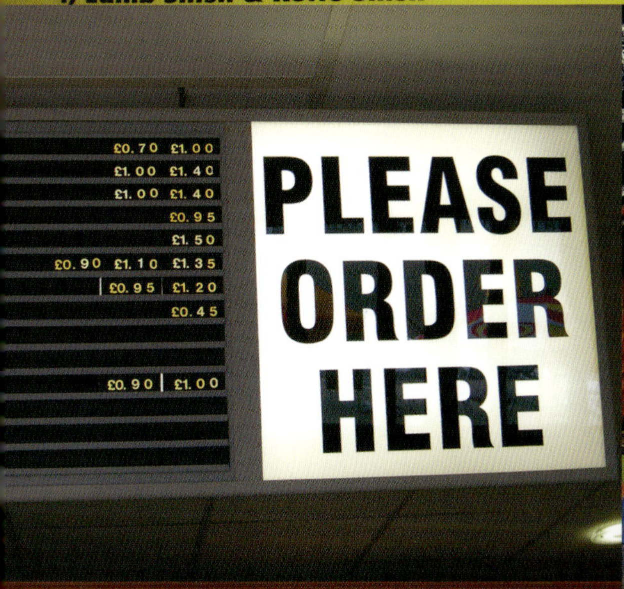
£0.70 £1.00
£1.00 £1.40
£1.00 £1.40
£0.95
£1.50
£0.90 £1.10 £1.35
£0.95 £1.20
£0.45
£0.90 £1.00
PLEASE ORDER HERE
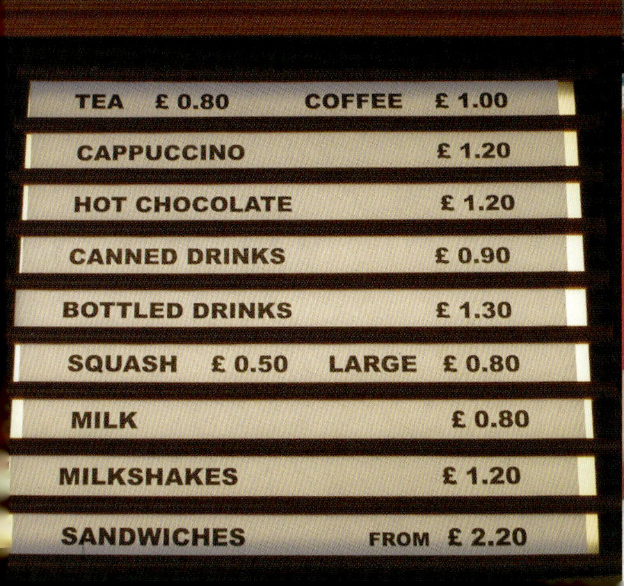
TEA £ 0.80 COFFEE £ 1.00
CAPPUCCINO £ 1.20
HOT CHOCOLATE £ 1.20
CANNED DRINKS £ 0.90
BOTTLED DRINKS £ 1.30
SQUASH £ 0.50 LARGE £ 0.80
MILK £ 0.80
MILKSHAKES £ 1.20
SANDWICHES FROM £ 2.20
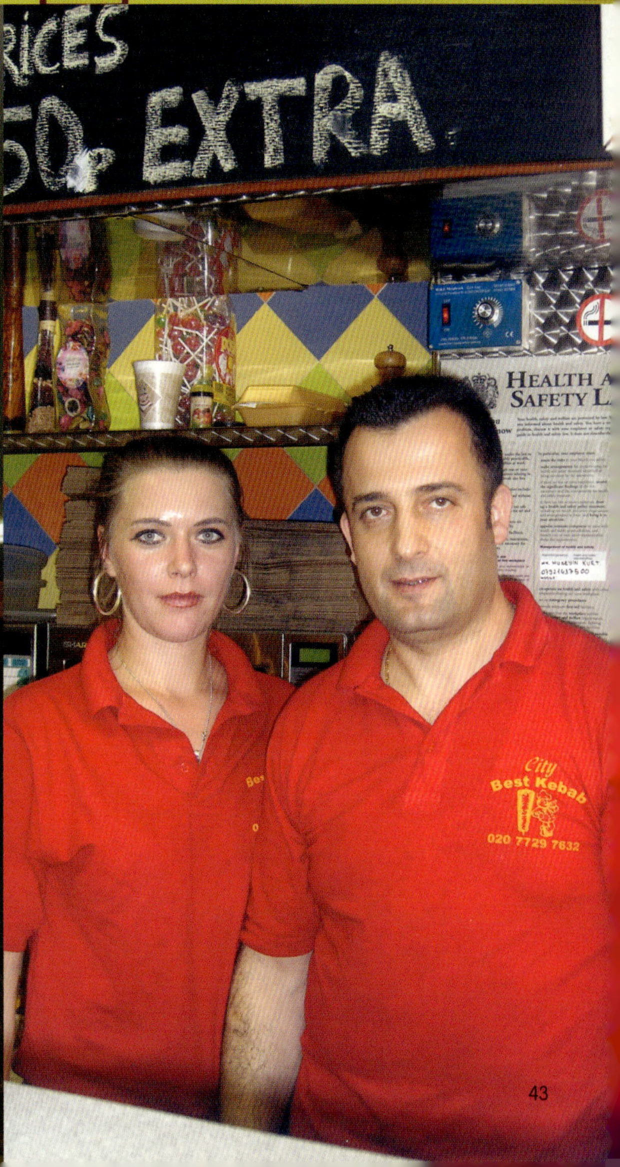
50p EXTRA
HEALTH A
SAFETY L
City
Best Kebab
020 7729 7632

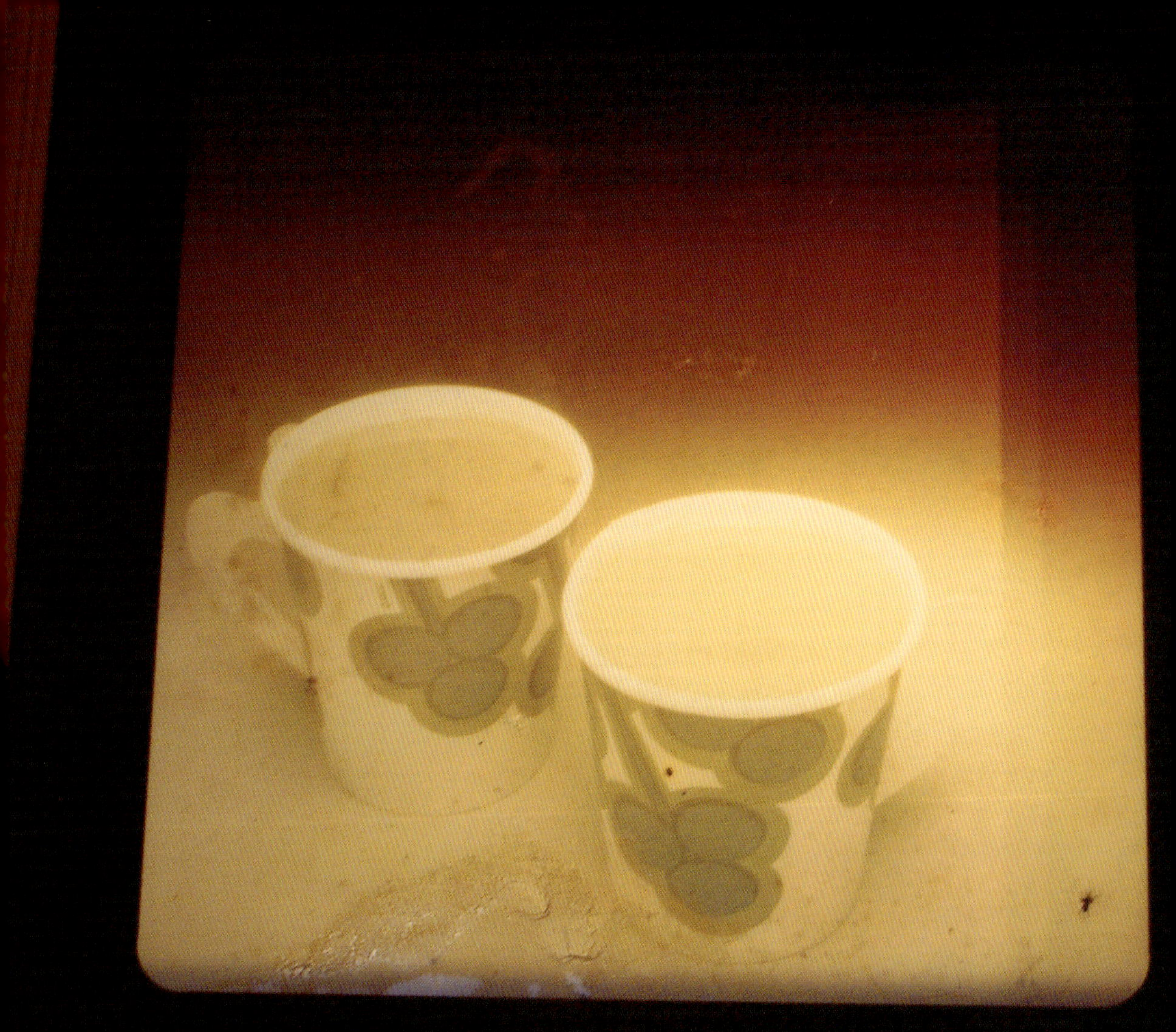

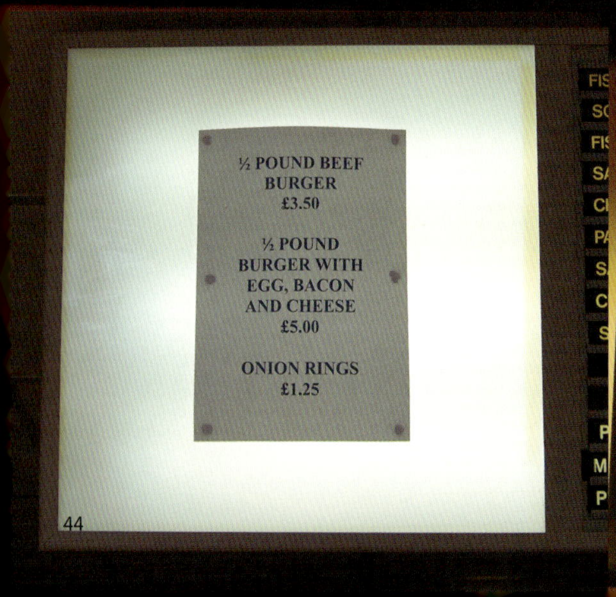
½ POUND BEEF
BURGER
£3.50
½ POUND
BURGER WITH
EGG, BACON
AND CHEESE
£5.00
ONION RINGS
£1.25

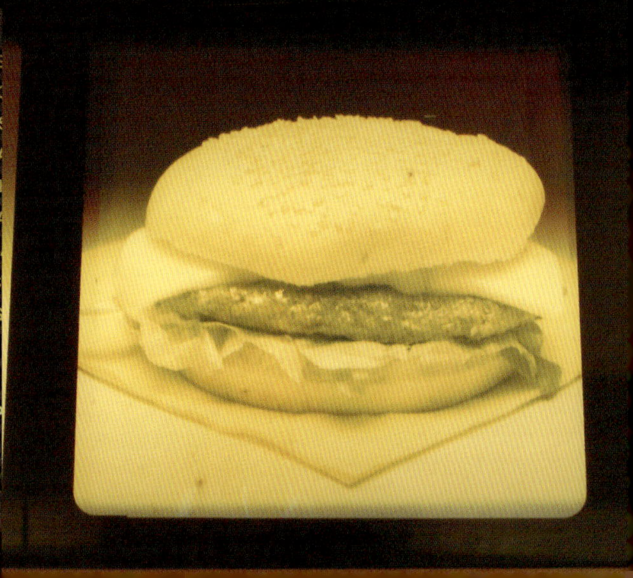

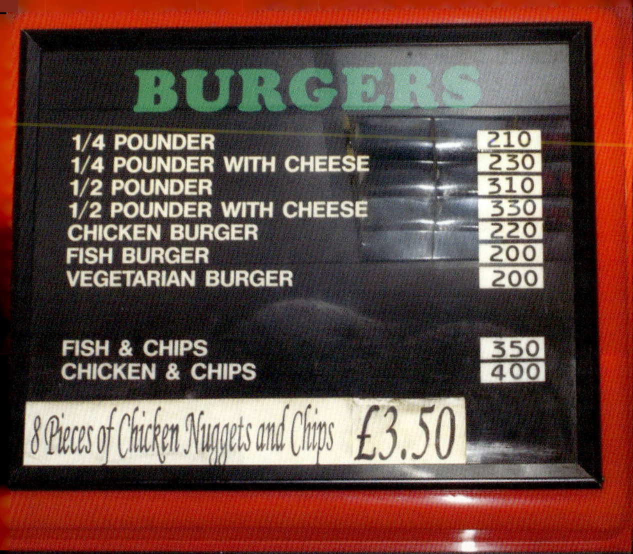
BURGERS
1/4 POUNDER 210
1/4 POUNDER WITH CHEESE 230
1/2 POUNDER 310
1/2 POUNDER WITH CHEESE 330
CHICKEN BURGER 220
FISH BURGER 200
VEGETARIAN BURGER 200
FISH & CHIPS 350
CHICKEN & CHIPS 400
8 Pieces of Chicken Nuggets and Chips £3.50

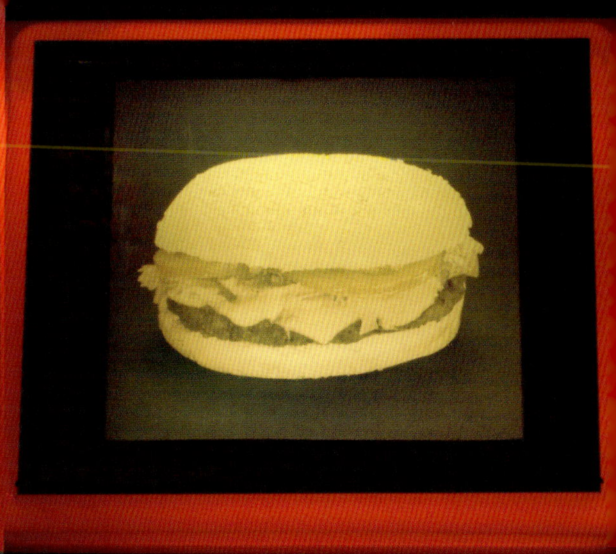

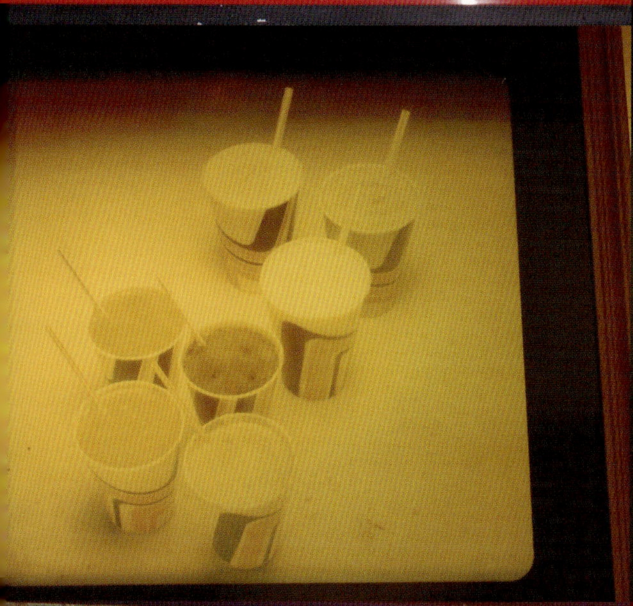

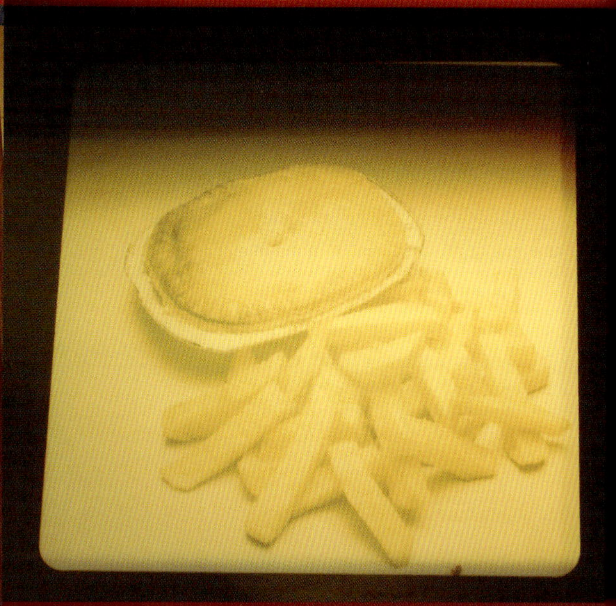

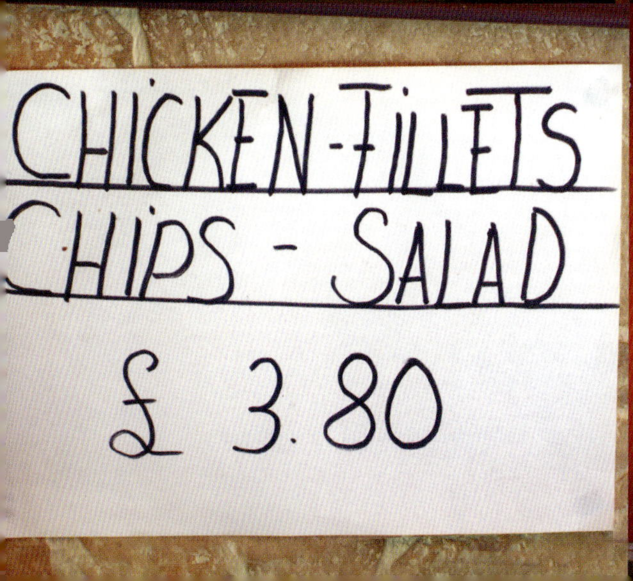
CHICKEN-FILLETS
CHIPS - SALAD
£ 3.80

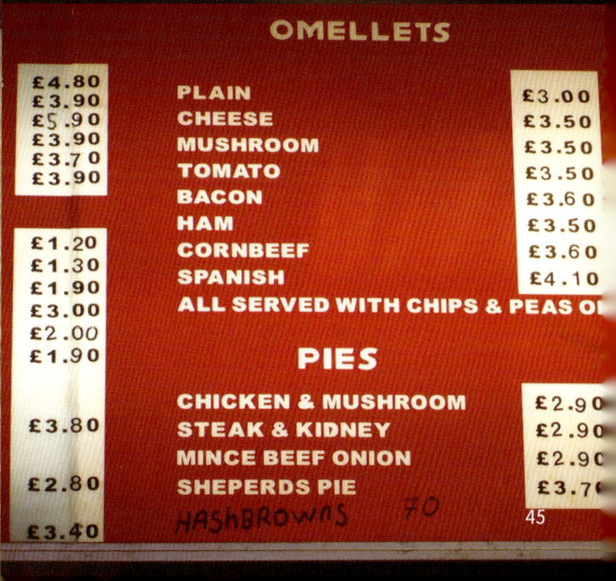
OMELLETS
£4.80
£3.90
£5.90
£3.90
£3.70
£3.90
PLAIN £3.00
CHEESE £3.50
MUSHROOM £3.50
TOMATO £3.50
BACON £3.60
HAM £3.50
CORNBEEF £3.60
SPANISH £4.10
£1.20
£1.30
£1.90
£3.00
£2.00
£1.90
ALL SERVED WITH CHIPS & PEAS
PIES
CHICKEN & MUSHROOM
STEAK & KIDNEY
MINCE BEEF ONION
SHEPERDS PIE
£3.80
£2.80
£3.40
HASHBROWNS 70

Yousef Sardaneh:

I was more happy four years ago than now. Ten years ago I was more happy than four years ago. I felt very good in that time, now we're struggling paying bills. Our life is a story, people taking drugs, smashing windows. One day about four years ago, one of our good customers came in. He ordered food, and then went next door to the other kebab shop, and because he had drugs he smashed all the windows and fridge. He came back in here and thought we'd hit him, so he started to break all the glass. He even put his head on the counter and said, "Cut my head, cut my head." After two weeks he came back in to apologise and said his friends had spiked his drink with drugs.

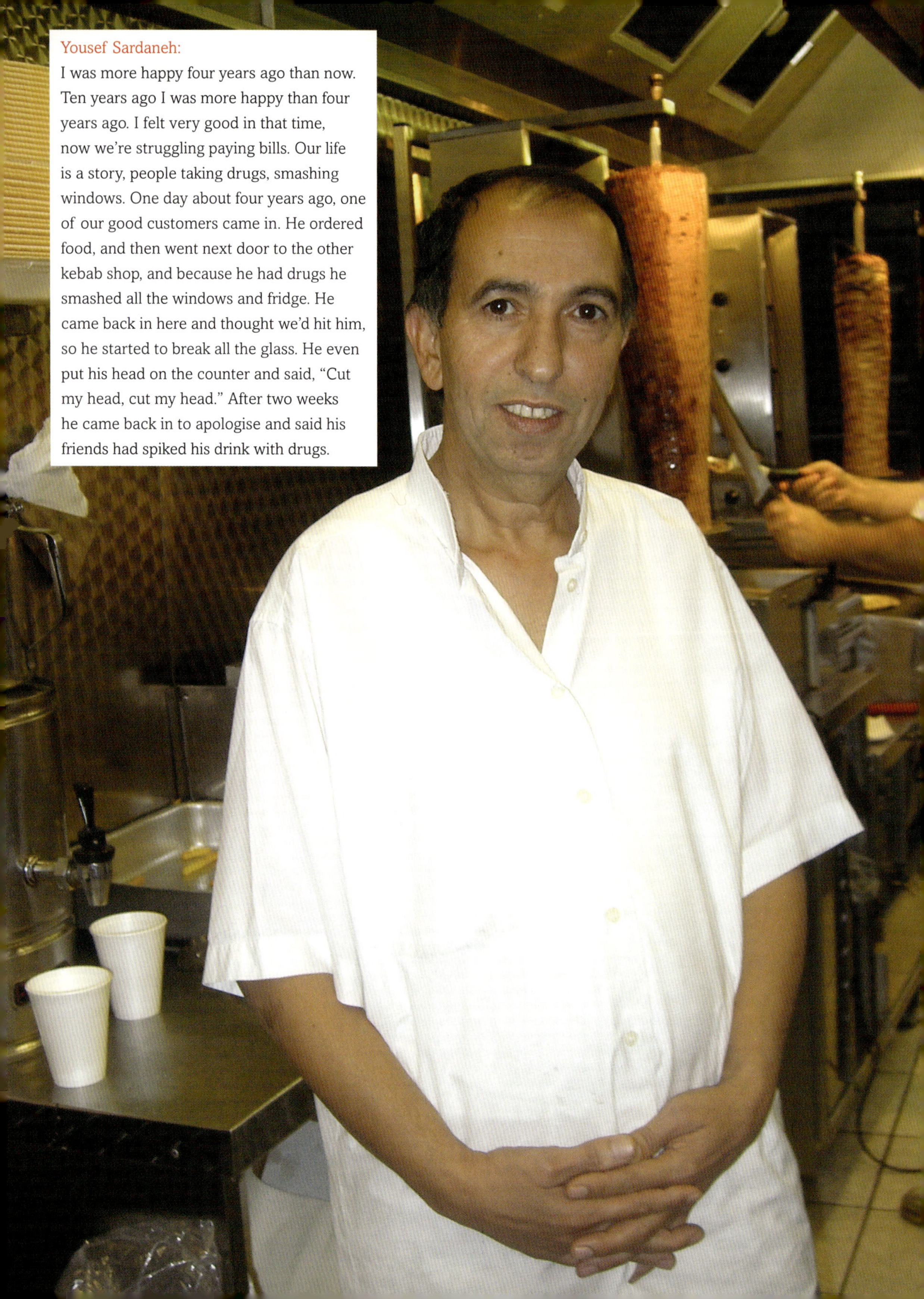

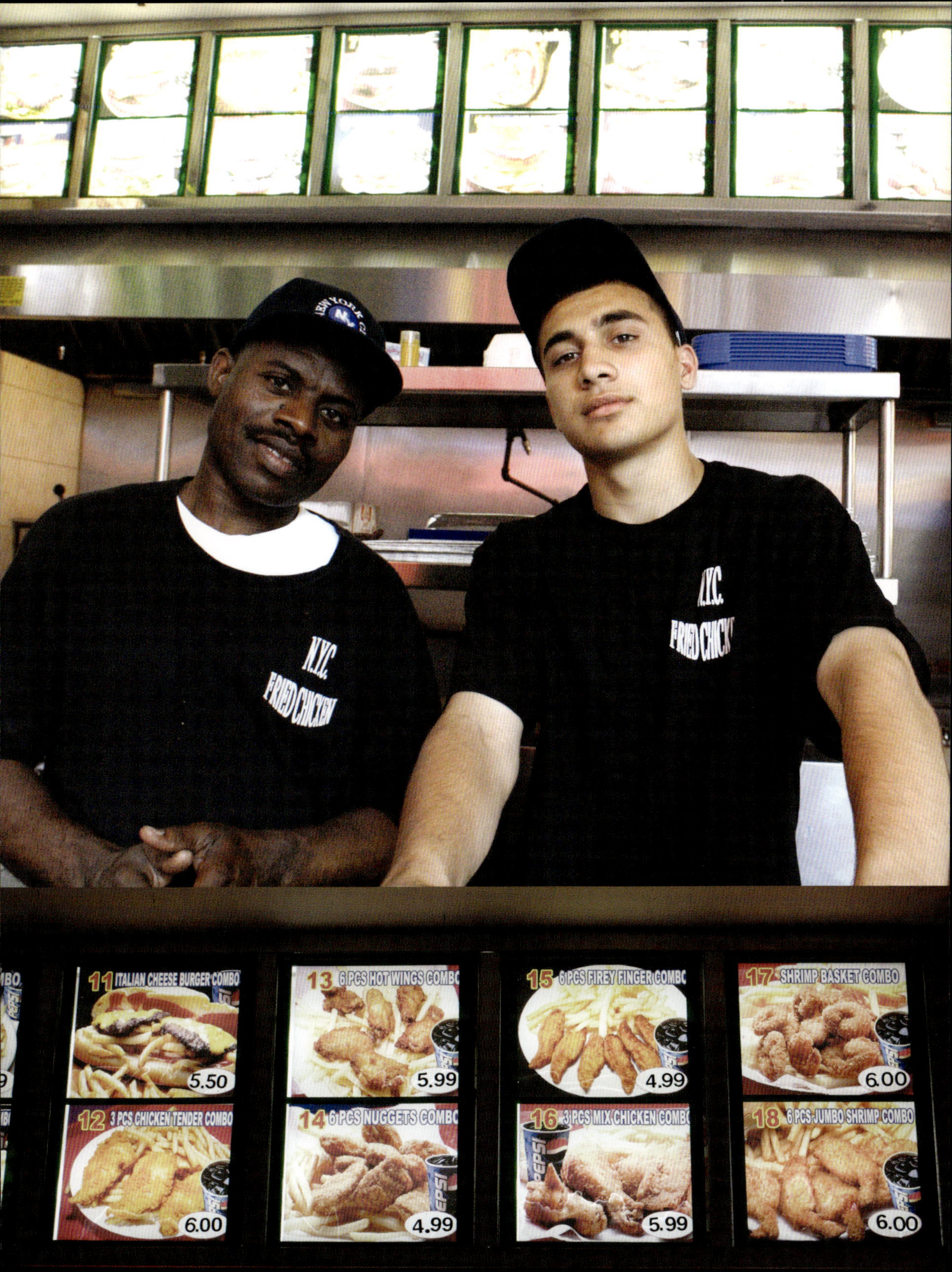
N.Y.C.
FRIED CHICKEN
11 ITALIAN CHEESE BURGER COMBO
5.50
13 6 PCS HOT WINGS COMBO
5.99
15 6 PCS FIREY FINGER COMBO
4.99
17 SHRIMP BASKET COMBO
6.00
12 3 PCS CHICKEN TENDER COMBO
6.00
14 6 PCS NUGGETS COMBO
4.99
16 3 PCS MIX CHICKEN COMBO
5.99
18 6 PCS JUMBO SHRIMP COMBO
6.00

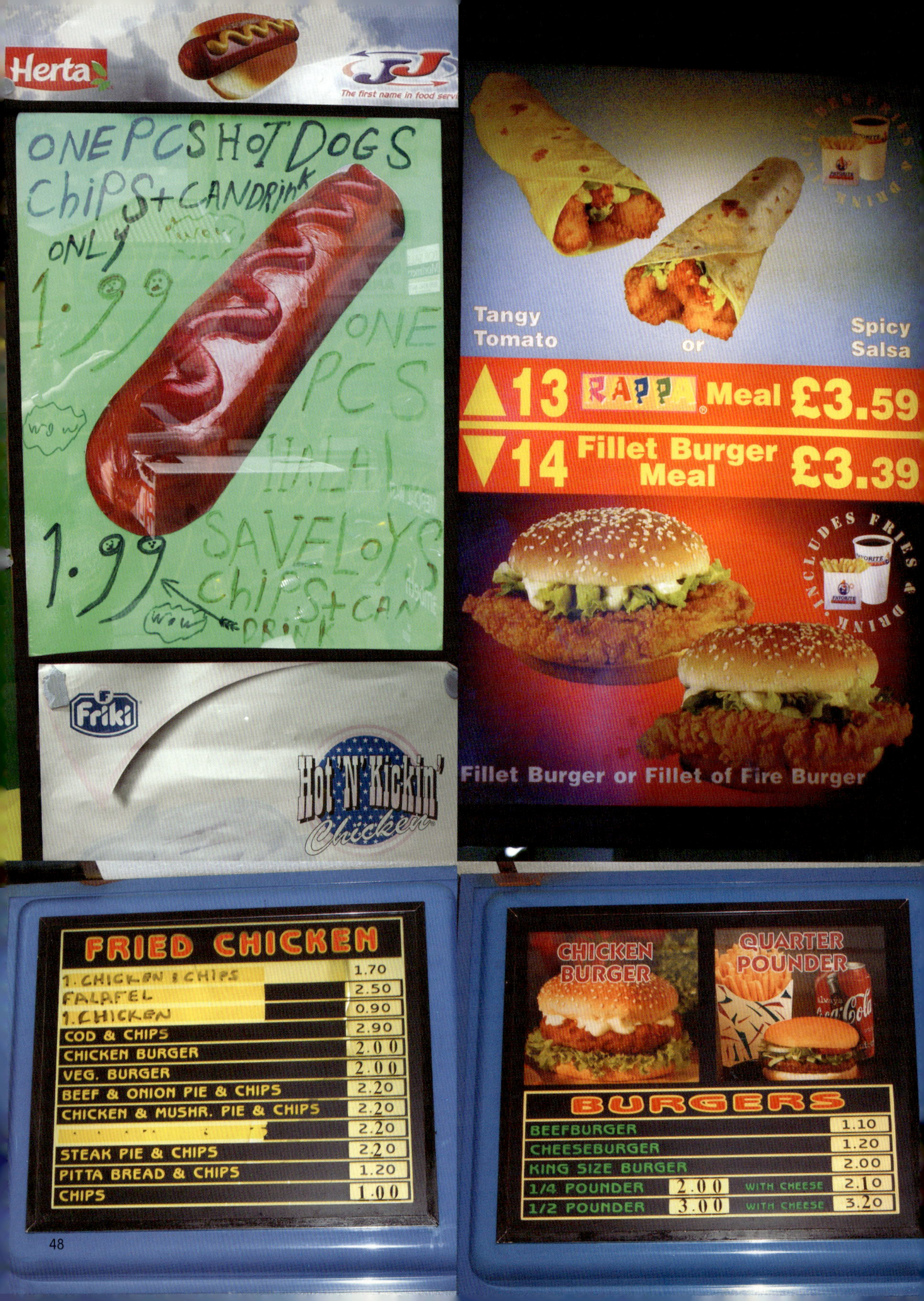
Herta
The first name in food servi
ONE PCS HOT DOGS
ChiPS + CANDRink
ONLY
1.99
ONE PCS HALAL SAVELOYS ChiPS + CAN DRINK
1.99
WOW
Friki
Hot 'N' Kickin' Chicken
Tangy Tomato
or
Spicy Salsa
13 RAPPA Meal £3.59
14 Fillet Burger Meal £3.39
INCLUDES FRIES & DRINK
Fillet Burger or Fillet of Fire Burger
FRIED CHICKEN
1. CHICKEN & CHIPS 1.70
FALAFEL 2.50
1. CHICKEN 0.90
COD & CHIPS 2.90
CHICKEN BURGER 2.00
VEG. BURGER 2.00
BEEF & ONION PIE & CHIPS 2.20
CHICKEN & MUSHR. PIE & CHIPS 2.20
2.20
STEAK PIE & CHIPS 2.20
PITTA BREAD & CHIPS 1.20
CHIPS 1.00
CHICKEN BURGER
QUARTER POUNDER
BURGERS
BEEFBURGER 1.10
CHEESEBURGER 1.20
KING SIZE BURGER 2.00
1/4 POUNDER 2.00 WITH CHEESE 2.10
1/2 POUNDER 3.00 WITH CHEESE 3.20

Rashid Rafiuqe Khan:

I work here part-time; I'm a self-employed painter and decorator. My boss is a brave man, he's working mostly night-time. One customer jumped over the counter and attacked him with a stool cutting his head. Would you like something to eat, drink?

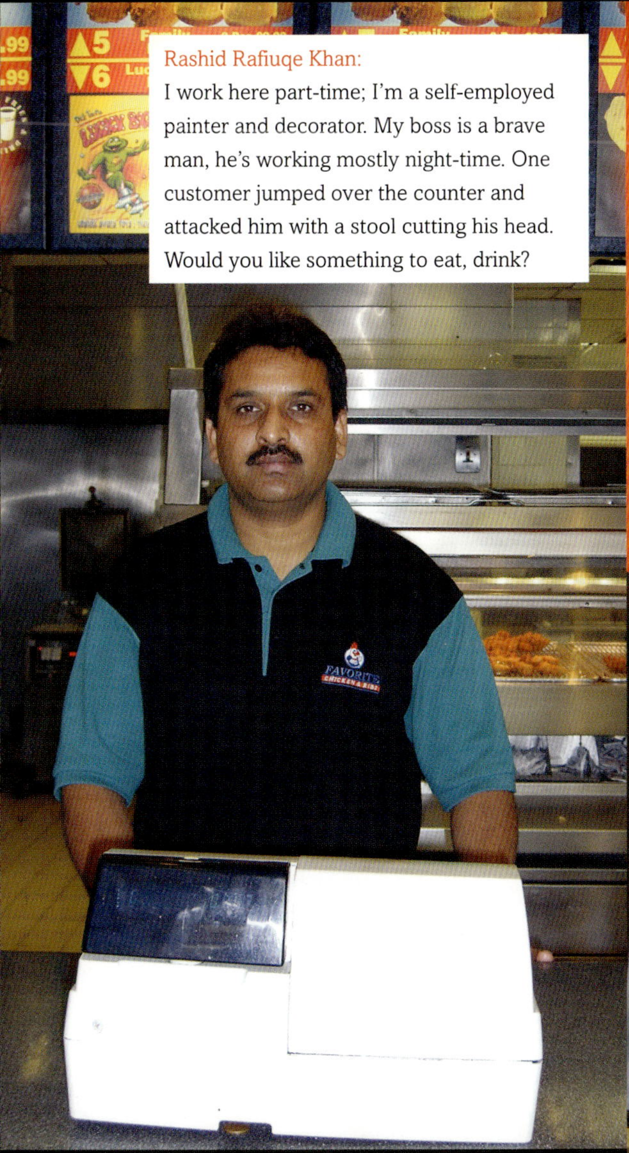

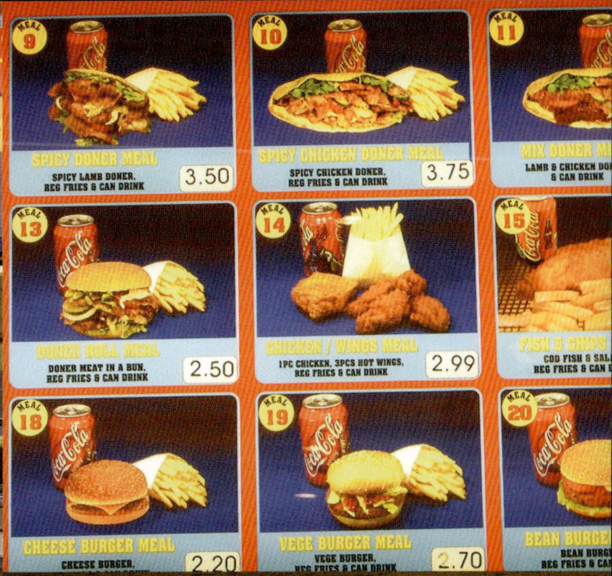

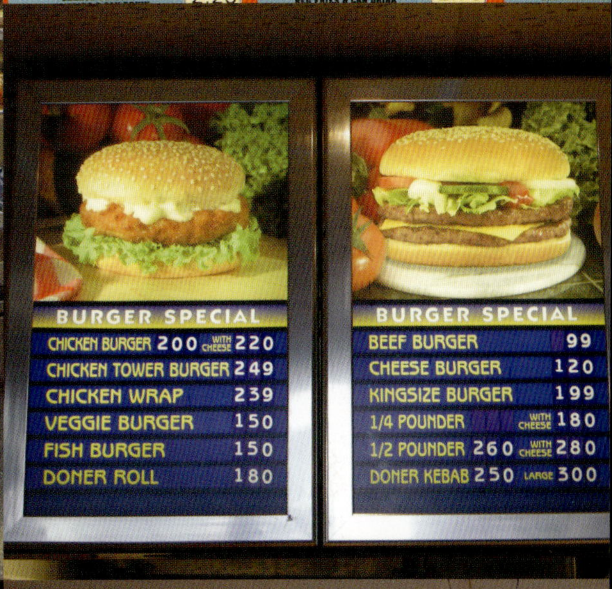

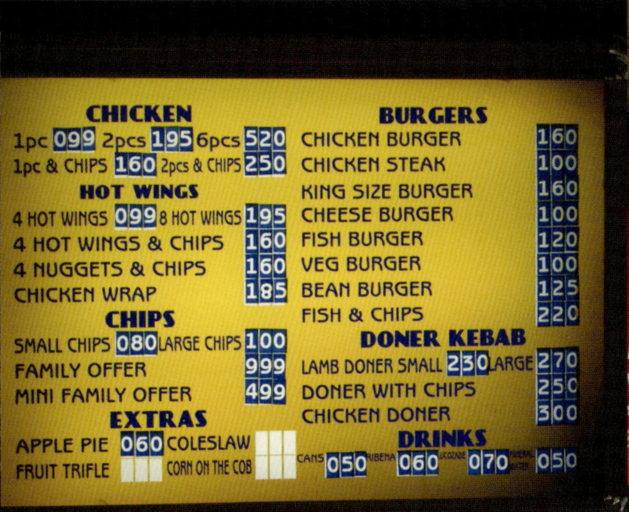

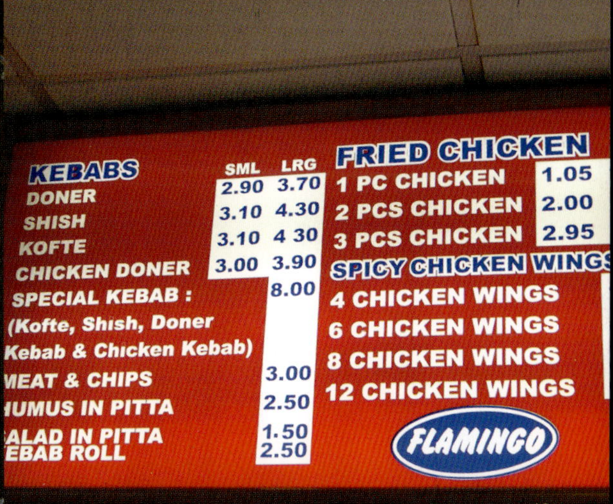

Muhayamin Karim:

The customers don't give you the chance to repeat the food order again, so you have to click it in your mind and serve it properly and nicely. Because there's lots of sauces like mayonnaise, ketchup, vinegar. Some people don't want mayonnaise, some people don't want ketchup and stuff y'know so lots of critical things to remember.

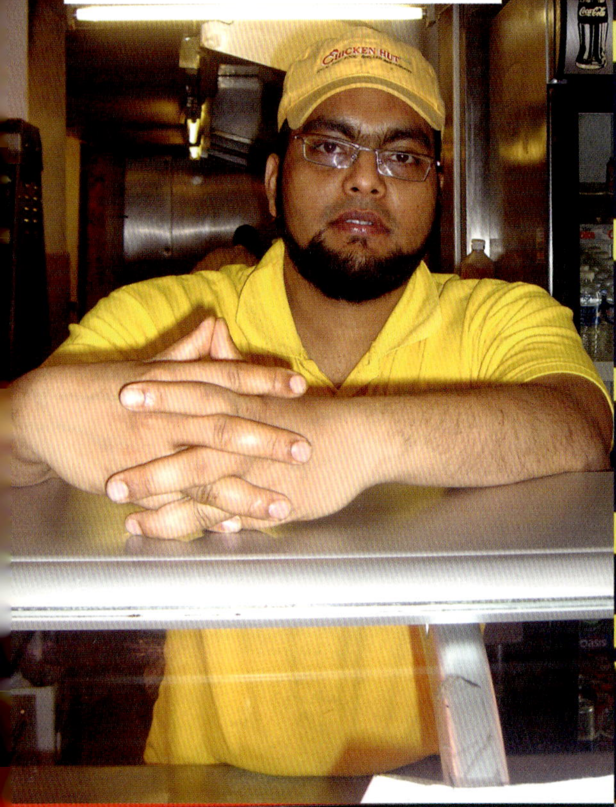

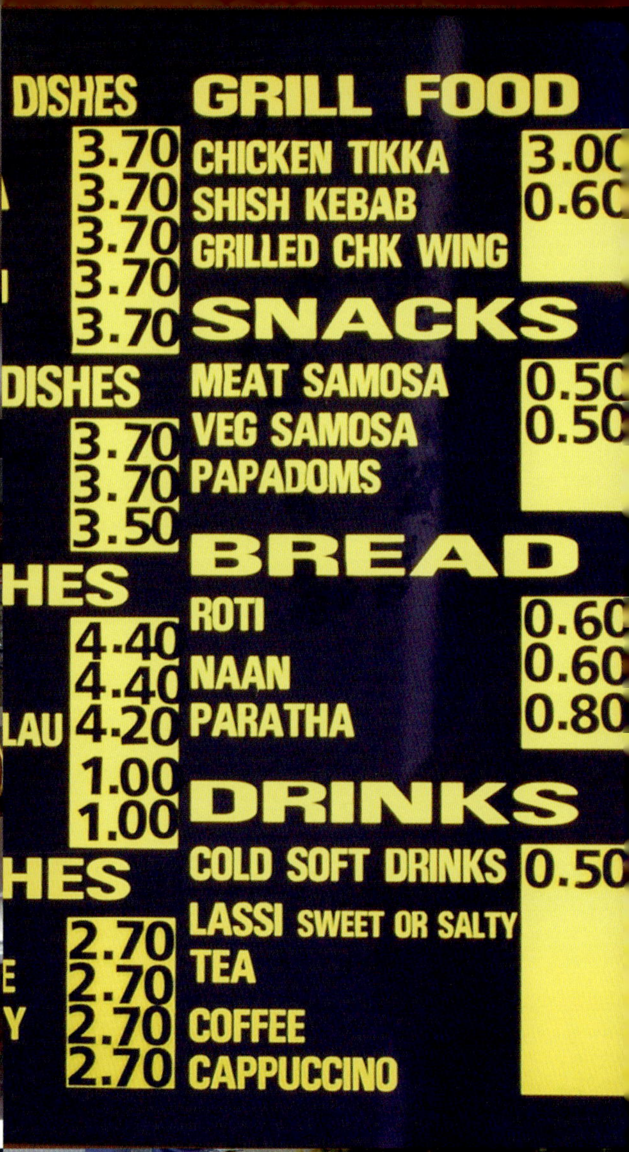

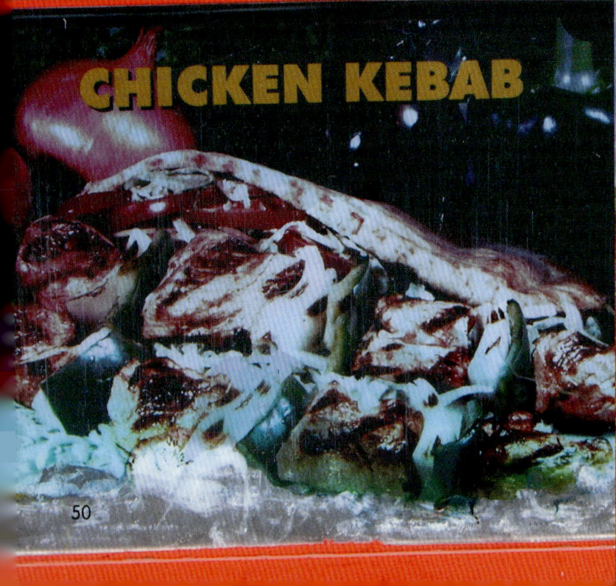

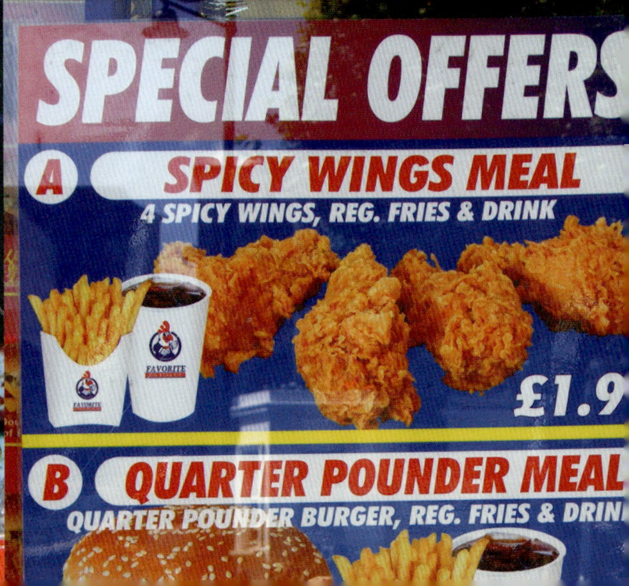

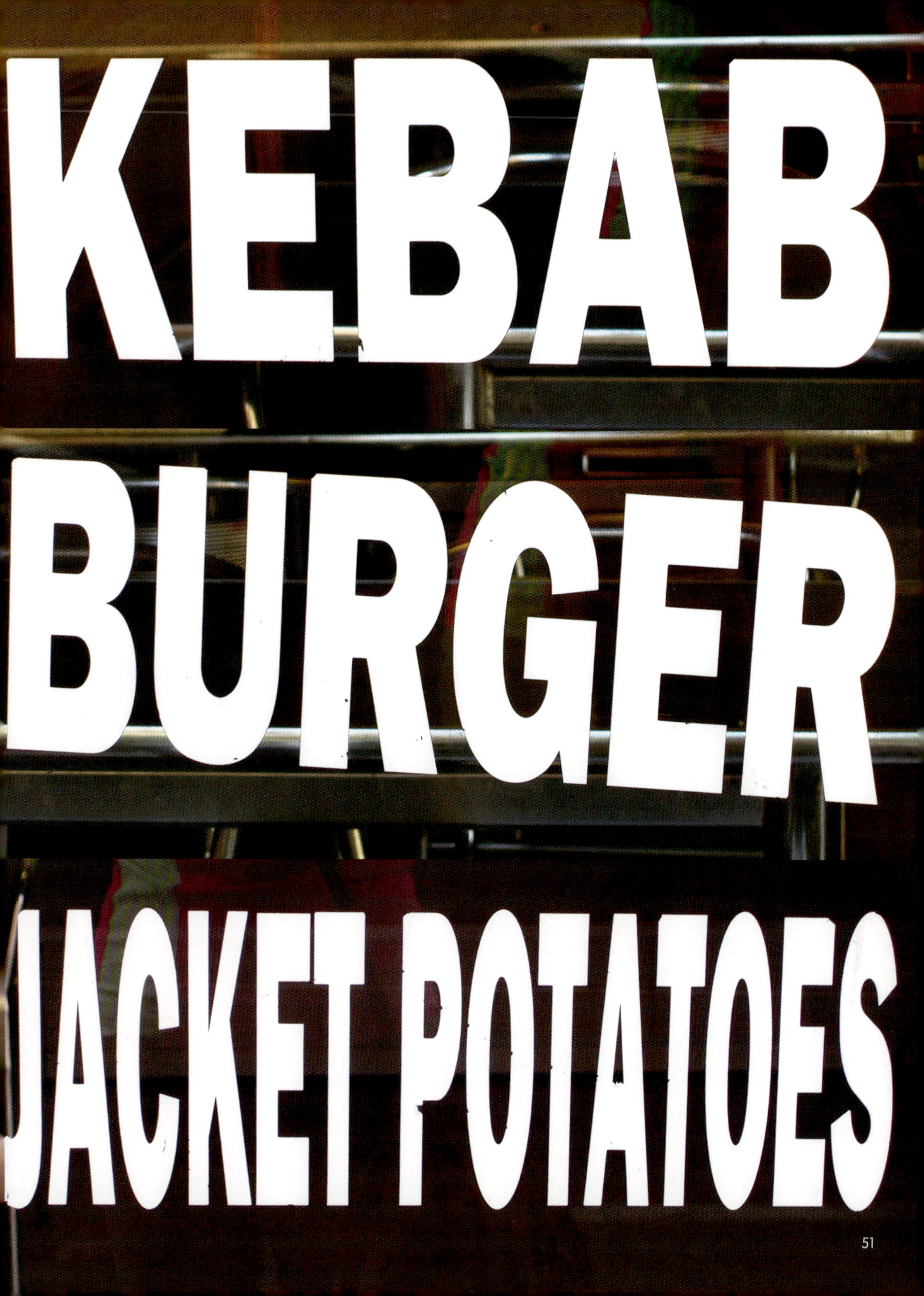
KEBAB
BURGER
JACKET POTATOES

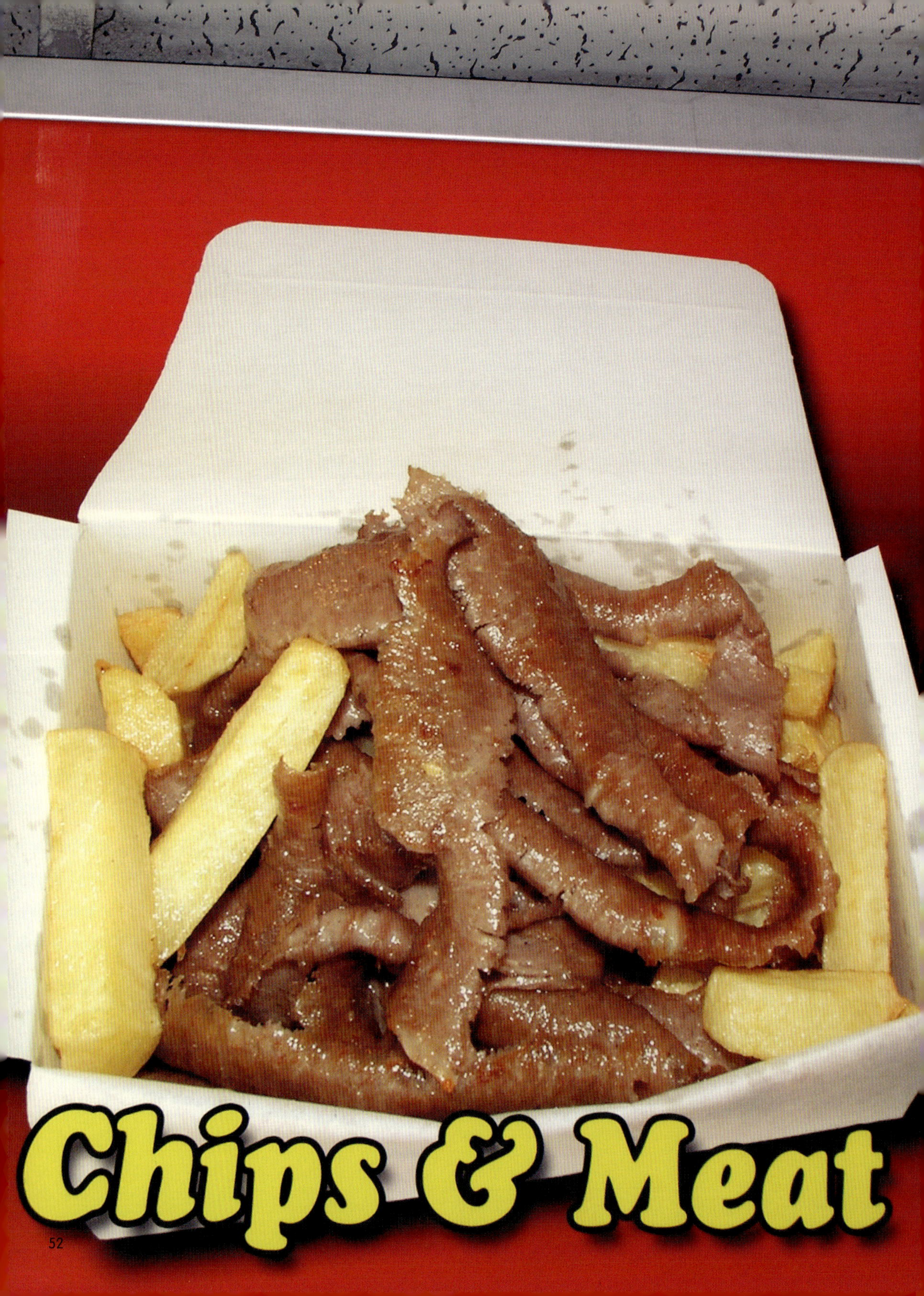

Chips & Meat

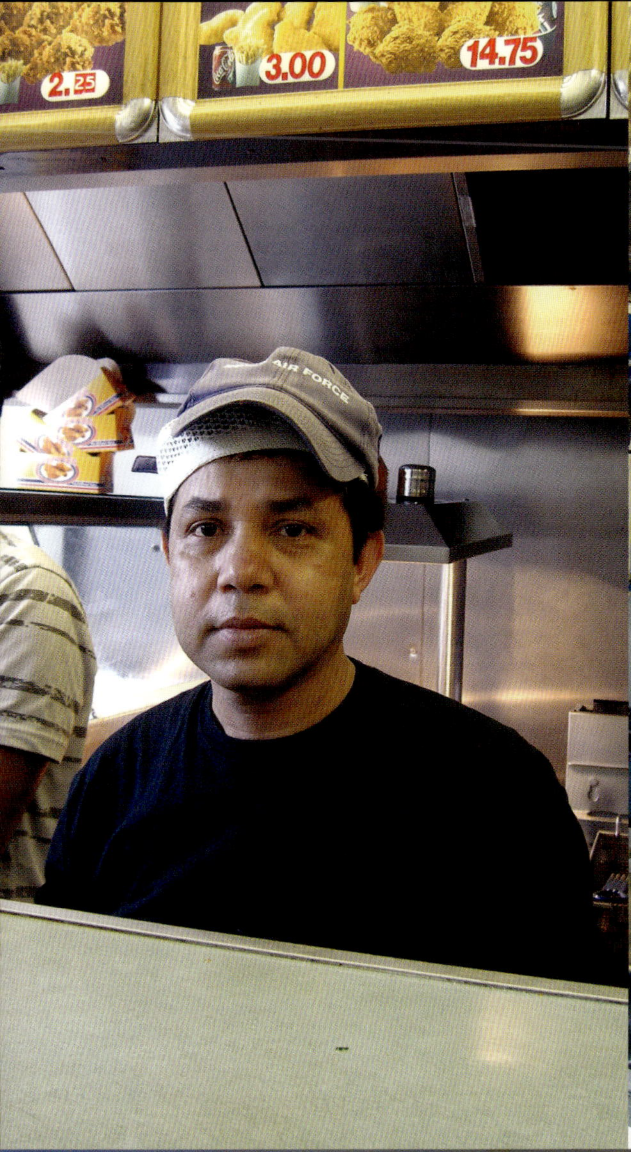

Fazli Caglar:

I've been here 14 years. (laughs) Sometimes good dealing with customers but sometimes stress, very hard, hard. Many customers come in stressed, after I feeling finished, after empty feeling. Aahh before ok, but now too hard you pay bill, bill, bill, I'm never going on holiday y'know, no money.

In my village in Turkey I looked after sheep, no worries no stress, no bills. Here everybody is stressed. My wife stress me, so I come here to forget and speak with the customers.

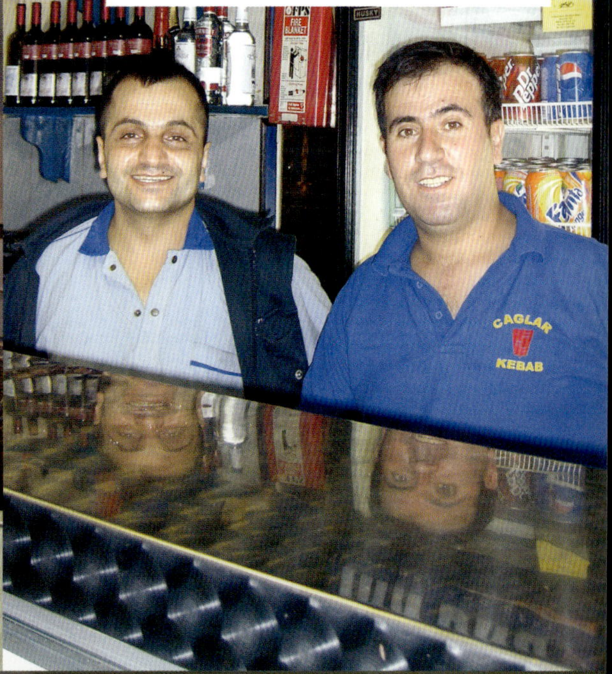

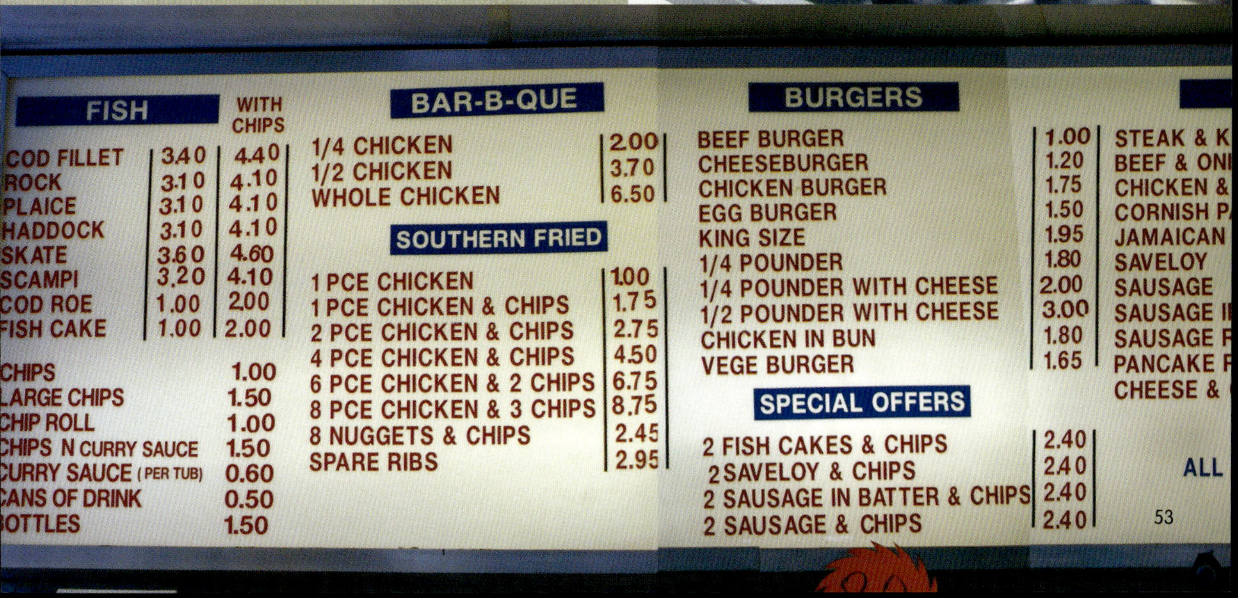

Amer Salim:

Lots of customers prefer me to serve them. They think maybe I'm serving them nicely, and it's my satisfaction as well. And if I'm not there some of them they ask, "Where is he?" If I'm in the kitchen they ask, "Please call him," it's many times it happens.

So would you like something to eat or drink? I'll make you some special tea, and I'll make some for me as well.

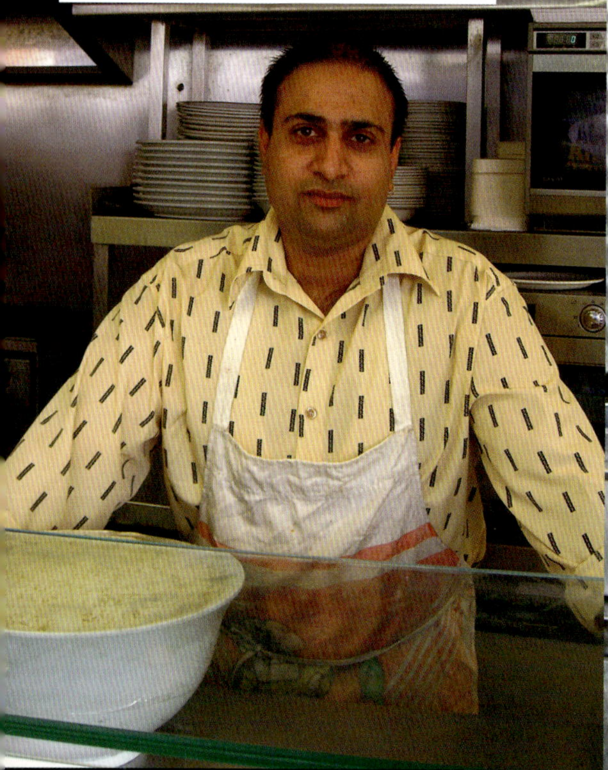

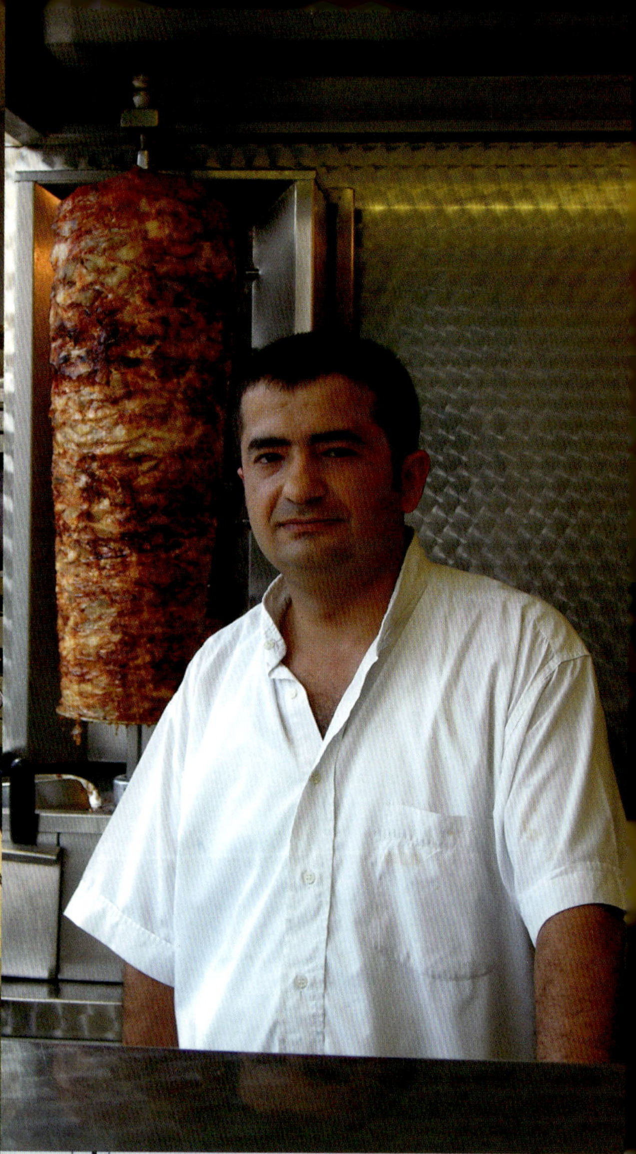

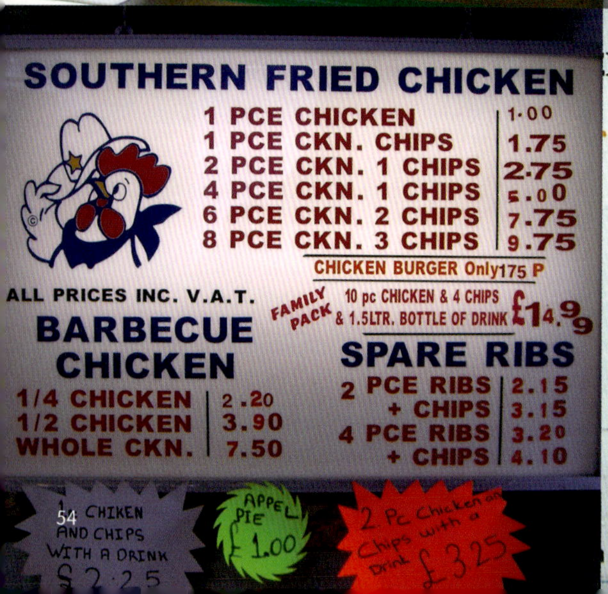

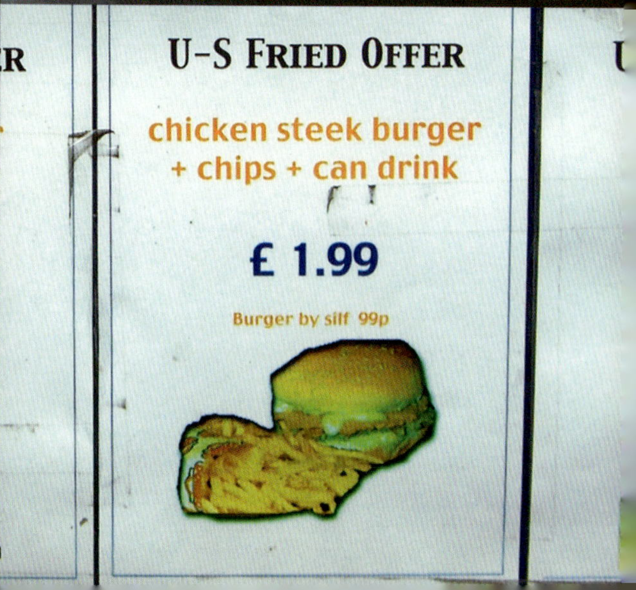

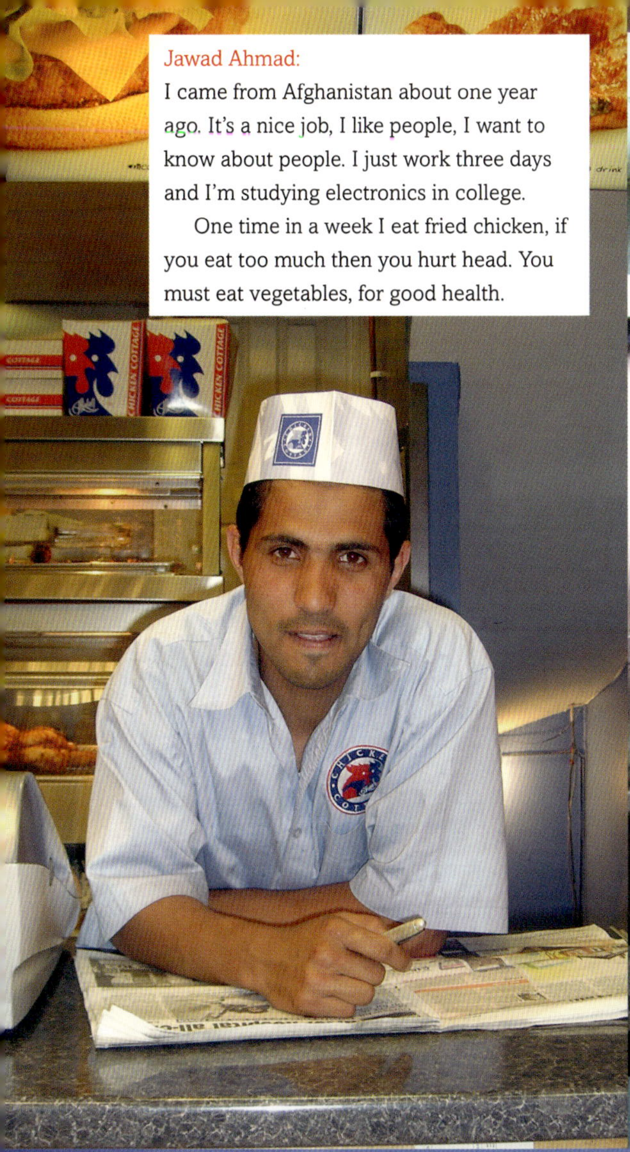

Jawad Ahmad:

I came from Afghanistan about one year ago. It's a nice job, I like people, I want to know about people. I just work three days and I'm studying electronics in college.

One time in a week I eat fried chicken, if you eat too much then you hurt head. You must eat vegetables, for good health.

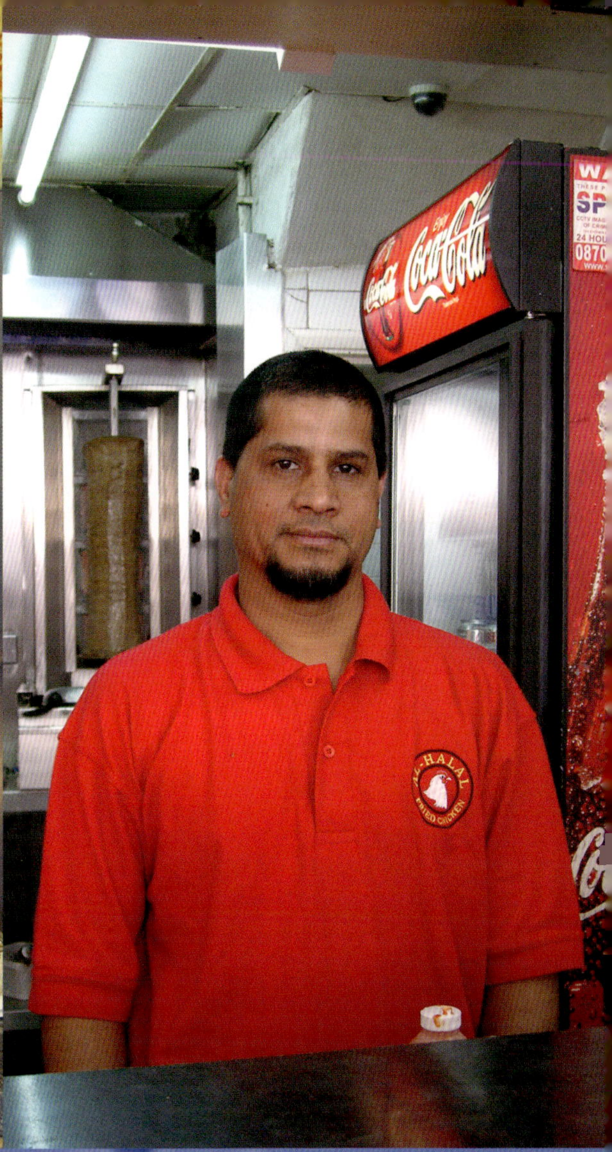

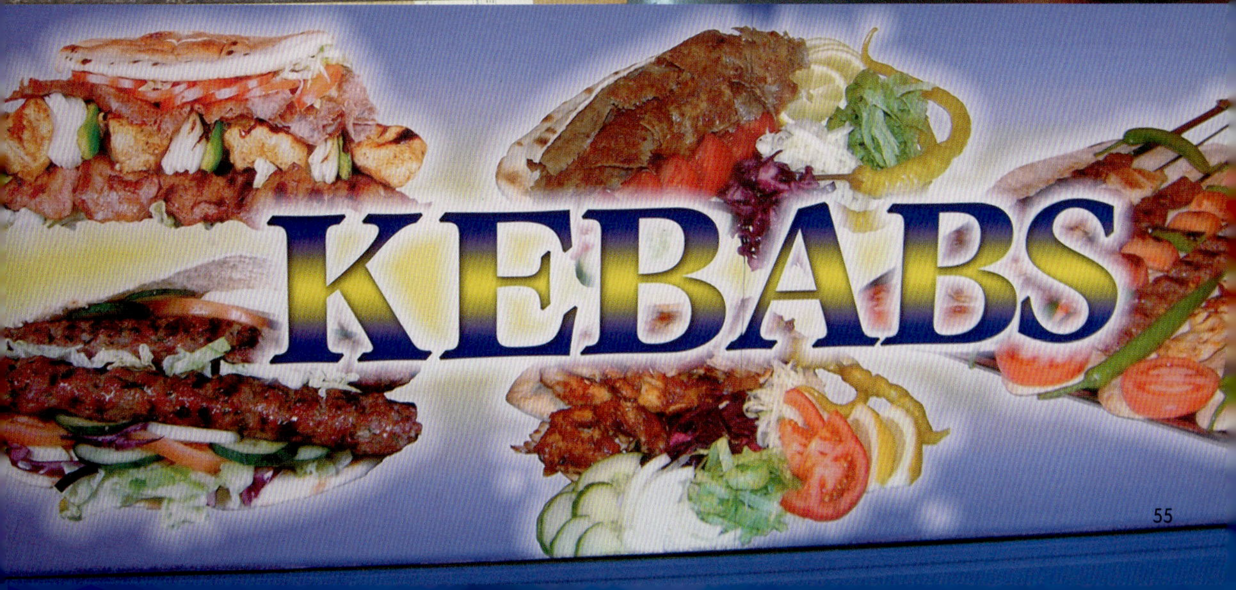

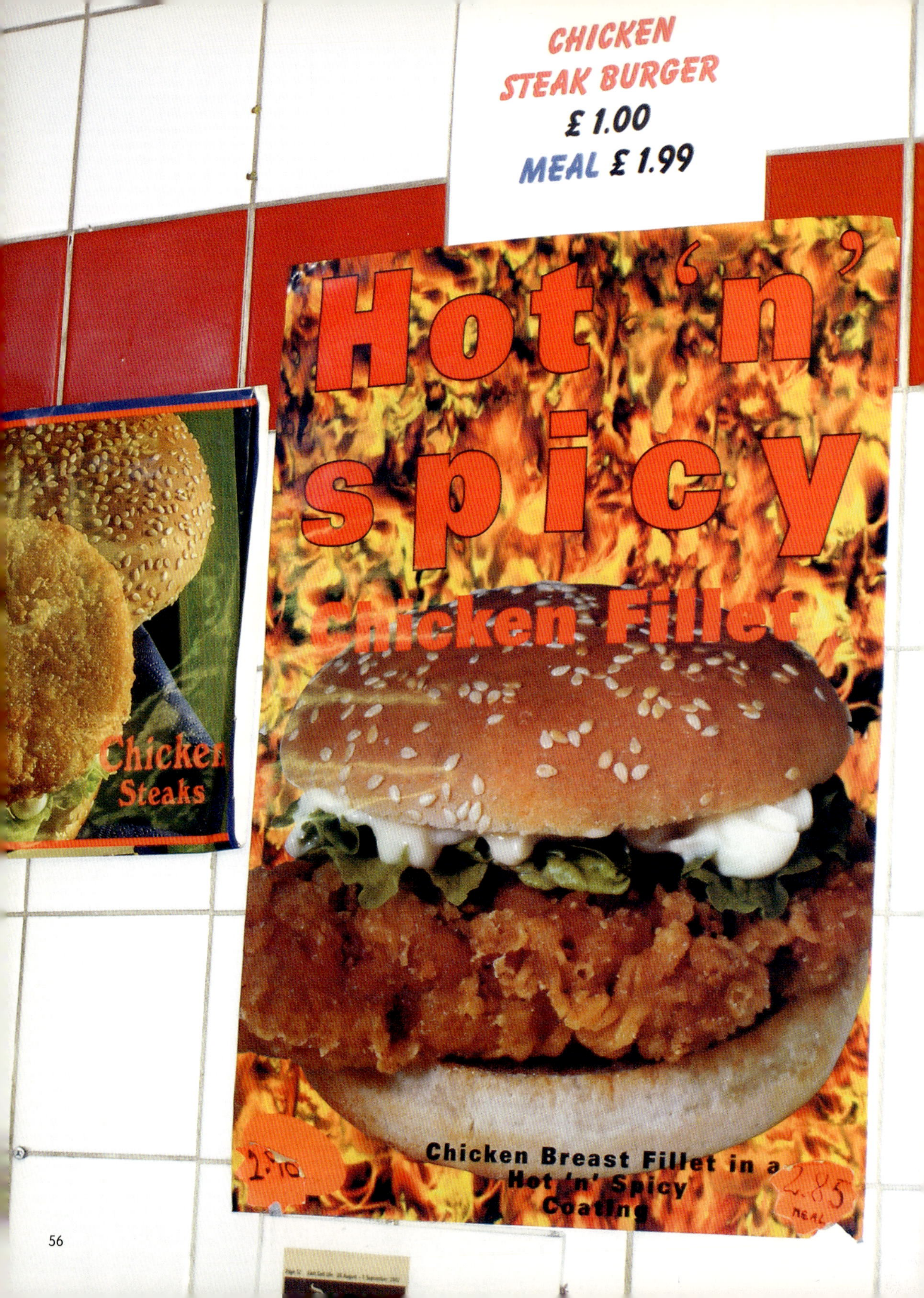
CHICKEN
STEAK BURGER
£ 1.00
MEAL £ 1.99
Hot 'n' spicy
Chicken Fillet
Chicken
Steaks
Chicken Breast Fillet in a
Hot 'n' Spicy
Coating
2.85
MEAL

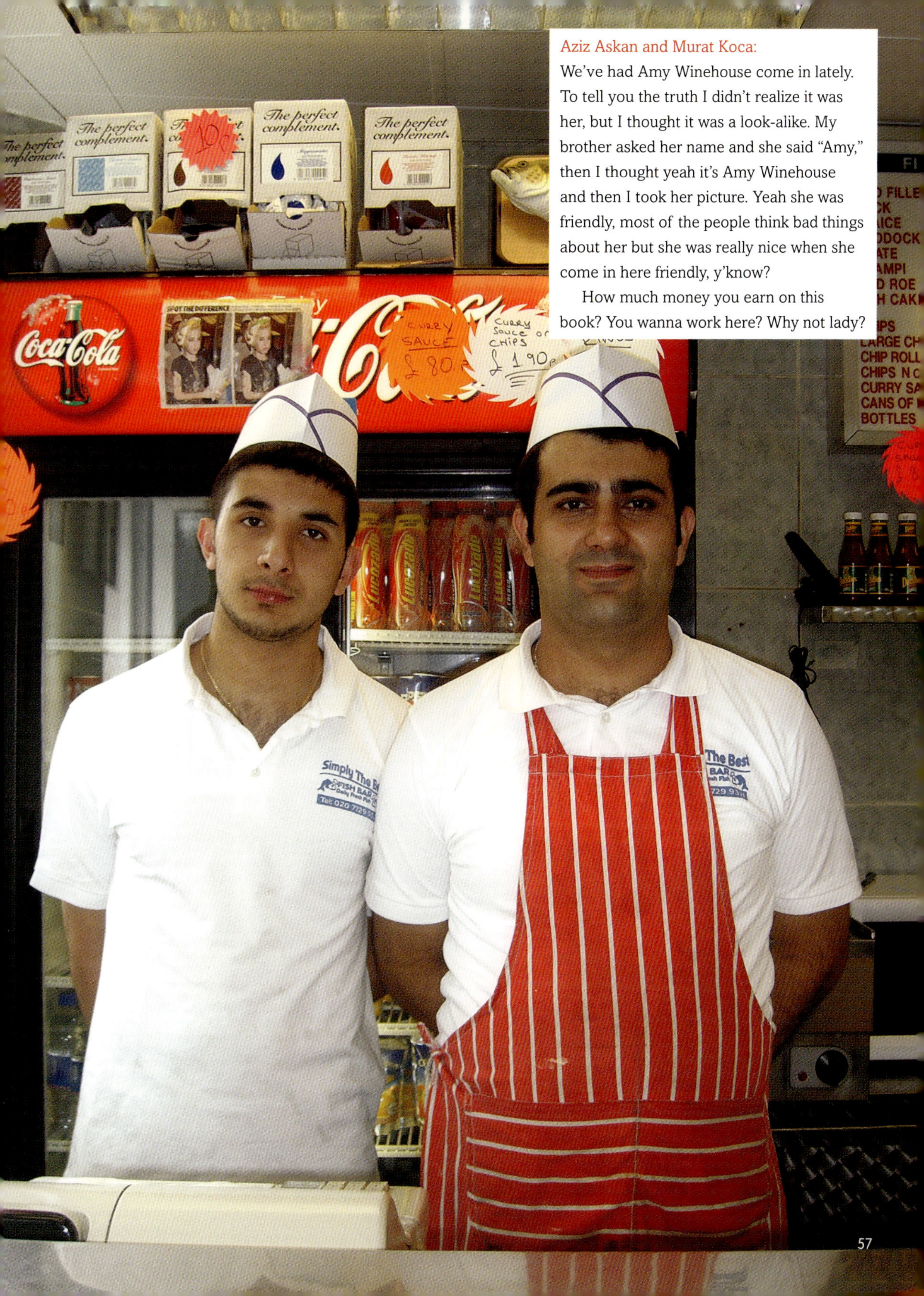

Aziz Askan and Murat Koca:

We've had Amy Winehouse come in lately. To tell you the truth I didn't realize it was her, but I thought it was a look-alike. My brother asked her name and she said "Amy," then I thought yeah it's Amy Winehouse and then I took her picture. Yeah she was friendly, most of the people think bad things about her but she was really nice when she come in here friendly, y'know?

How much money you earn on this book? You wanna work here? Why not lady?

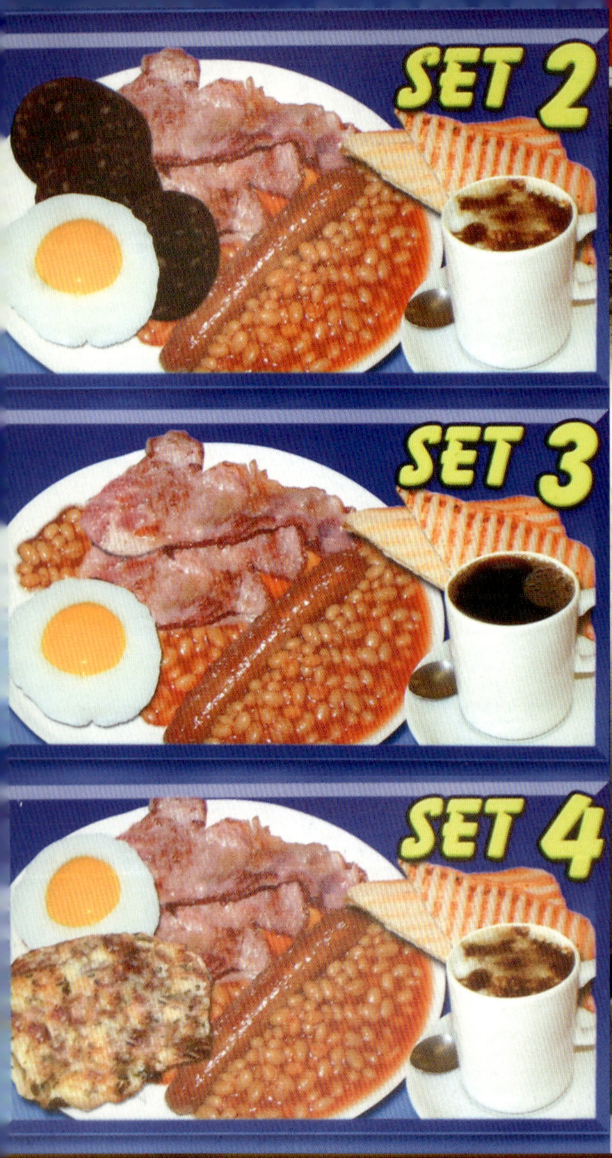
SET 2
SET 3
SET 4

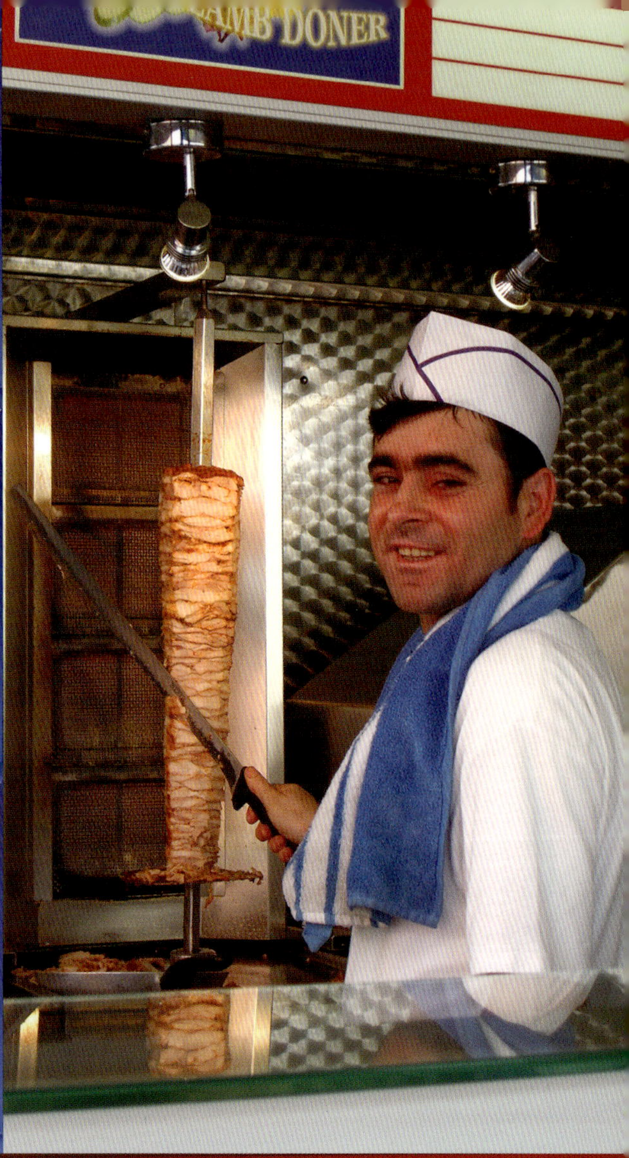
LAMB DONER

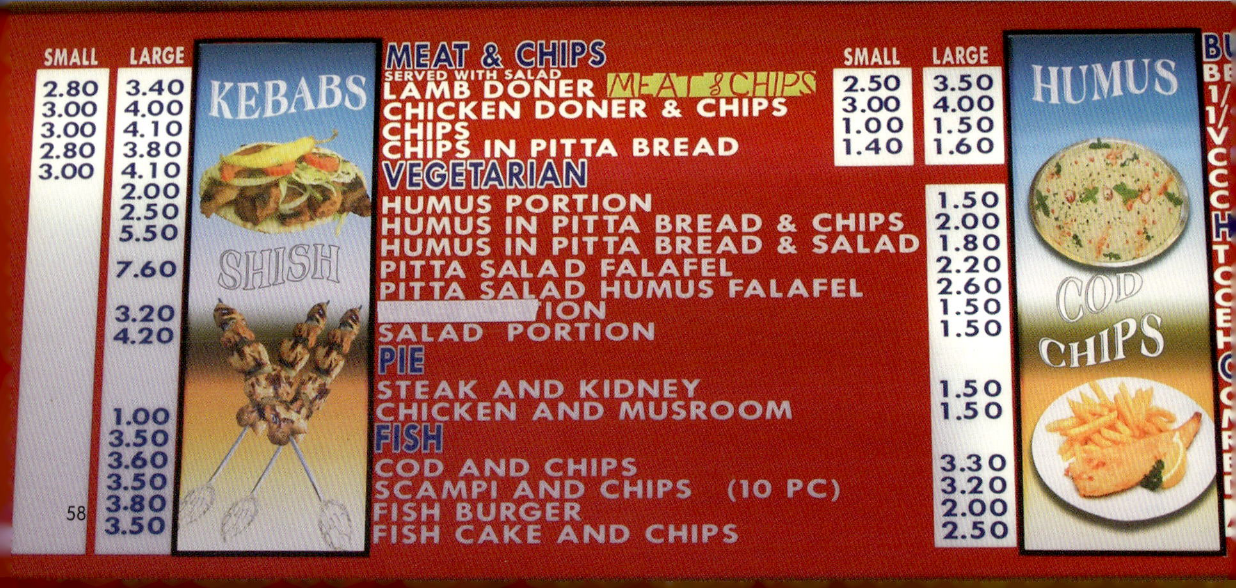
SMALL
LARGE
2.80
3.00
3.00
2.80
3.00
3.40
4.00
4.10
3.80
4.10
2.00
2.50
5.50
7.60
3.20
4.20
1.00
3.50
3.60
3.50
3.80
3.50
KEBABS
SHISH
MEAT & CHIPS
SERVED WITH SALAD
LAMB DONER
MEAT & CHIPS
CHICKEN DONER & CHIPS
CHIPS
CHIPS IN PITTA BREAD
VEGETARIAN
HUMUS PORTION
HUMUS IN PITTA BREAD & CHIPS
HUMUS IN PITTA BREAD & SALAD
PITTA SALAD FALAFEL
PITTA SALAD HUMUS FALAFEL
ION
SALAD PORTION
PIE
STEAK AND KIDNEY
CHICKEN AND MUSROOM
FISH
COD AND CHIPS
SCAMPI AND CHIPS (10 PC)
FISH BURGER
FISH CAKE AND CHIPS
SMALL
LARGE
2.50
3.00
1.00
1.40
3.50
4.00
1.50
1.60
1.50
2.00
1.80
2.20
2.60
1.50
1.50
1.50
1.50
3.30
3.20
2.00
2.50
HUMUS
COD
CHIPS

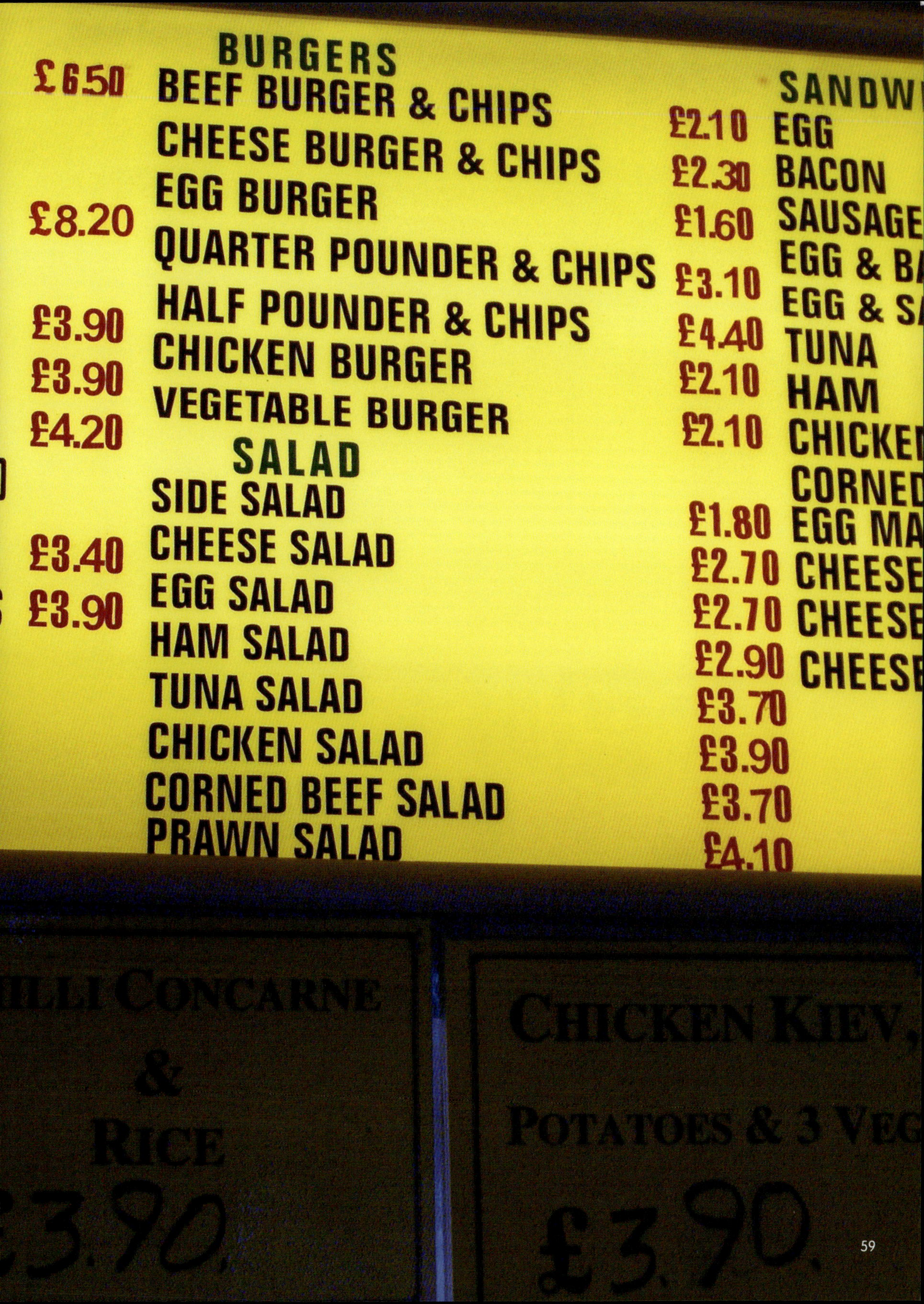

BURGERS
£6.50 BEEF BURGER & CHIPS
CHEESE BURGER & CHIPS
EGG BURGER
£8.20 QUARTER POUNDER & CHIPS
HALF POUNDER & CHIPS
£3.90 CHICKEN BURGER
£3.90 VEGETABLE BURGER
£4.20
SALAD
SIDE SALAD
£3.40 CHEESE SALAD
£3.90 EGG SALAD
HAM SALAD
TUNA SALAD
CHICKEN SALAD
CORNED BEEF SALAD
PRAWN SALAD
£2.10 EGG
£2.30 BACON
£1.60
£3.10
£4.40 TUNA
£2.10 HAM
£2.10
£1.80
£2.70
£2.70
£2.90
£3.70
£3.90
£3.70
£4.10
&
RICE
POTATOES & 3
£3.90

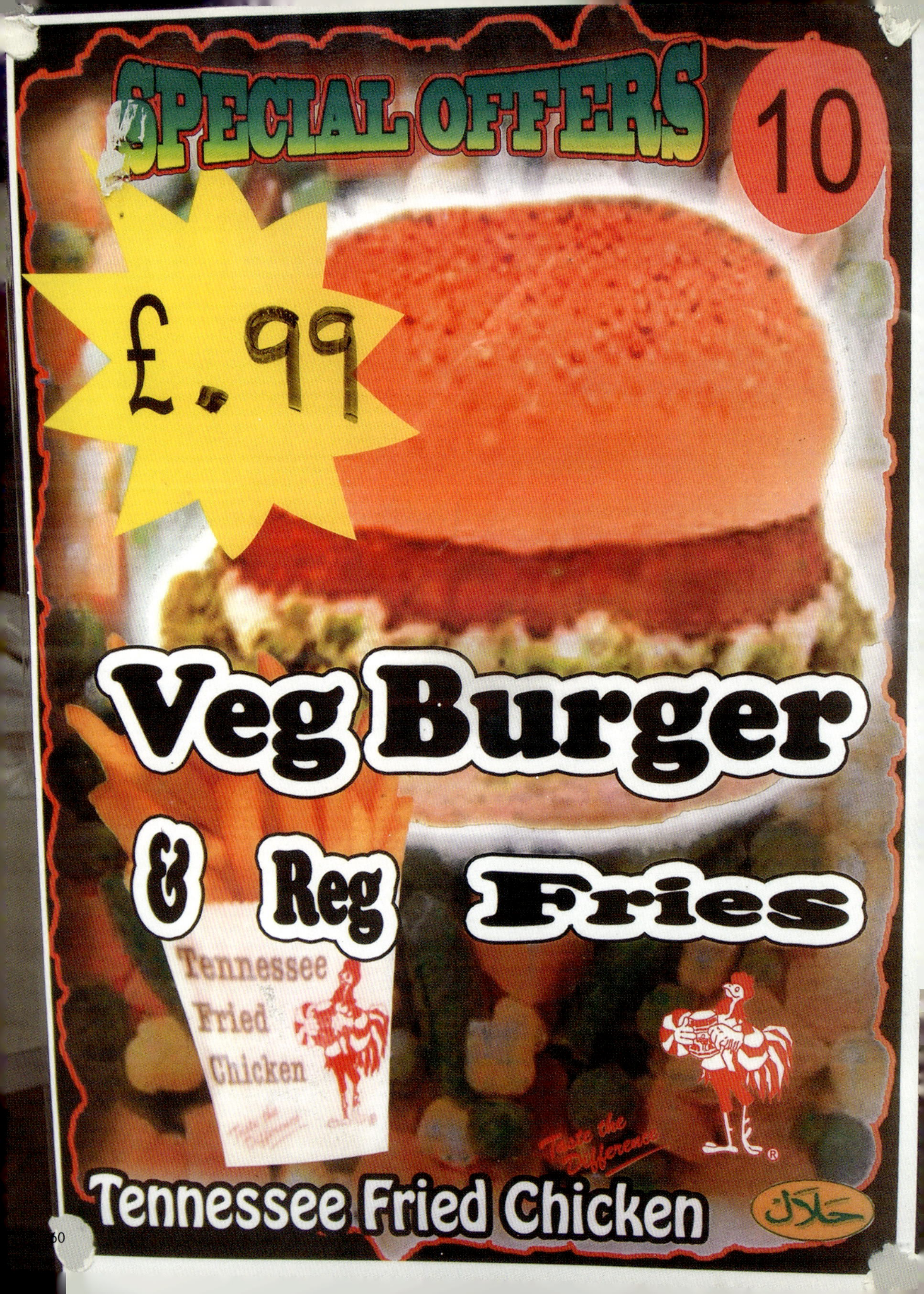
SPECIAL OFFERS
10
£.99
Veg Burger
& Reg Fries
Tennessee
Fried
Chicken
Taste the Difference
Tennessee Fried Chicken
حلال

Mohammed Waif:

When the weather is nice, I like watching all the ladies, you know what I mean? (laughs) The brilliant thing is chatting with the customers, you see a lot of different people every day. Even if they're being rude, you have to be cool, otherwise you can't do business. I don't like to cook, even when I'm not working I eat at fast food shops.

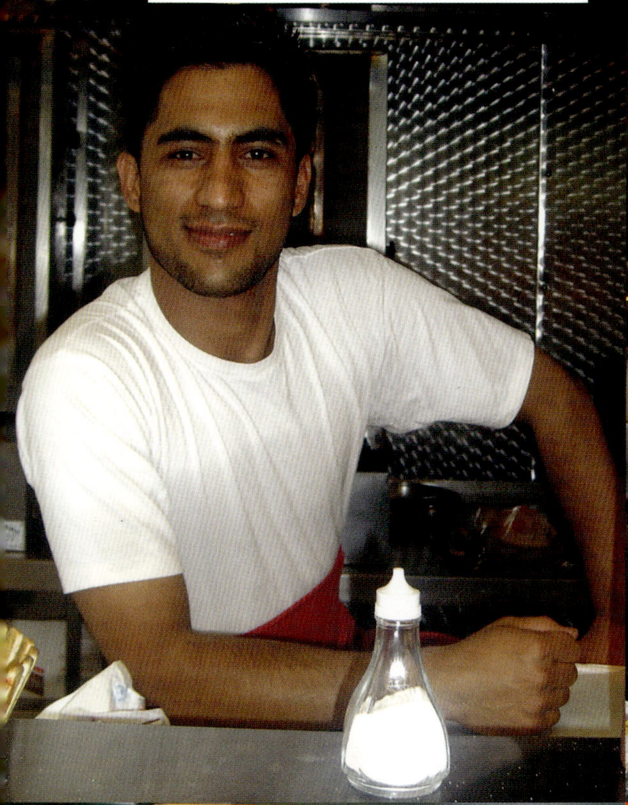

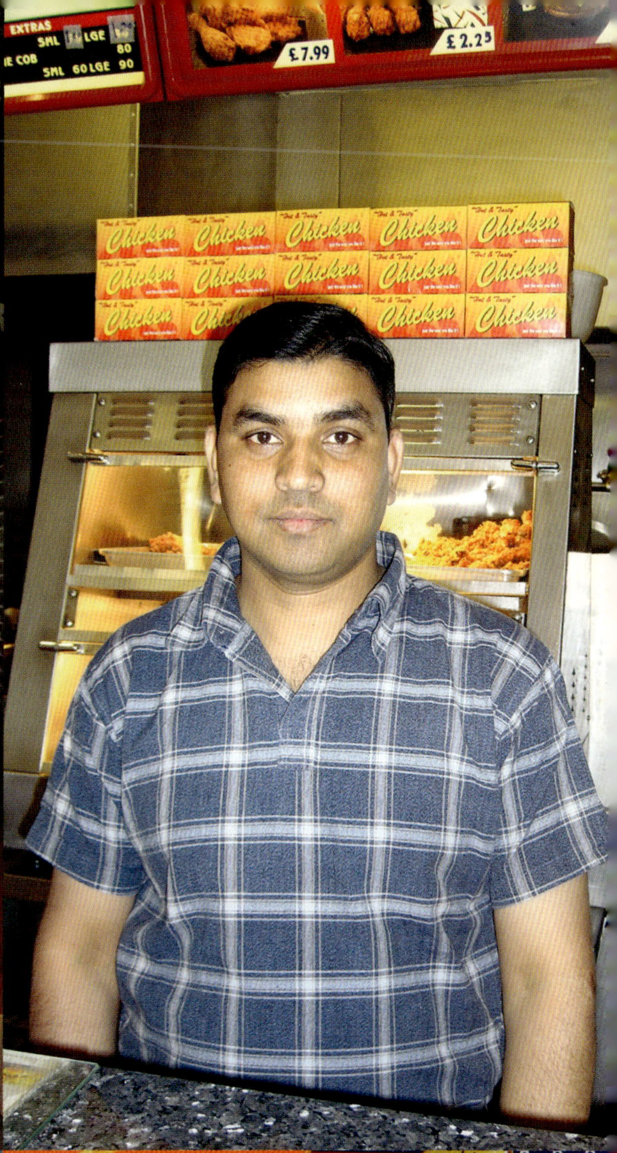

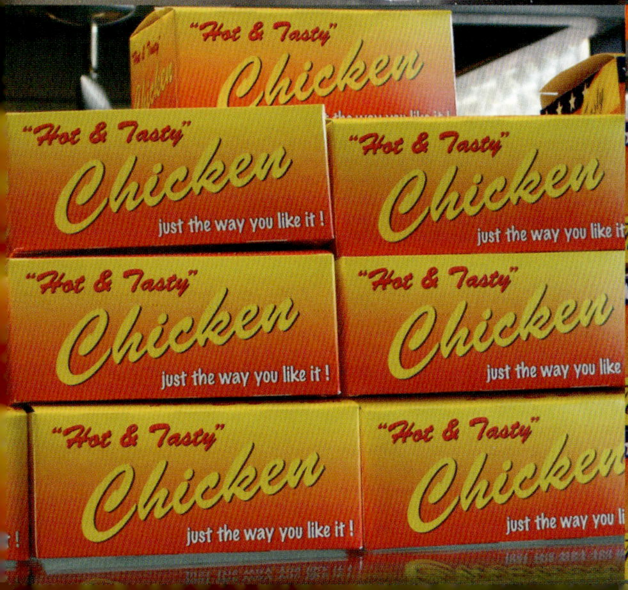

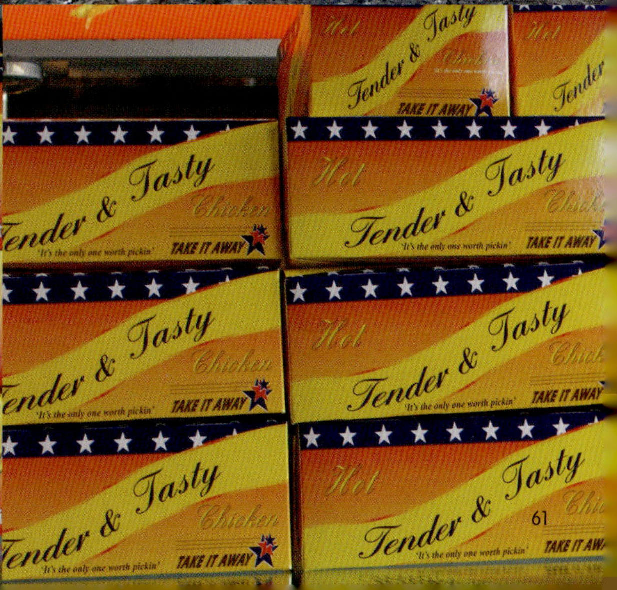

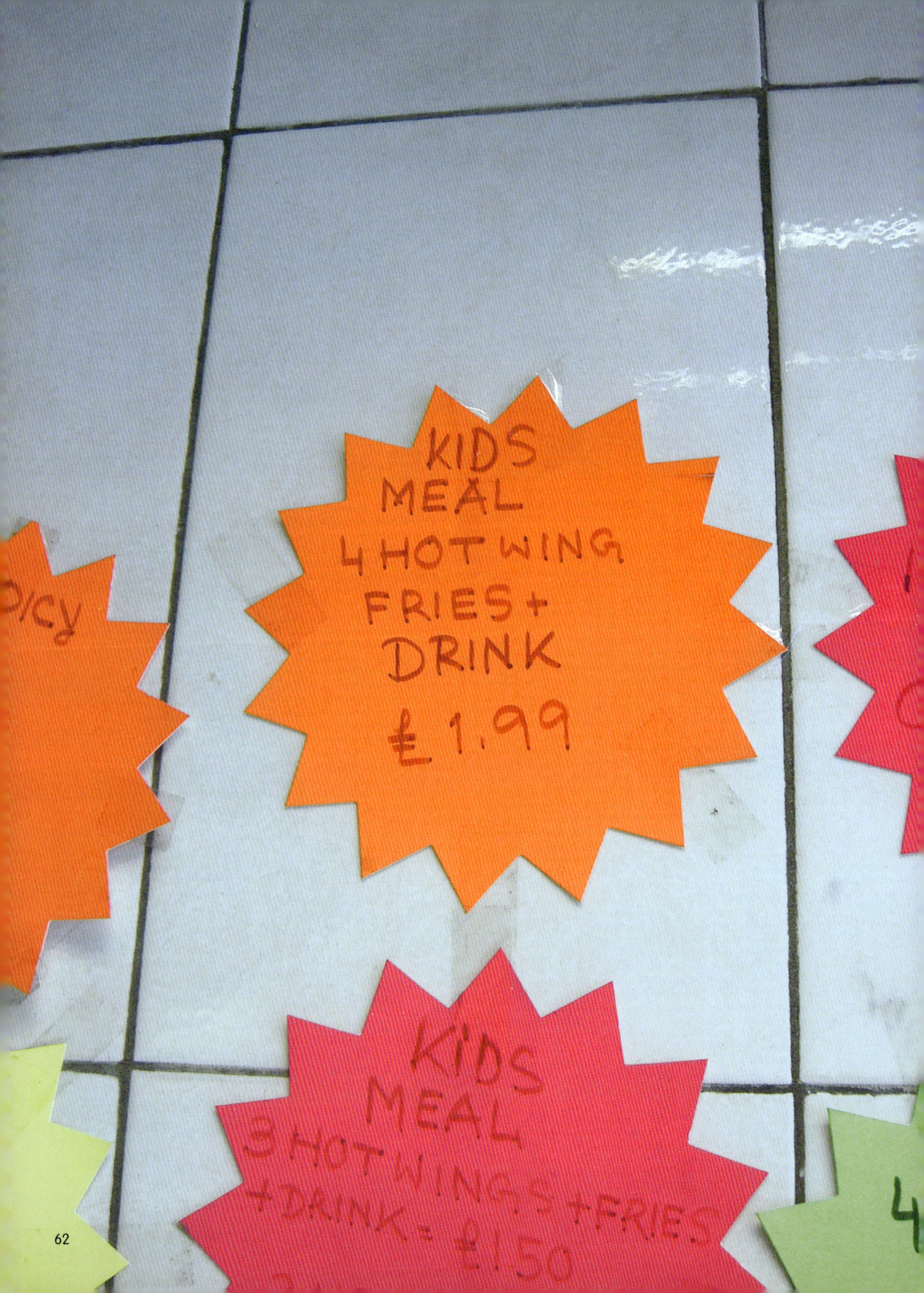
KIDS
MEAL
4 HOT WING
FRIES +
DRINK
£1.99
KIDS
MEAL
3 HOT WINGS + FRIES
+ DRINK = £1.50

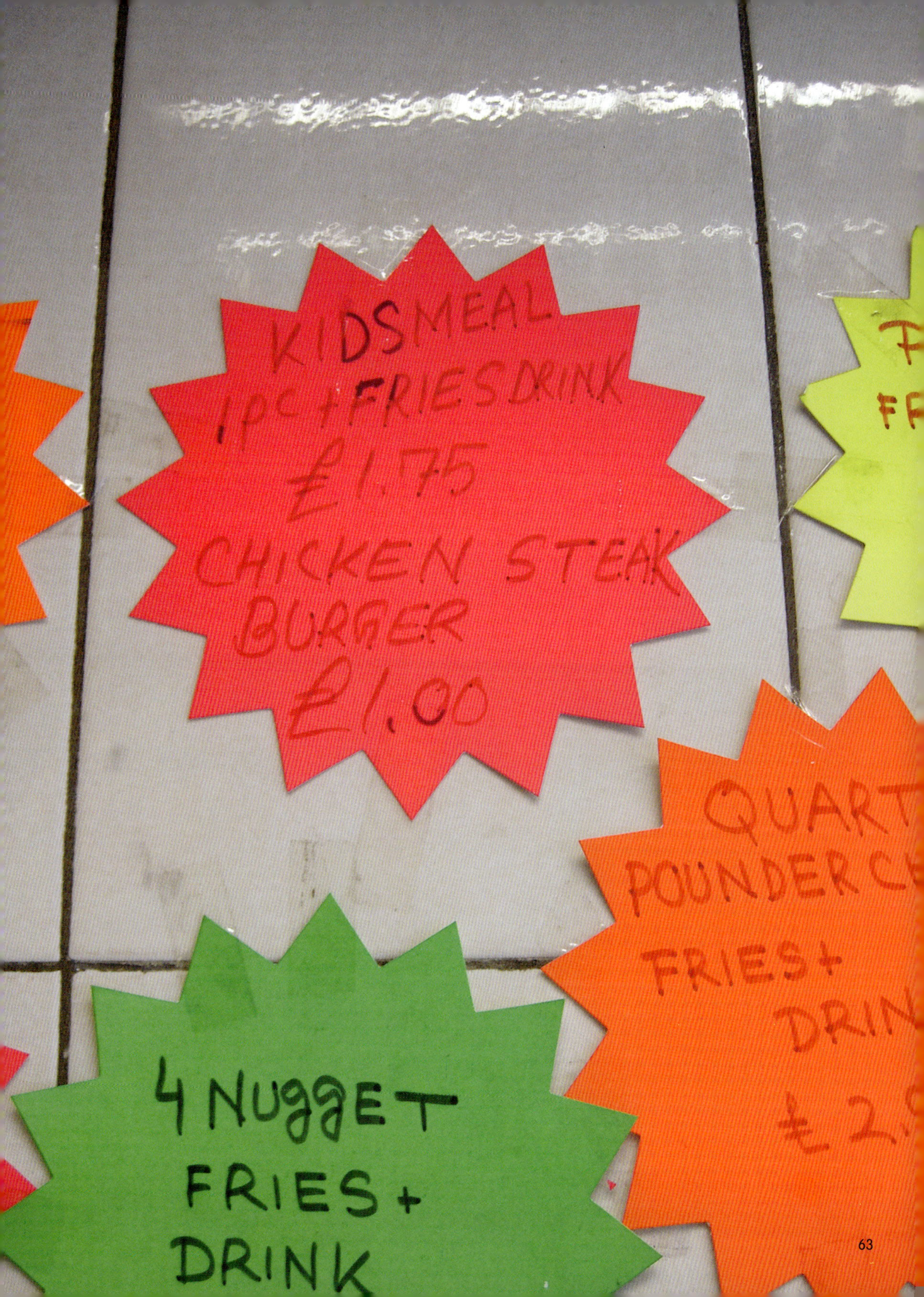
KIDSMEAL
1PC+FRIES DRINK
£1.75
CHICKEN STEAK
BURGER
£1.00
4 NUGGET
FRIES+
DRINK
FRIES+

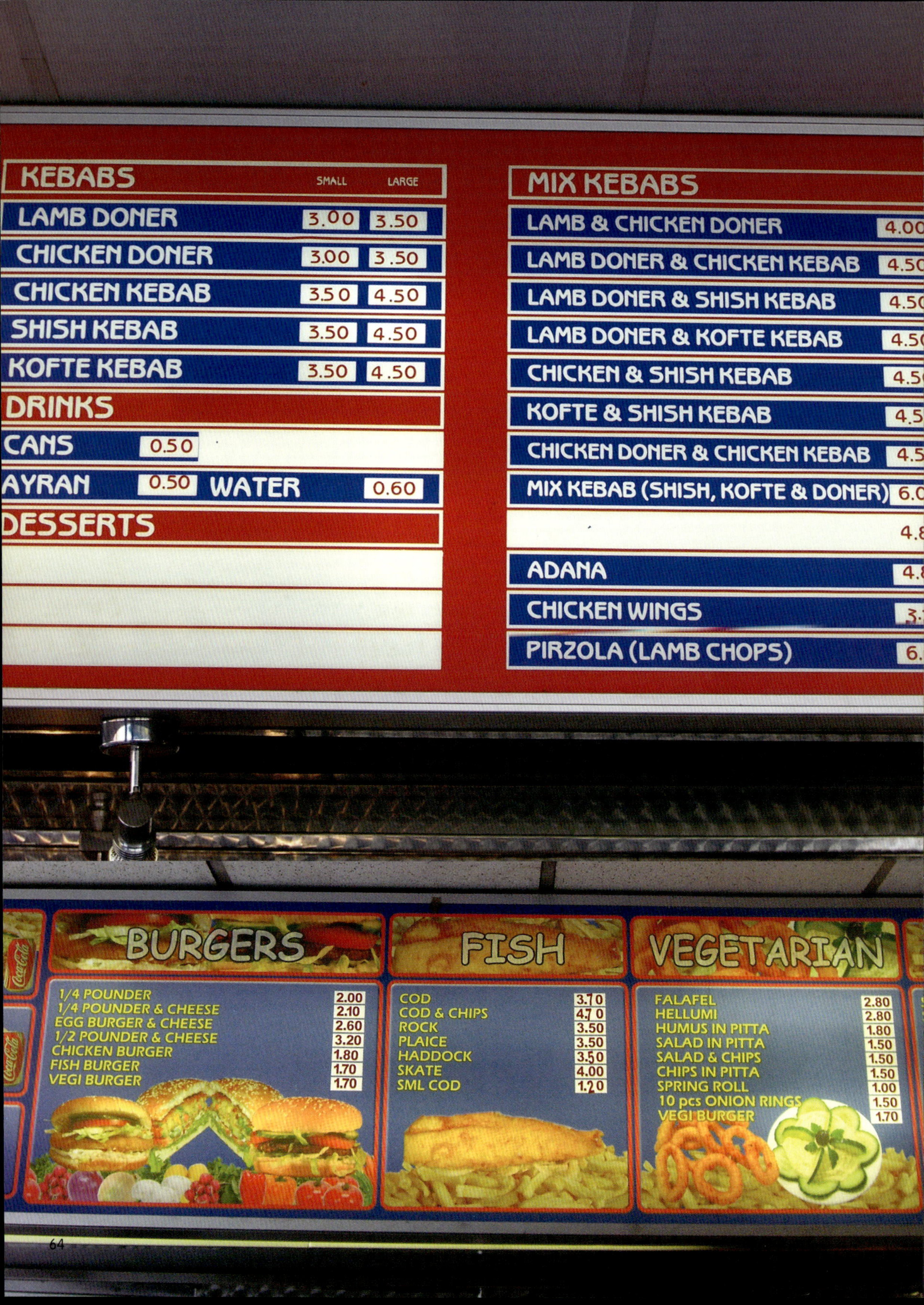
KEBABS
SMALL
LARGE
LAMB DONER 3.00 3.50
CHICKEN DONER 3.00 3.50
CHICKEN KEBAB 3.50 4.50
SHISH KEBAB 3.50 4.50
KOFTE KEBAB 3.50 4.50
DRINKS
CANS 0.50
AYRAN 0.50
WATER 0.60
DESSERTS
MIX KEBABS
LAMB & CHICKEN DONER 4.00
LAMB DONER & CHICKEN KEBAB 4.50
LAMB DONER & SHISH KEBAB 4.50
LAMB DONER & KOFTE KEBAB 4.50
CHICKEN & SHISH KEBAB 4.5
KOFTE & SHISH KEBAB 4.5
CHICKEN DONER & CHICKEN KEBAB 4.5
MIX KEBAB (SHISH, KOFTE & DONER) 6.0
4.8
ADANA 4.8
CHICKEN WINGS
PIRZOLA (LAMB CHOPS) 6.
BURGERS
1/4 POUNDER 2.00
1/4 POUNDER & CHEESE 2.10
EGG BURGER & CHEESE 2.60
1/2 POUNDER & CHEESE 3.20
CHICKEN BURGER 1.80
FISH BURGER 1.70
VEGI BURGER 1.70
FISH
COD 3.70
COD & CHIPS 4.70
ROCK 3.50
PLAICE 3.50
HADDOCK 3.50
SKATE 4.00
SML COD 1.20
VEGETARIAN
FALAFEL 2.80
HELLUMI 2.80
HUMUS IN PITTA 1.80
SALAD IN PITTA 1.50
SALAD & CHIPS 1.50
CHIPS IN PITTA 1.50
SPRING ROLL 1.00
10 pcs ONION RINGS 1.50
VEGI BURGER 1.70

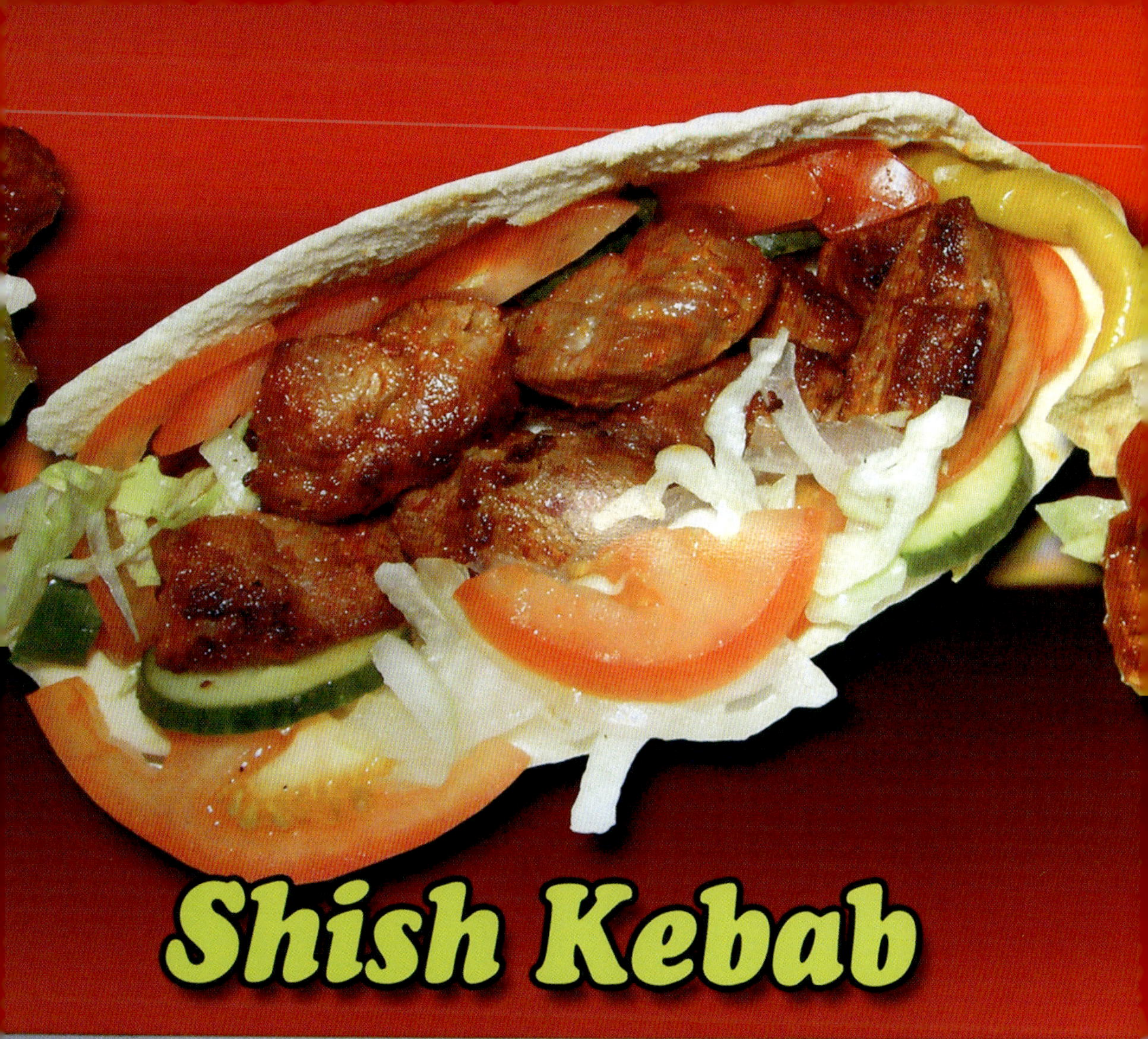

1 pc. CHICKEN
Chips + Can Drink

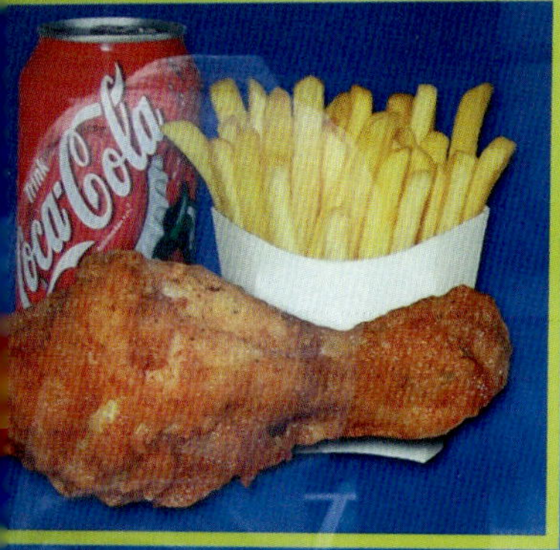

2 pcs.CHICKEN
+ Chips + Can Drink

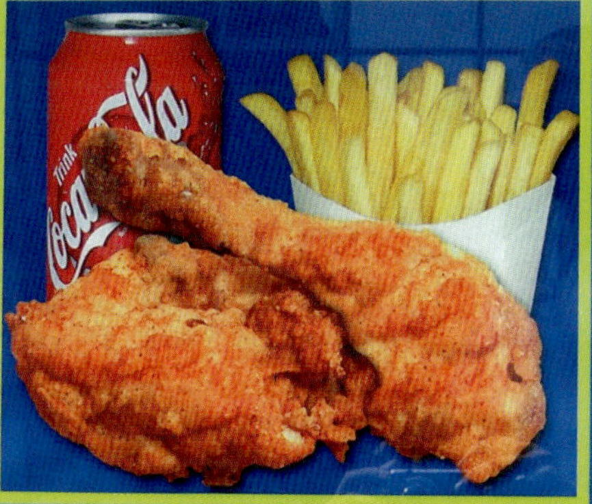

2 pcs.CHICKEN
2 pcs. WINGS
+ Chips + Can Drink

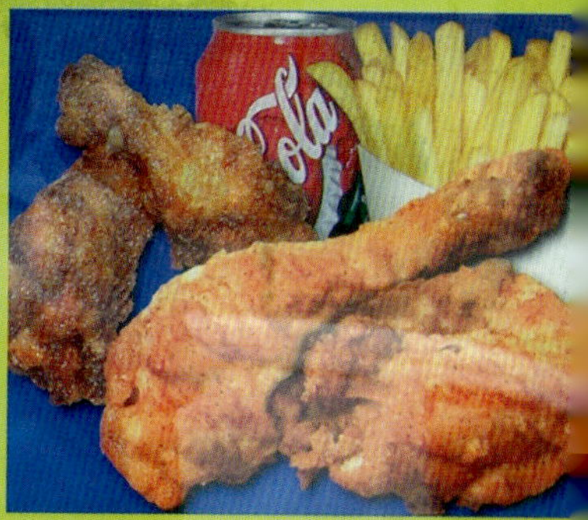

5 pcs. WINGS
+ Chips + Can Drink

4 pcs.CHICKEN
3 pcs.WINGS
3 pcs.NUGGETS

CHICKEN BURGER
+ Chips + Can Drin

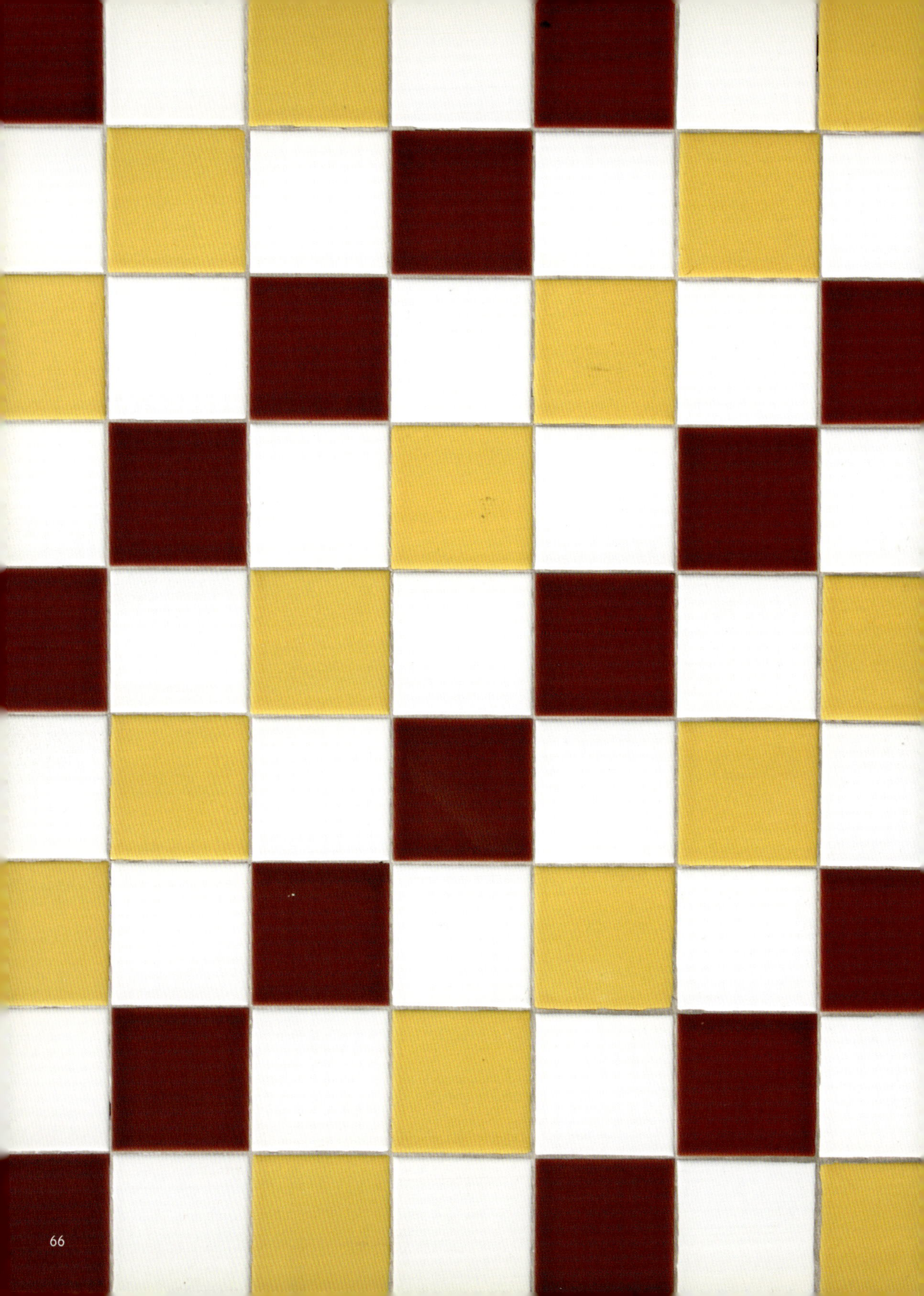

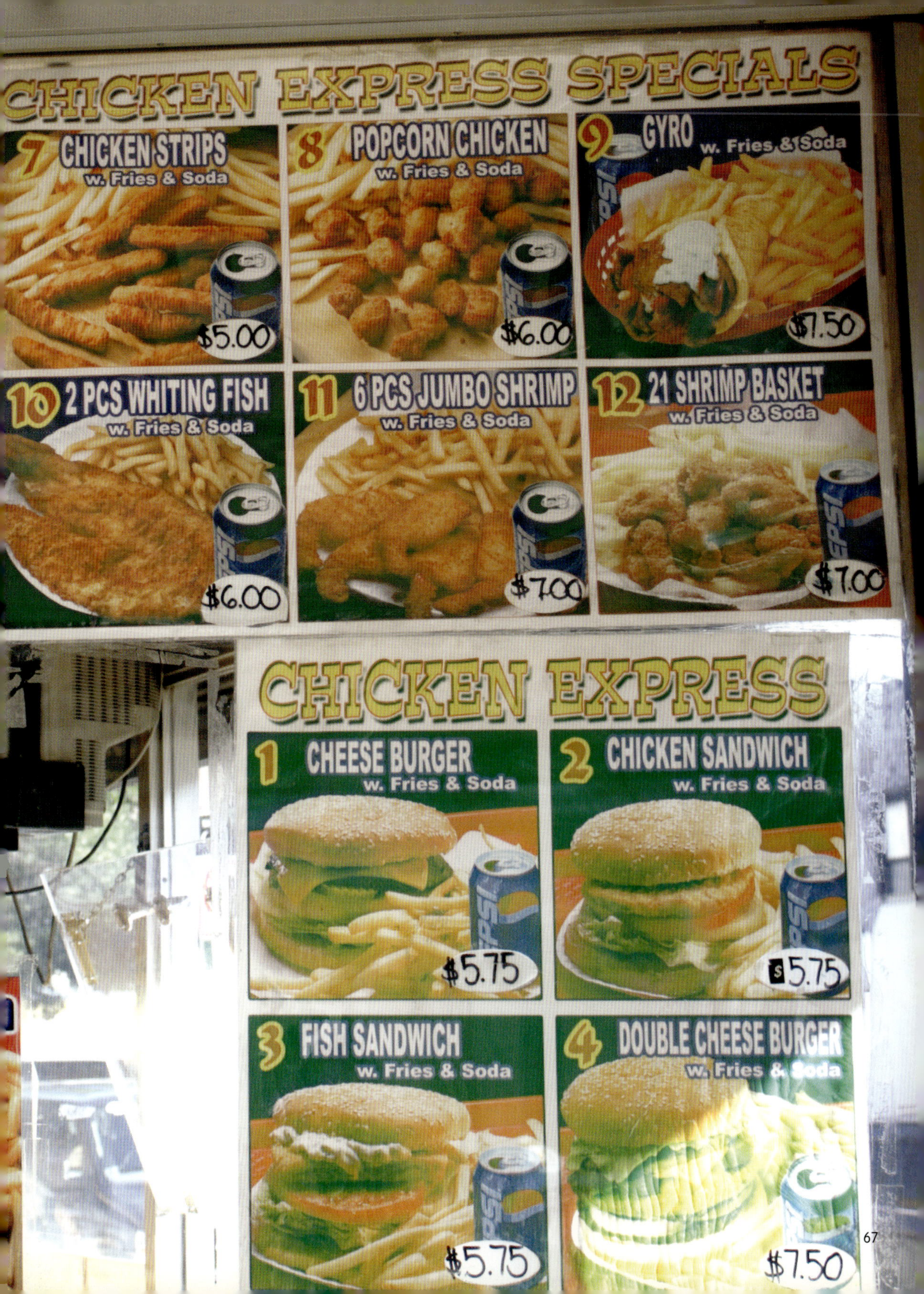
CHICKEN EXPRESS SPECIALS
7 CHICKEN STRIPS
w. Fries & Soda
$5.00
8 POPCORN CHICKEN
w. Fries & Soda
$6.00
9 GYRO
w. Fries & Soda
$7.50
10 2 PCS WHITING FISH
w. Fries & Soda
$6.00
11 6 PCS JUMBO SHRIMP
w. Fries & Soda
$7.00
12 21 SHRIMP BASKET
w. Fries & Soda
$7.00
CHICKEN EXPRESS
1 CHEESE BURGER
w. Fries & Soda
$5.75
2 CHICKEN SANDWICH
w. Fries & Soda
$5.75
3 FISH SANDWICH
w. Fries & Soda
$5.75
4 DOUBLE CHEESE BURGER
w. Fries & Soda
$7.50

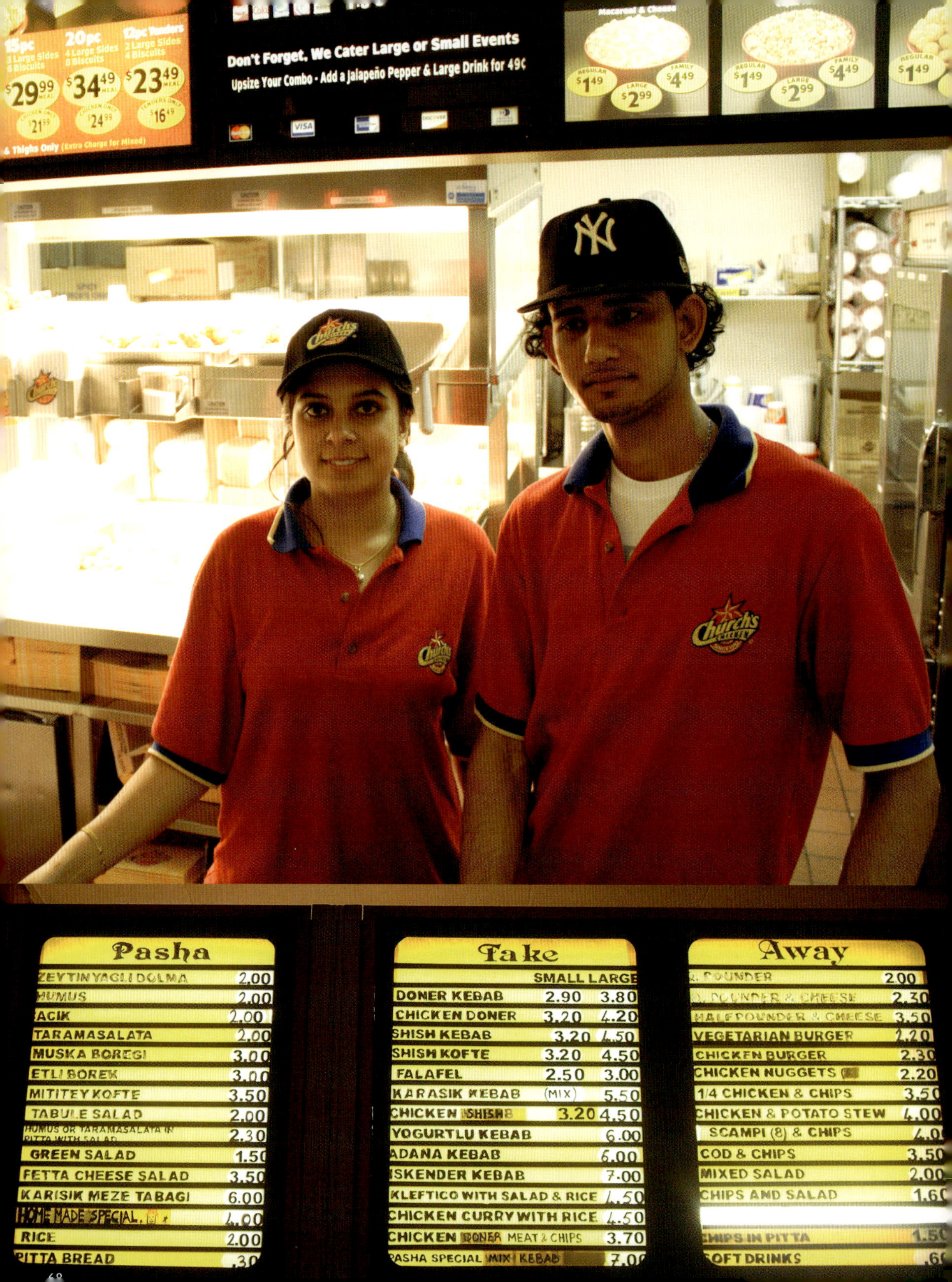

Don't Forget, We Cater Large or Small Events
Upsize Your Combo - Add a Jalapeño Pepper & Large Drink for 49¢
Pasha
ZEYTINYAGLI DOLMA 2.00
HUMUS 2.00
TARAMASALATA 2.00
MUSKA BOREGI 3.00
ETLI BOREK 3.00
MITITEY KOFTE 3.50
TABULE SALAD 2.00
GREEN SALAD 1.50
FETTA CHEESE SALAD 3.50
KARISIK MEZE TABAGI 6.00
HOME MADE SPECIAL 4.00
RICE 2.00
PITTA BREAD
Take
SMALL LARGE
DONER KEBAB 2.90 3.80
CHICKEN DONER 3.20 4.20
SHISH KEBAB 3.20 4.50
SHISH KOFTE 3.20 4.50
FALAFEL 2.50 3.00
KARASIK KEBAB (MIX) 5.50
YOGURTLU KEBAB 6.00
ADANA KEBAB 6.00
ISKENDER KEBAB 7.00
KLEFTICO WITH SALAD & RICE 4.50
CHICKEN CURRY WITH RICE 4.50
Away
VEGETARIAN BURGER 1.20
CHICKEN BURGER 2.30
CHICKEN NUGGETS 2.20
1/4 CHICKEN & CHIPS 3.50
CHICKEN & POTATO STEW 4.00
COD & CHIPS 3.50
MIXED SALAD 2.00
CHIPS AND SALAD 1.60

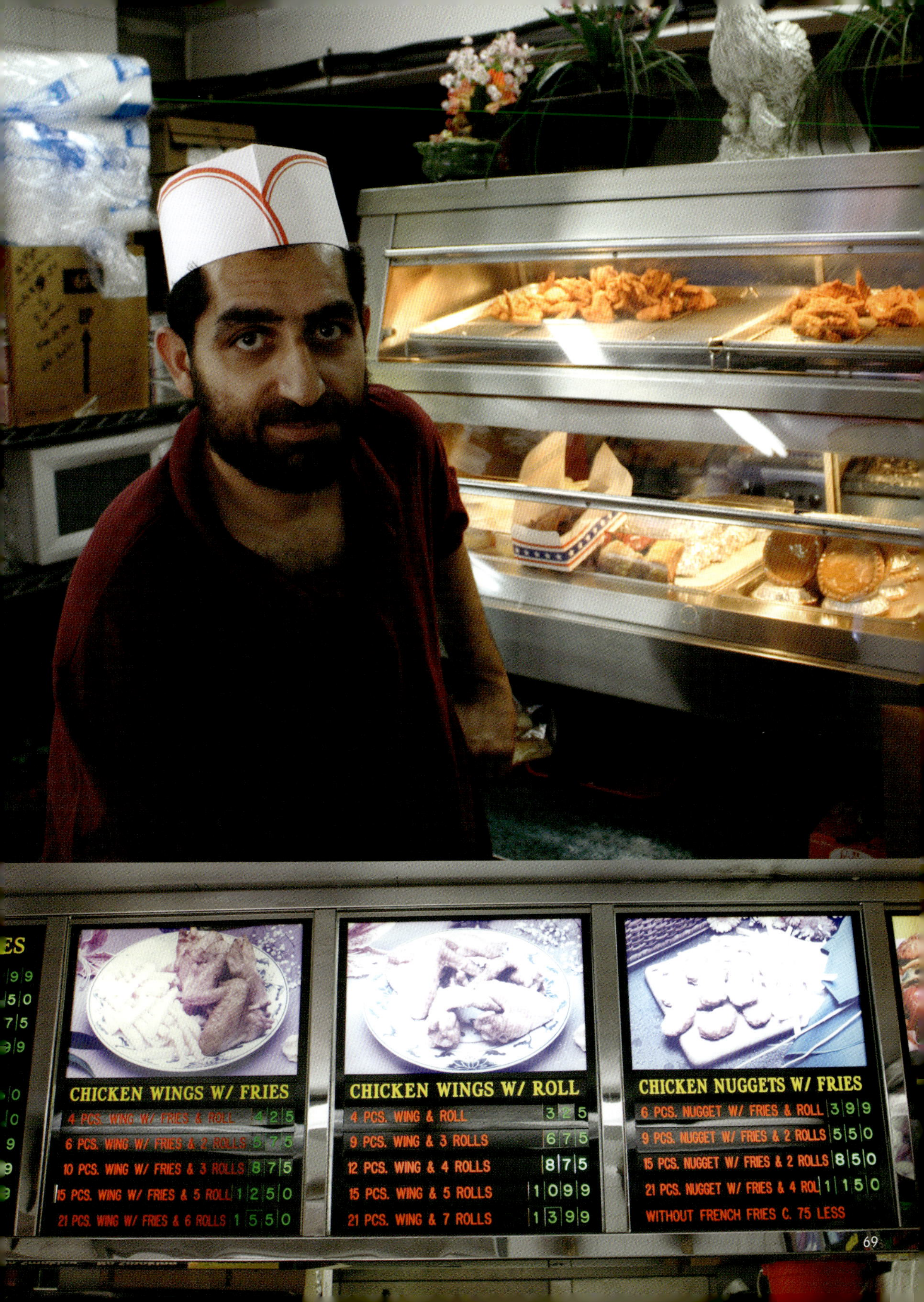
CHICKEN WINGS W/ FRIES
4 PCS. WING W/ FRIES & ROLL 425
6 PCS. WING W/ FRIES & 2 ROLLS 575
10 PCS. WING W/ FRIES & 3 ROLLS 875
15 PCS. WING W/ FRIES & 5 ROLL 1250
21 PCS. WING W/ FRIES & 6 ROLLS 1550
CHICKEN WINGS W/ ROLL
4 PCS. WING & ROLL 325
9 PCS. WING & 3 ROLLS 675
12 PCS. WING & 4 ROLLS 875
15 PCS. WING & 5 ROLLS 1099
21 PCS. WING & 7 ROLLS 1399
CHICKEN NUGGETS W/ FRIES
6 PCS. NUGGET W/ FRIES & ROLL 399
9 PCS. NUGGET W/ FRIES & 2 ROLLS 550
15 PCS. NUGGET W/ FRIES & 2 ROLLS 850
21 PCS. NUGGET W/ FRIES & 4 ROL 1150
WITHOUT FRENCH FRIES C. 75 LESS

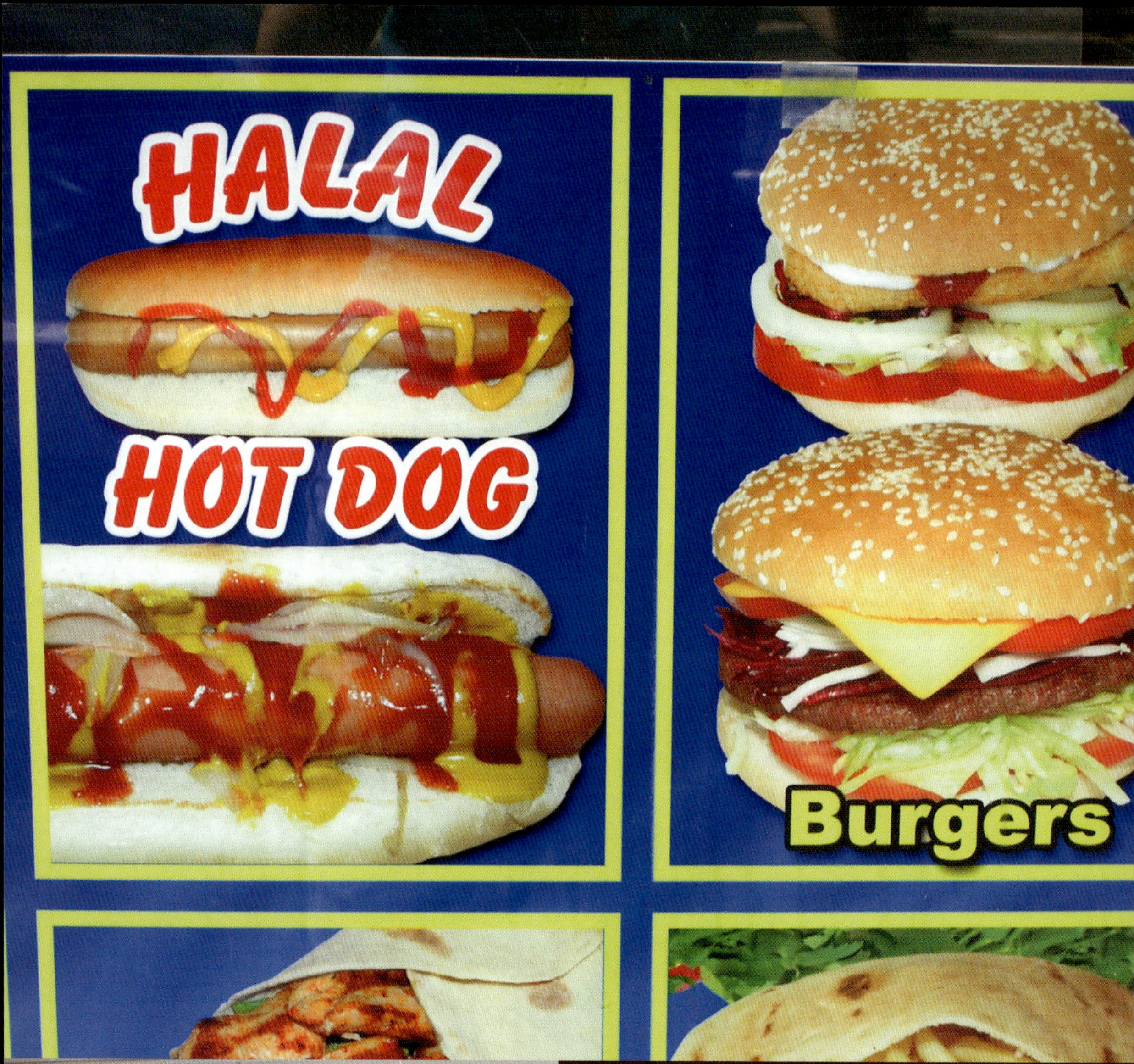

HALAL
HOT DOG
Burgers

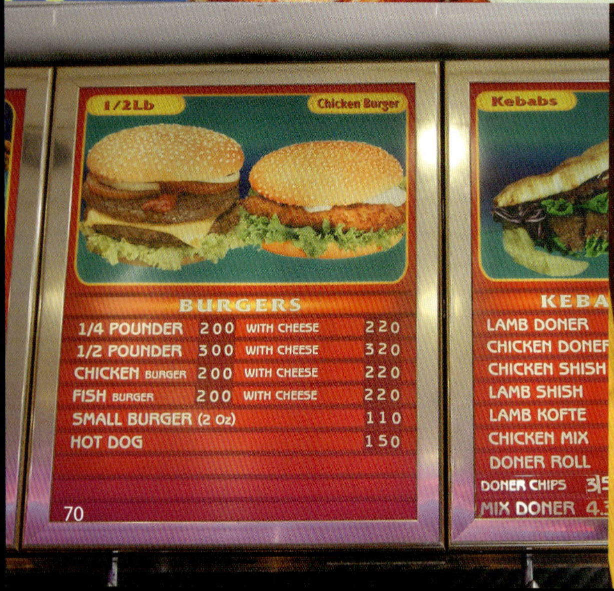

1/2Lb
Chicken Burger
Kebabs
BURGERS
1/4 POUNDER 200 WITH CHEESE 220
1/2 POUNDER 300 WITH CHEESE 320
CHICKEN BURGER 200 WITH CHEESE 220
FISH BURGER 200 WITH CHEESE 220
SMALL BURGER (2 Oz) 110
HOT DOG 150
LAMB DONER
CHICKEN SHISH
LAMB SHISH
LAMB KOFTE
CHICKEN MIX
DONER ROLL
DONER CHIPS
MIX DONER

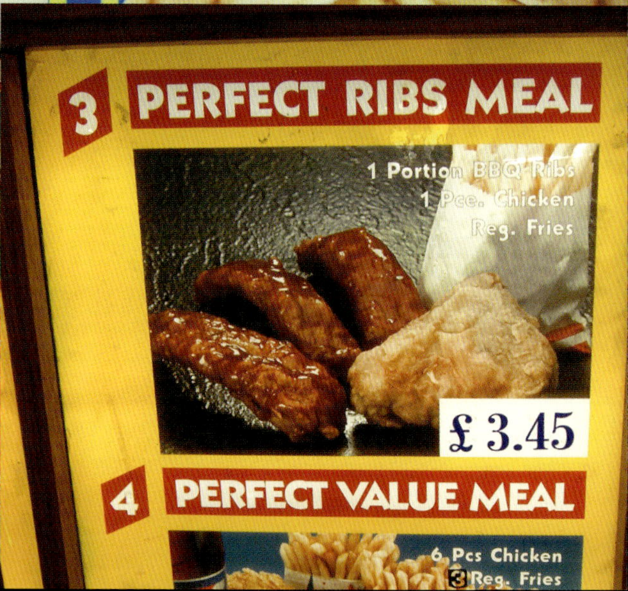

3 PERFECT RIBS MEAL
1 Portion BBQ Ribs
1 Pce. Chicken
Reg. Fries
£ 3.45
4 PERFECT VALUE MEAL
6 Pcs Chicken
Reg. Fries

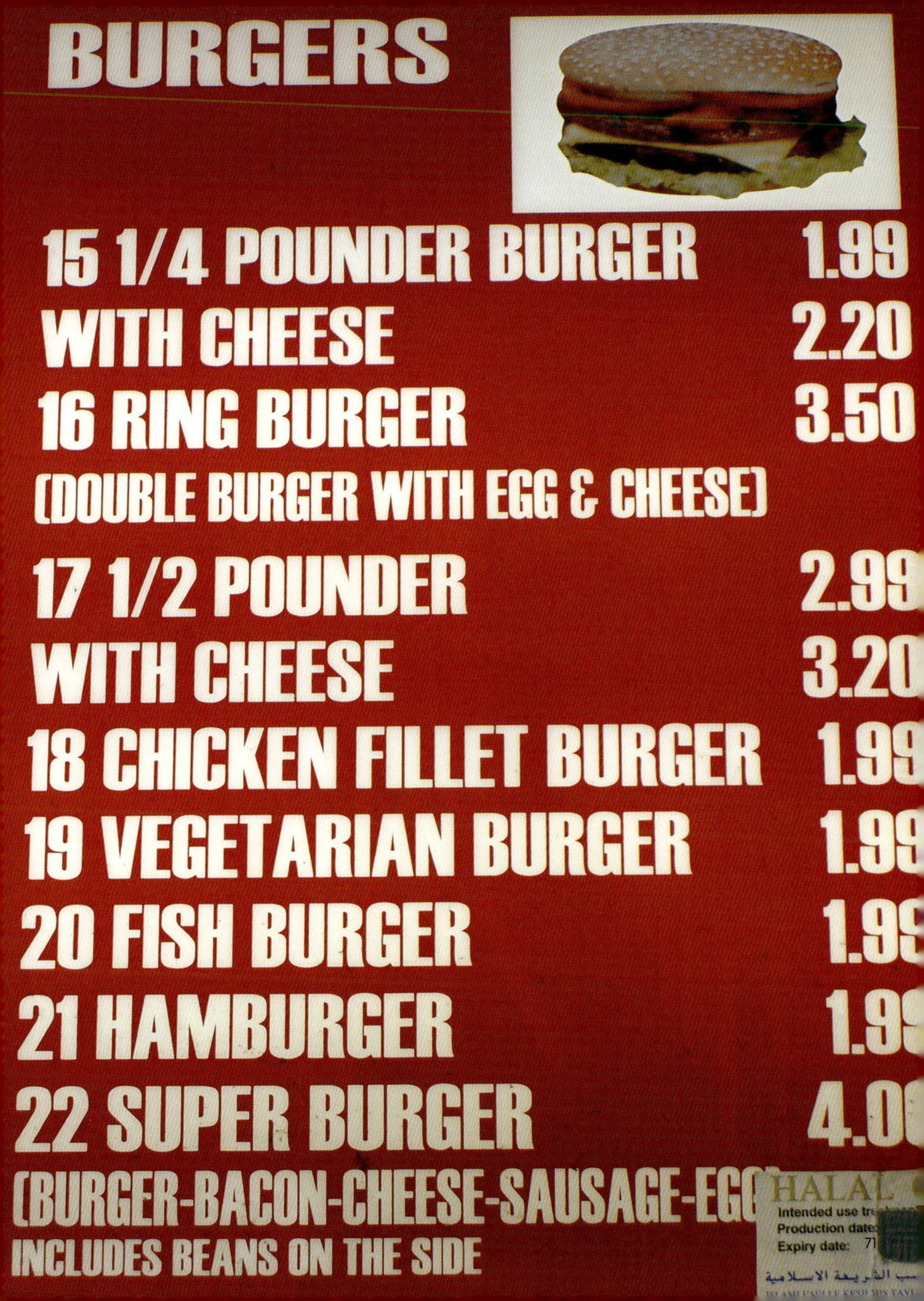
BURGERS
15 1/4 POUNDER BURGER 1.99
WITH CHEESE 2.20
16 RING BURGER 3.50
(DOUBLE BURGER WITH EGG & CHEESE)
17 1/2 POUNDER 2.99
WITH CHEESE 3.20
18 CHICKEN FILLET BURGER 1.99
19 VEGETARIAN BURGER 1.99
20 FISH BURGER 1.99
21 HAMBURGER 1.99
22 SUPER BURGER 4.0
(BURGER-BACON-CHEESE-SAUSAGE-EG
INCLUDES BEANS ON THE SIDE
HALAL
Intended use
Production date
Expiry date:

SIGN MAKERS

AND DESIGNERS

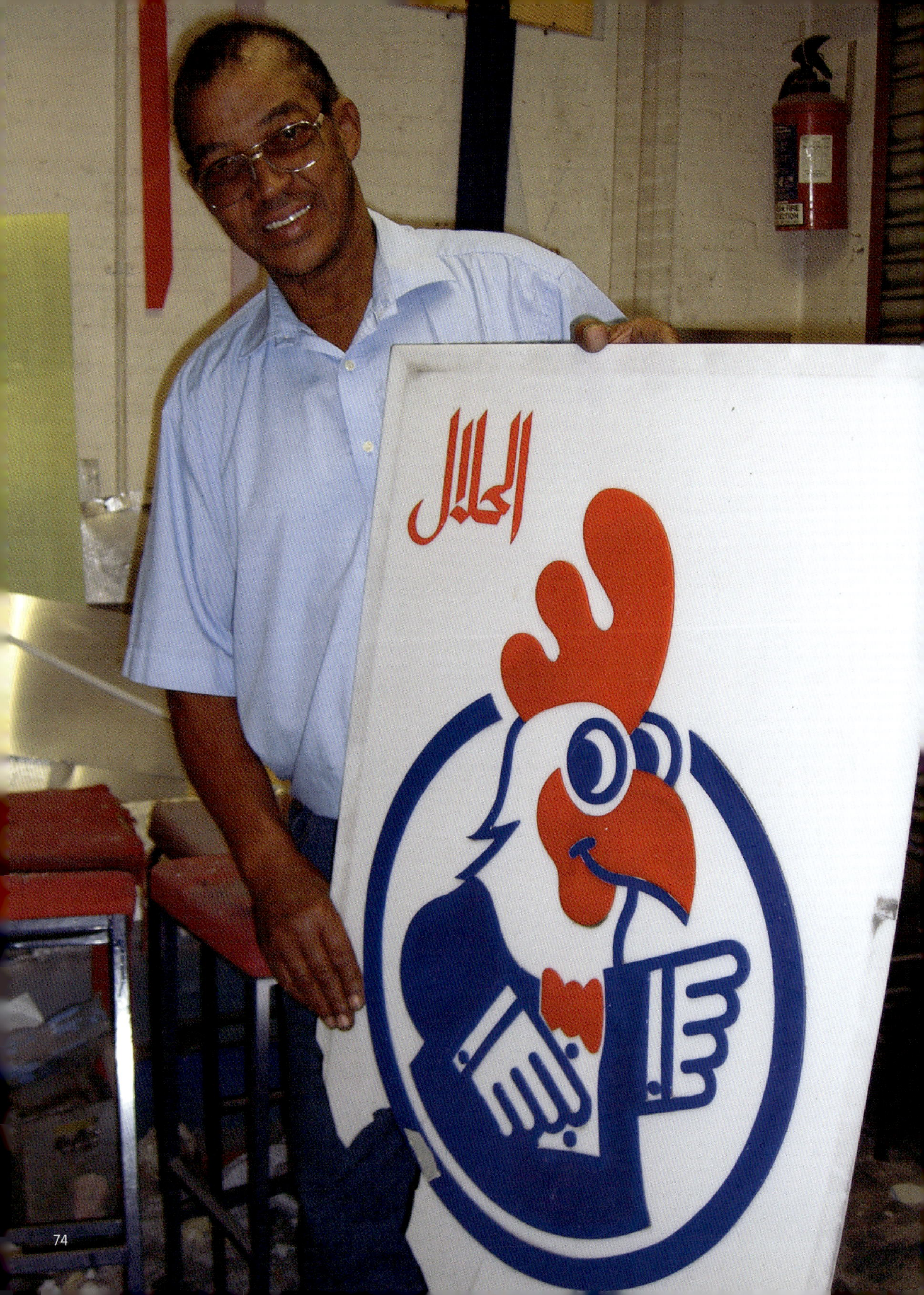
الحلال

Mr Chicken

Interview with Morris Cassanova (a.k.a. Mr Chicken).

Siāron: Could you tell me about MBC (Morris Benjamin Cassanova) Signs and how you started it?

Morris: MBC Signs started back in 1979, somewhere along that line. I used to work for a company by the name of Red Circus Signs in Harrow Road, but while working for them they moved out close to Heathrow airport and the distance was too far for me to travel. And so I got myself some premises in Kingsland Road and I set up from there. One or two workers, people used to follow me around. I mean I've got a chap downstairs called John and he's been with me from since he left school, from the age of 15 and he's in his late 40s.

It was very hard for us to get in with some of the major fried chicken companies...the bigger boys don't want to know. A lot of it was back-handers, he'll stick with one company because he's getting a ticket to Wembley or Wimbledon or something like that, and we were not in a position to make those sorts of offers. So the majority of work which we got was by recommendation from other people, other satisfied companies. We were able to continue business by what we call trade work, namely from some of the larger companies. In them days it was your ClowerGen, your Red Circus Signs, your Night Electrics and what have you. We used to do a lot of trade work for them, a lot of the car companies and banks. Night Electrics had those covered but they had a lot, even when B&Q first started they got a lot of work from them but they were unable to turn it out on time, so whatever overflow they had we usually do it for them as trade work. Admittedly we had to go in a little bit cheaper than if we were pricing it ourselves, but at the end of the day we were in it just to make a living, so it didn't matter. But as time goes on we tried to satisfy all our customers that we deal with no matter how big or small, and we managed to satisfy them and everything has been by way of recommendation.

Siāron: So all the Perfect Fried Chicken and the bigger companies, that came in time did it?

Morris: Yeah, the chicken world or the fast food world started taking over in a big way about ten years ago, no the early 90s. A lot of people who were franchises say from Kentucky Fried Chicken or something like that, maybe were feeling the squeeze. They feel as though they were working for Kentucky Fried Chicken and y'know Kentucky is so strict, whatever they says goes. And so a lot of them come out of the franchise because they know how to prepare the chicken and how to do that and what have you, a lot of them branch off and call themselves different names. So that's why we get all these different names now. Some of them who've gone on like Sams Fried Chicken and things like that they've grown bigger and they're now letting people use their name of which they charge a certain amount.

Some of the areas are so saturated with chicken shops, y'know what I mean? I blame the council to be honest to a certain extent, for letting a shop be within in a certain y'know. I feel sorry for some of them, when I put up a sign here today for somebody and then next week somebody wants me to put up another sign virtually next door. They're going to struggle to make ends meet. So eventually what's happening is that instead of some of the shops just doing chicken alone they diversify to things like pizza, burgers, kebabs, so you can go into one shop and you get four different types of menu as apposed to just chicken alone. Whereas, back to Kentucky Fried Chicken, they would not allow something like that to happen. People like Favorite Fried Chicken, they have got bigger over the years. They've got quite a few outlets, and even them tried to become like Kentucky Fried Chicken by not letting the franchisee do anything else apart from chicken, even them in certain areas has allowed certain things to carry on because they notice that the people are struggling to make ends meet. All they want is their money at the end of the day so they allow them to y'know maybe start selling pizzas, start selling burgers and what have you.

Siâron: Sometimes you'll get a chicken logo appearing for Chicken Cottage and then you have virtually the same logo for Orlando Fried Chicken, how does that work?

Morris: People do copy logos as they go along. We design a hell of a lot of logos for chicken shops of which we've never registered any of them, and if these names are not registered people just use them, right? And people like Chicken Cottage and things like that, you'll see they have a ™ at the end of each of their logos. It's registered, so anyone trying to copy that, although they look similar in appearance if you look at it, it's completely different, there's no interlocking chickens or halal sign and things like that. Everything's different. The majority of the logos you see floating about we came up with.

Siâron: Yeah, your nickname is Mr Chicken, which is why I got hold of you. Quite a few different chicken and kebab shop owners referred to you by it!

Morris: (laughing) All of these in your book, I did.

Siâron: In London, how much of the signage would you say you're responsible for?

Morris: I would say 90% of the logos that's been used out there now, was originally designed by ourselves. People see them and try to change them around a little bit, and you will see somewhere along the line somebody will have something looking similar to that. It's not all about the bits and pieces that goes with it, they will automatically try to copy it.

Siâron: There's lots of mimicking America going on isn't there?

Morris: Yeah, yeah the majority of shop owners out there they want for some reason or other, because Kentucky Fried Chicken is an American company, they wants to give the impression that they are linked with the American fast food chain. In the past Kentucky usually have a little logo, a little slogan, "American Recipe," people used to copy that. I mean a lot of people still try, and we say, "Oh that's old fashioned, people not using that again." Because they try to pull the wool over people's eyes, you get your Dallas, it's American, you get your California, it's American, you get your Mississippi it's American, and so forth and so on, and people just use those names to link with America just as well as they're using their recipe, y'know. You hardly ever see a sign saying English Fried Chicken, or with an English name or anything like that.

Siâron: You've already mentioned how the menus aren't neccessarily very American anymore?

Morris: No it's not so American anymore, because people eventually found out it doesn't matter anymore, once the product is good and it's selling that's all people is interested in. In the early days when Kentucky first came over everyone was brain-washed, y'know? It's American and it's good, it's gotta be good because it's American. It's not just chicken shops it's pizza, too. You get people like Domino Pizza or Pizza Hut. You find other little shops they learn how to do pizza and wise up to it, once the quality of your product is good you've got companies like Perfect Fried Chicken, which looks different and changes their logo.

Siâron: In all your years working, have you got any funny stories?

Morris: (laughing) My brain is a little bit fuzzy now. We had one, over at Lewisham and he chose the

(continued on page 79)

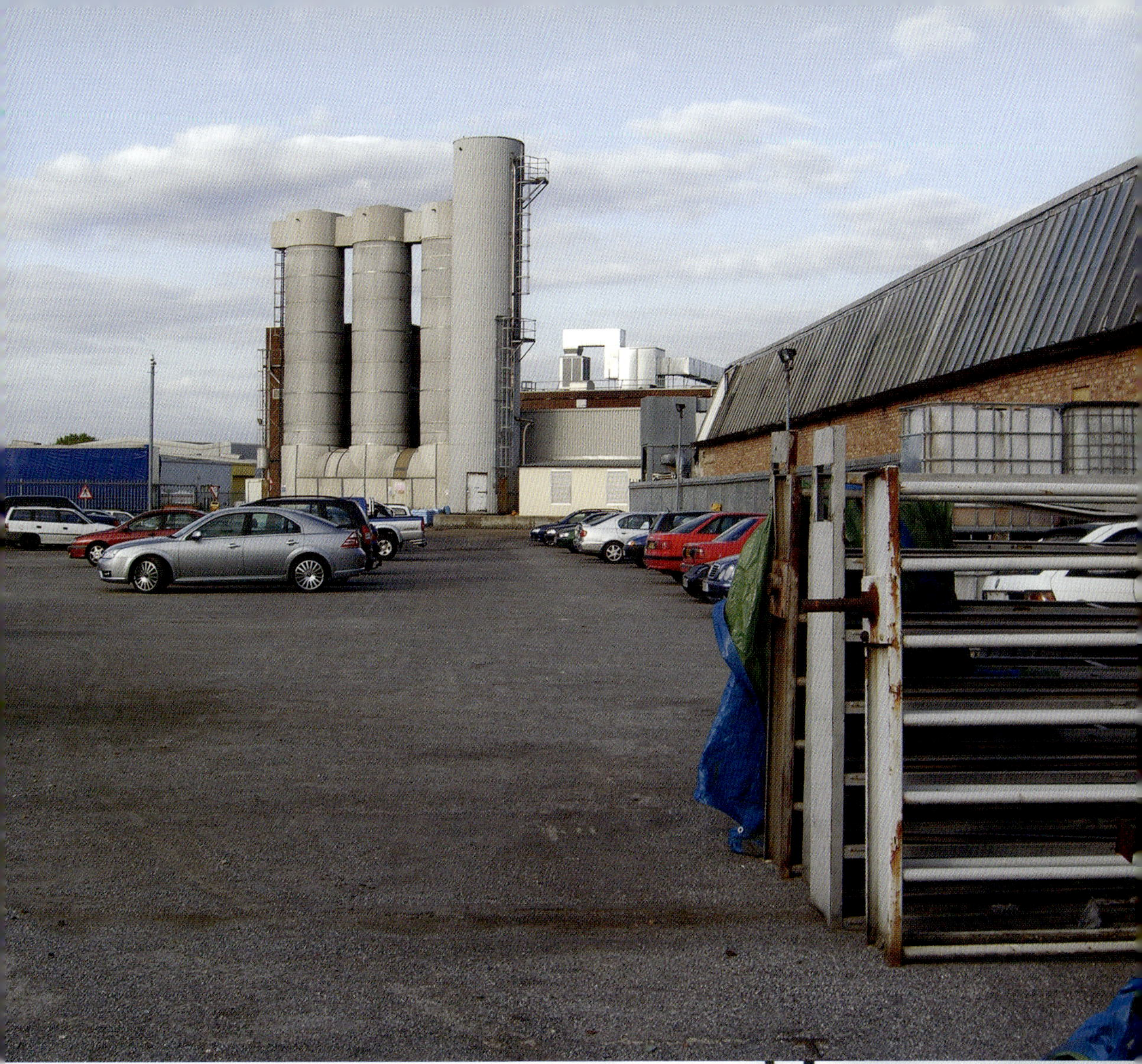

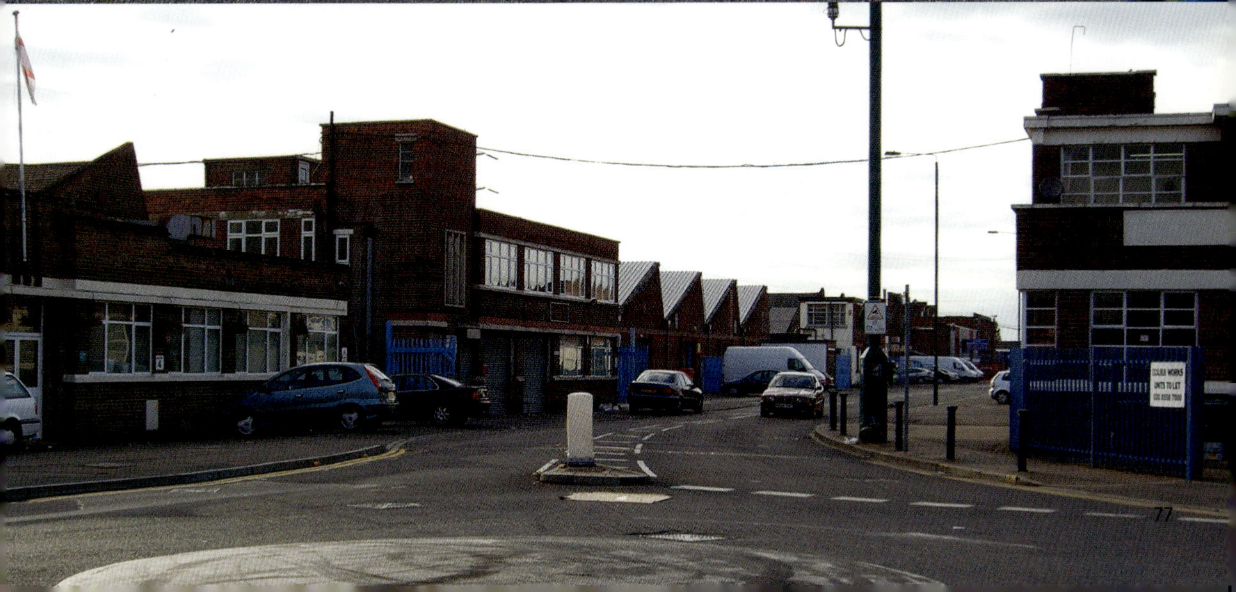

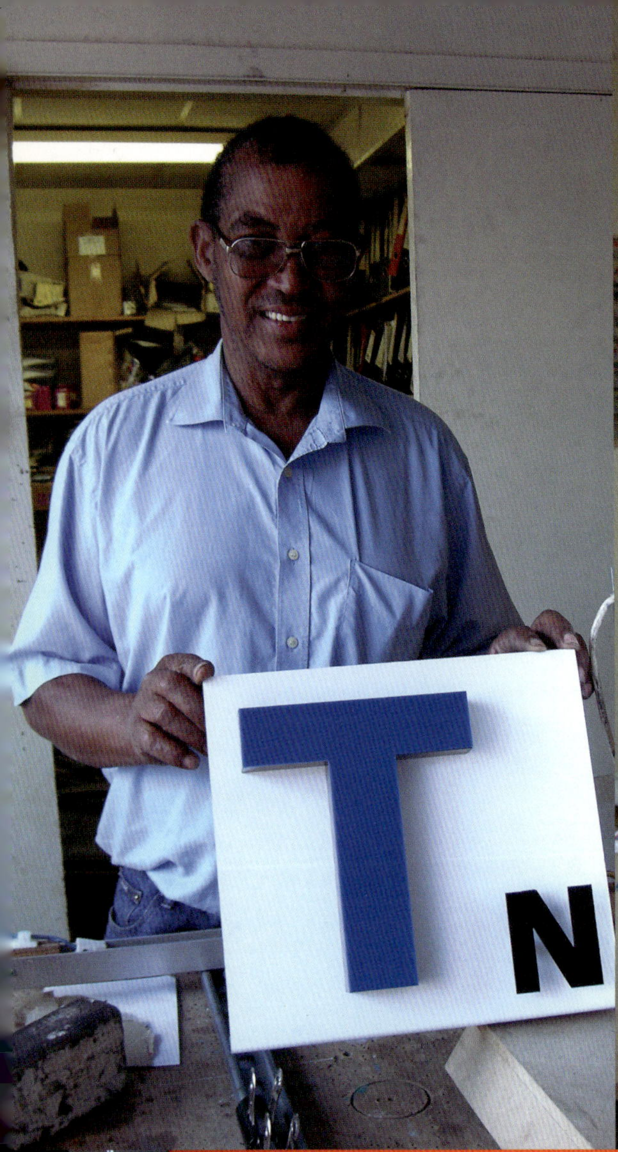
T
N

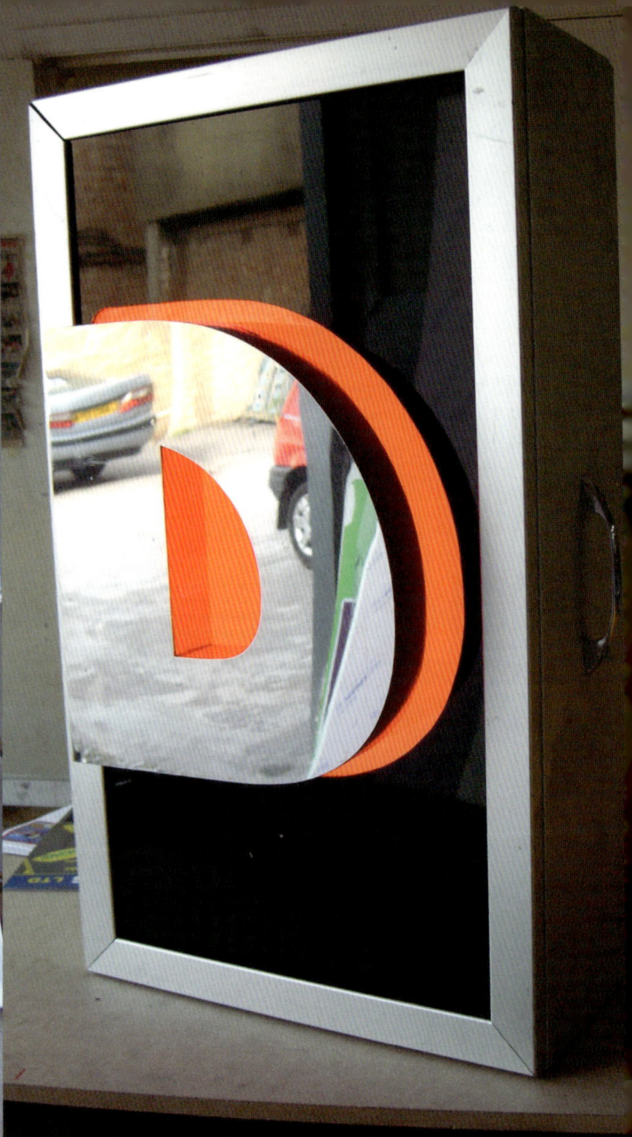
D

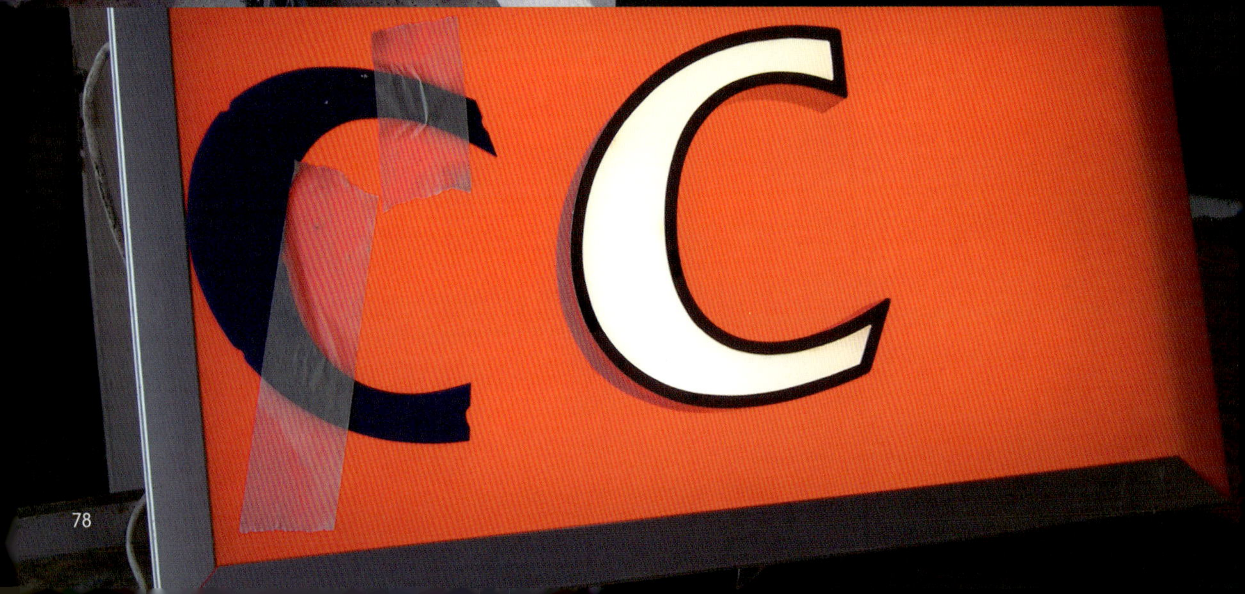
C
C

computer age and computer images and things like that. The guy wanted the name Chicken Dot Com. What's that? That's the name he wanted. We managed to talk him out of it, y'know. Chicken Dot Com. I was like "Are you some company to repair Chickens?!" (laughs)

There was a bloke as well, near Brixton that way. He wanted his chicken shop, originally he was Dallas, but he wanted to come out of Dallas and wants to use his son's name. But on the signboard itself there was hardly anything about chicken. It was more like the life of his son, because he wanted all of his pictures all over the sign, y'know? I suppose because he's so proud of him that's what he wanted. But it was nothing to do with chicken at all it was mainly just to do with the life story of his son. If you drove past there you wouldn't think it was a chicken shop. After two or three years he was closed down because nobody was taking much notice. You can only try and advise people when they come along to you in things like that. You don't think that's right, you've been in the trade for so many years that don't sound right, y'know? Some people, it takes a hell of a lot to convince them of that, y'know! (laughs)

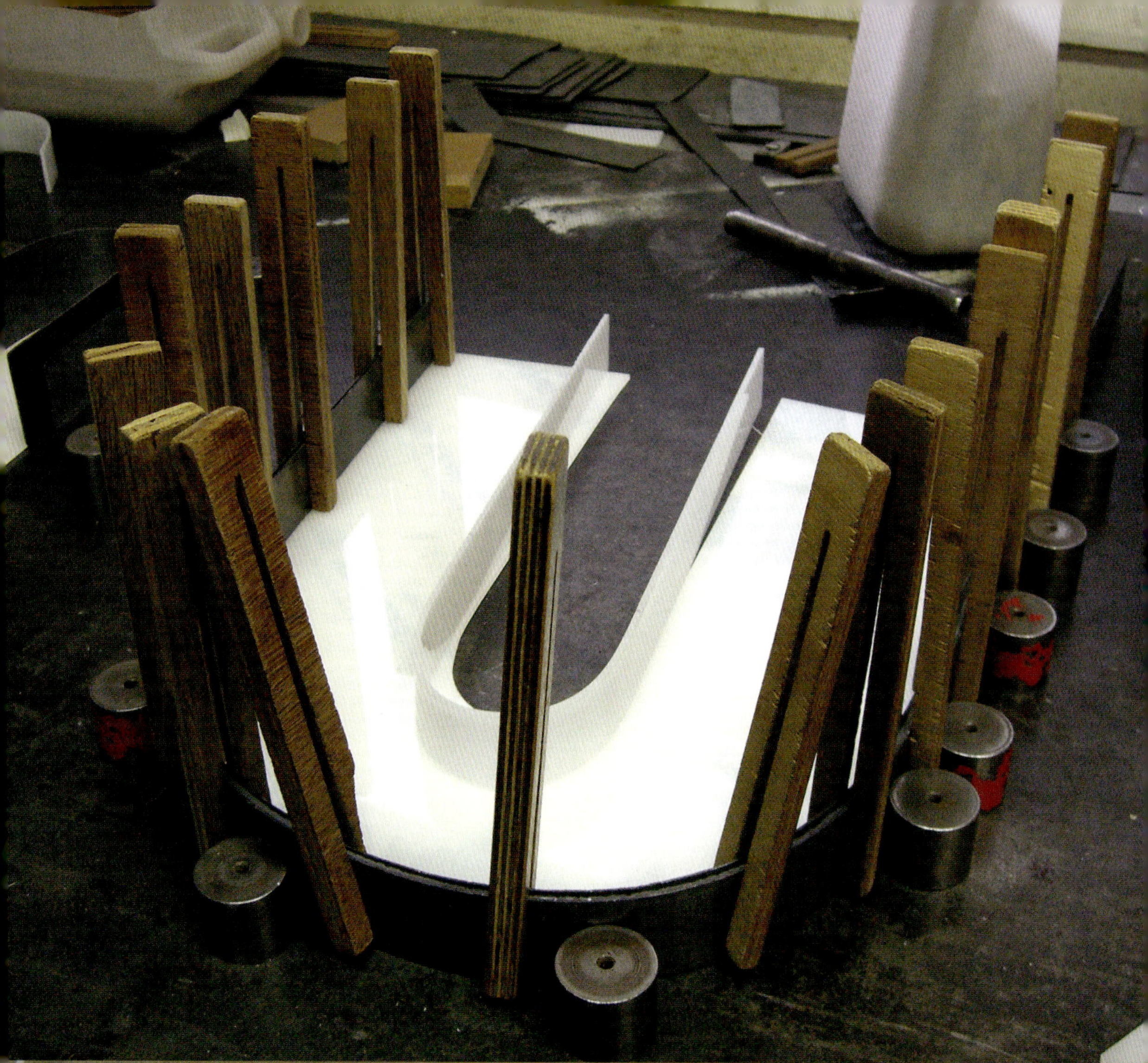

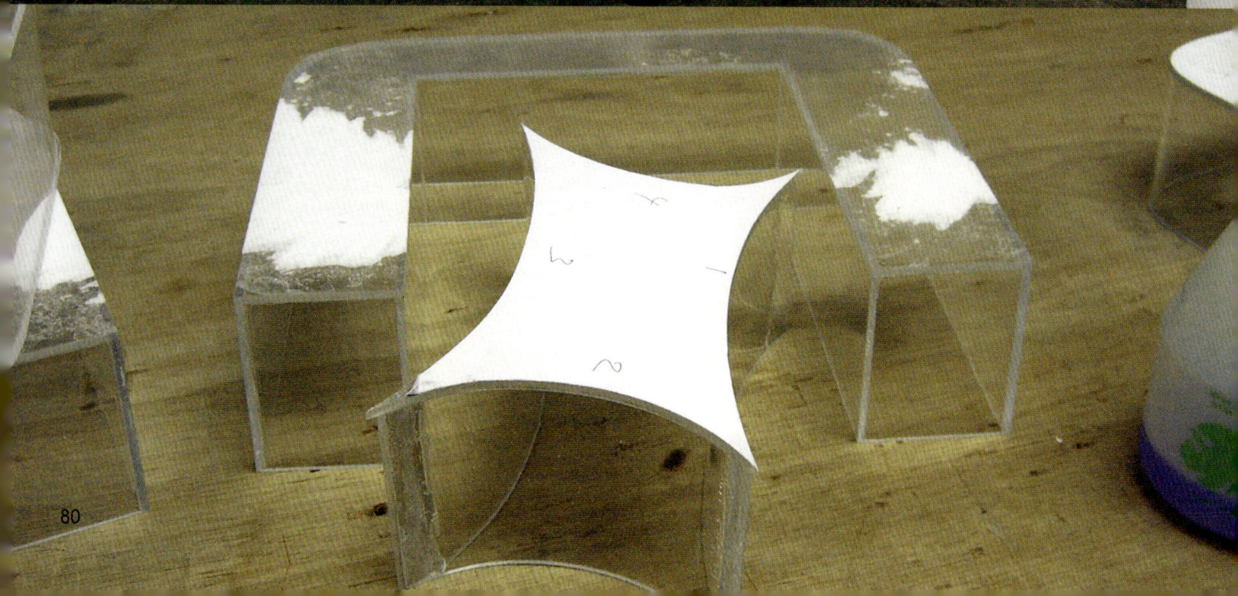

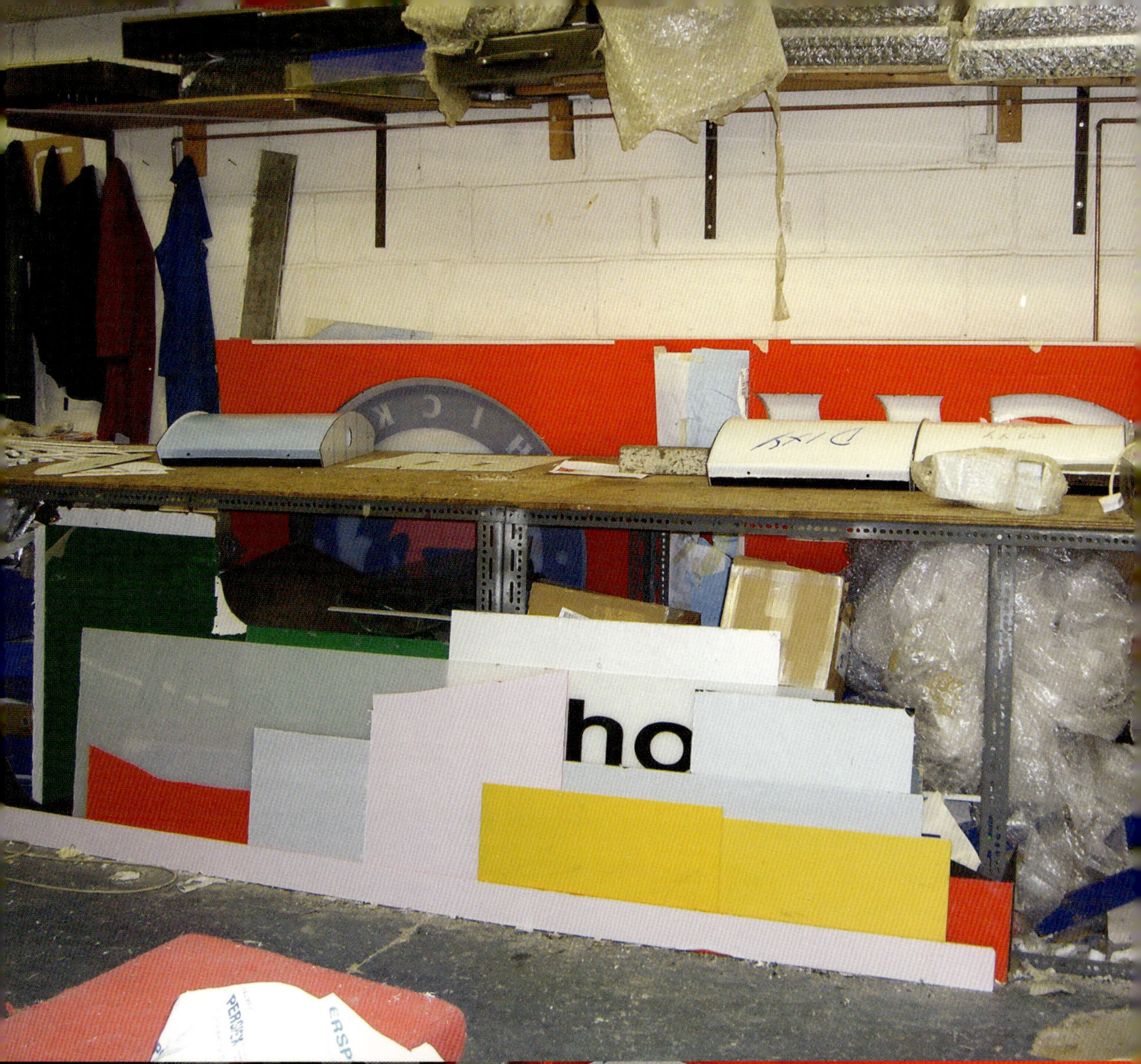

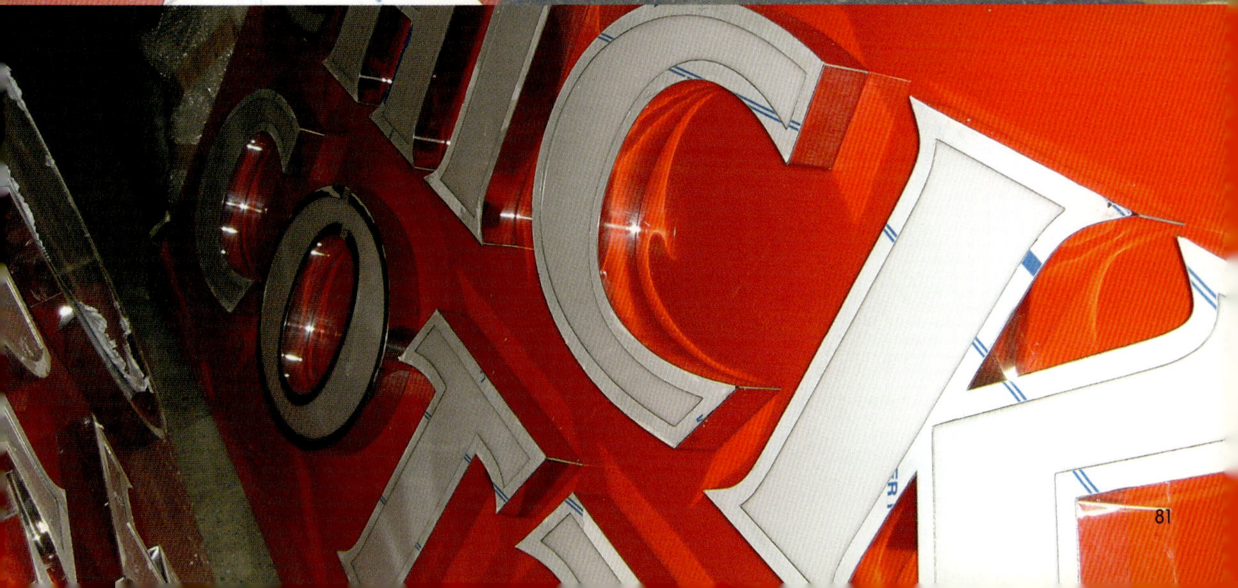

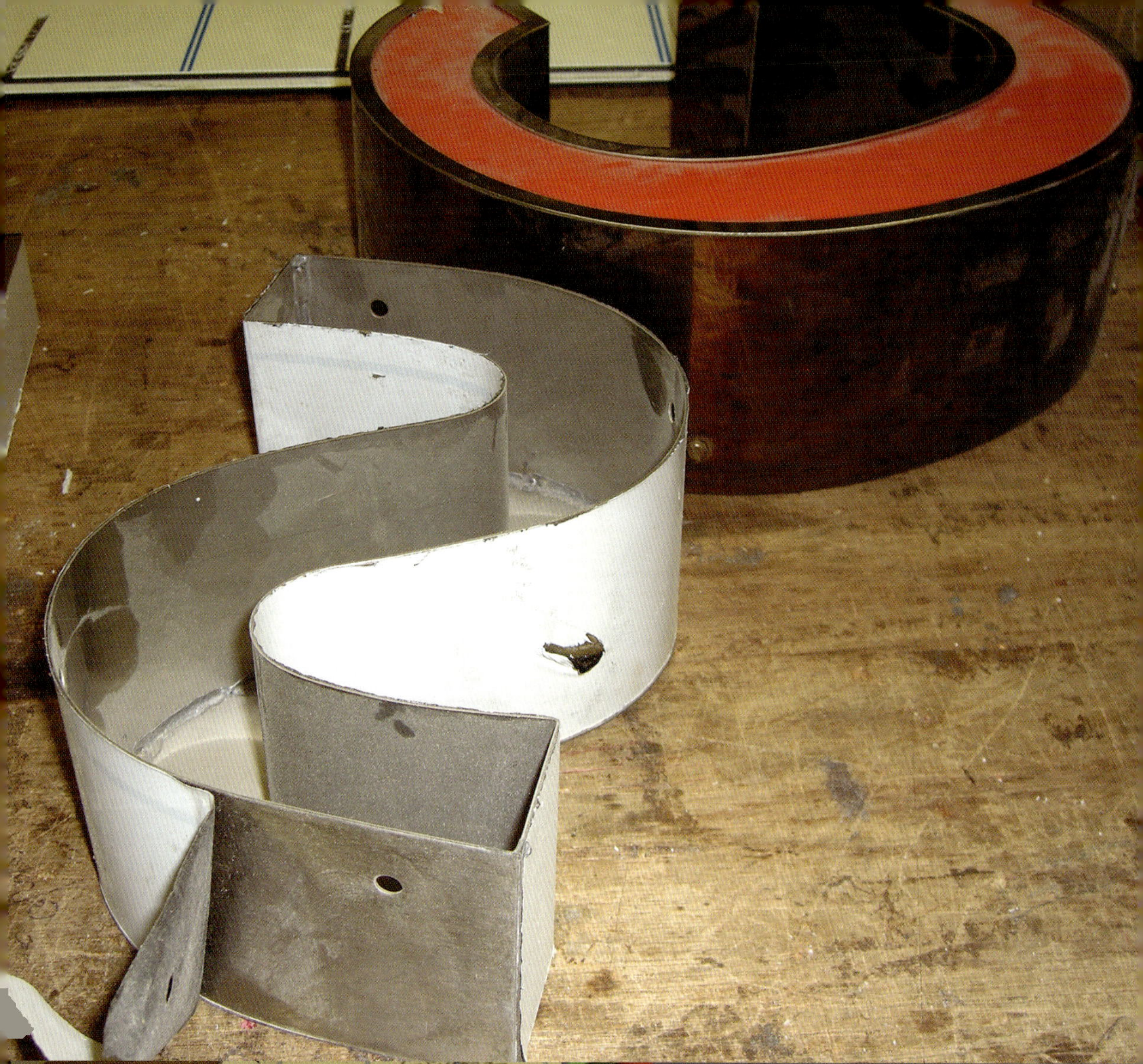

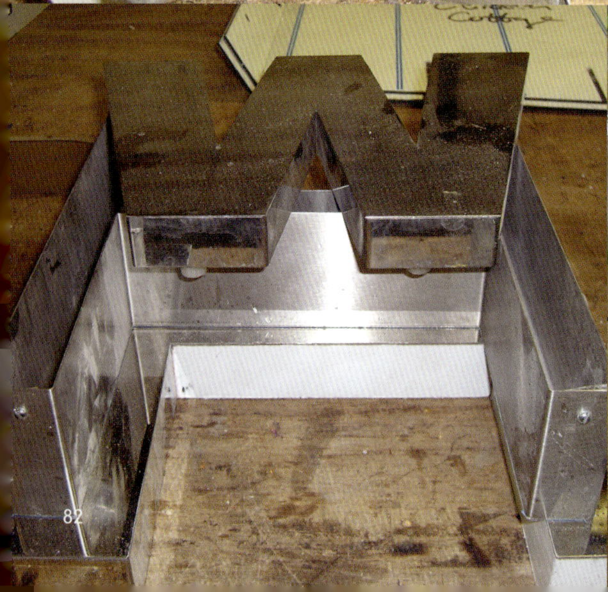

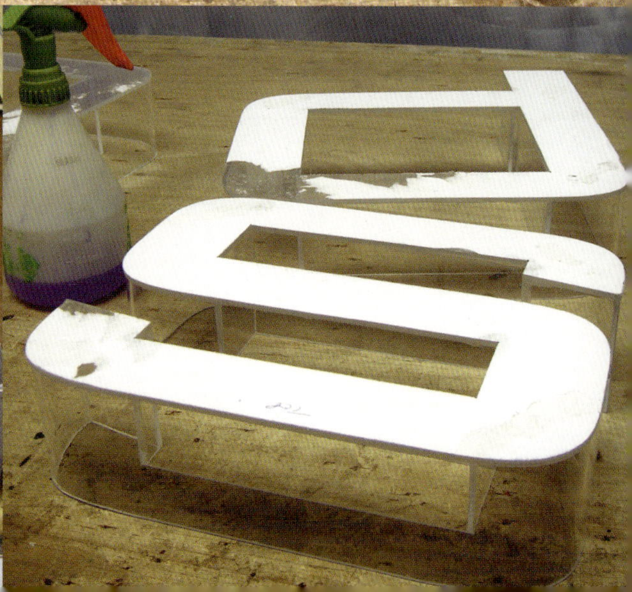

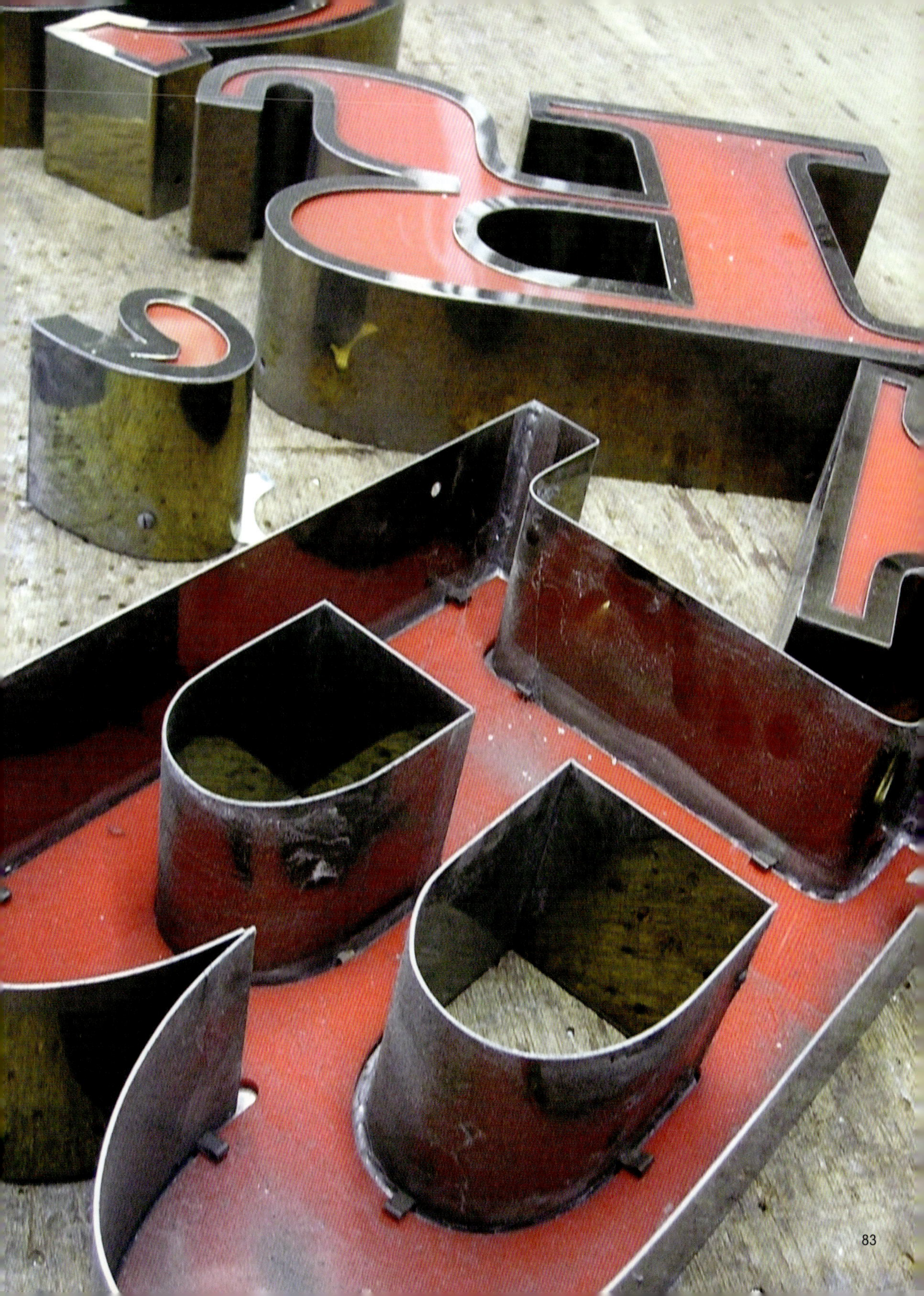

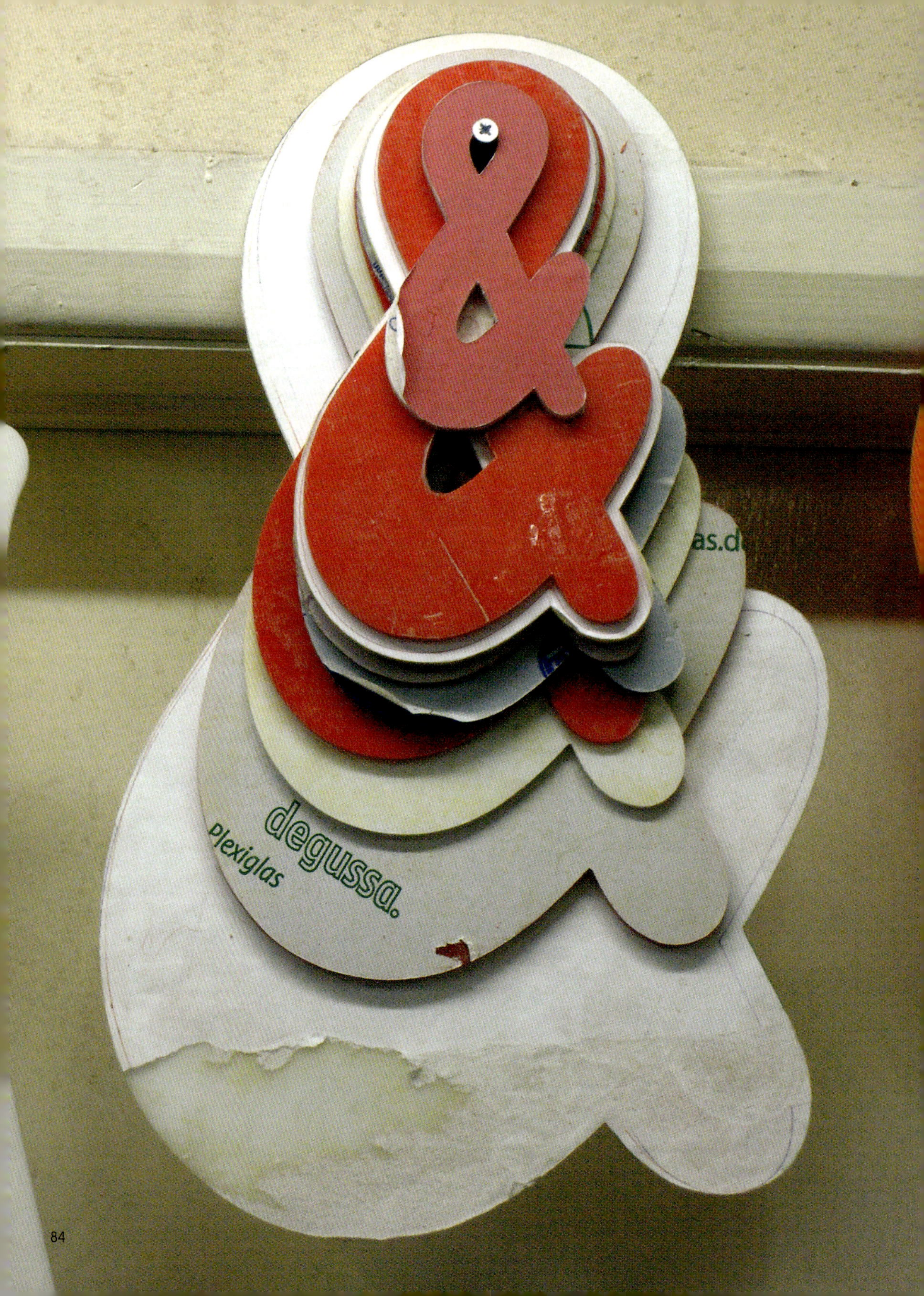
degussa.
Plexiglas

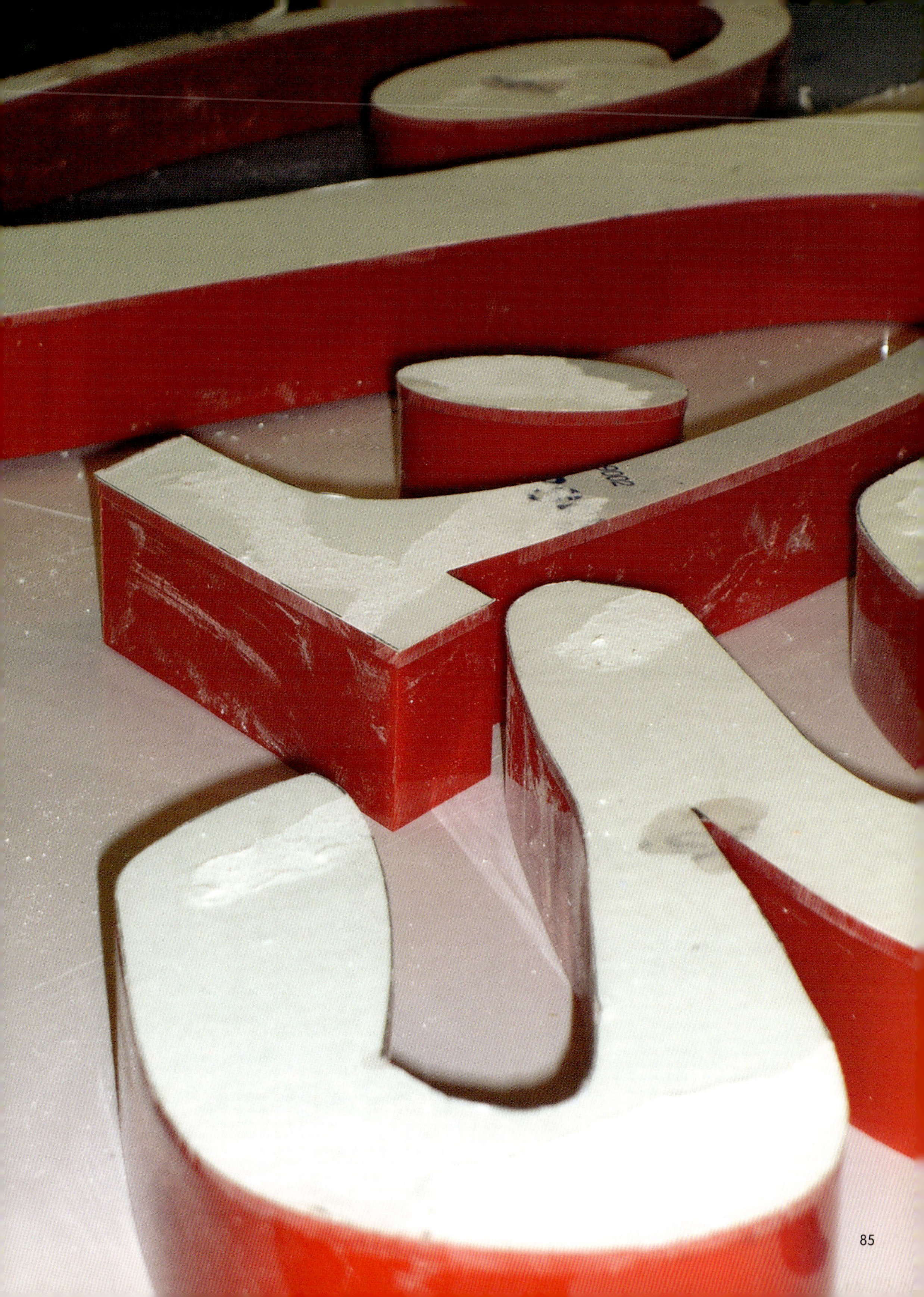

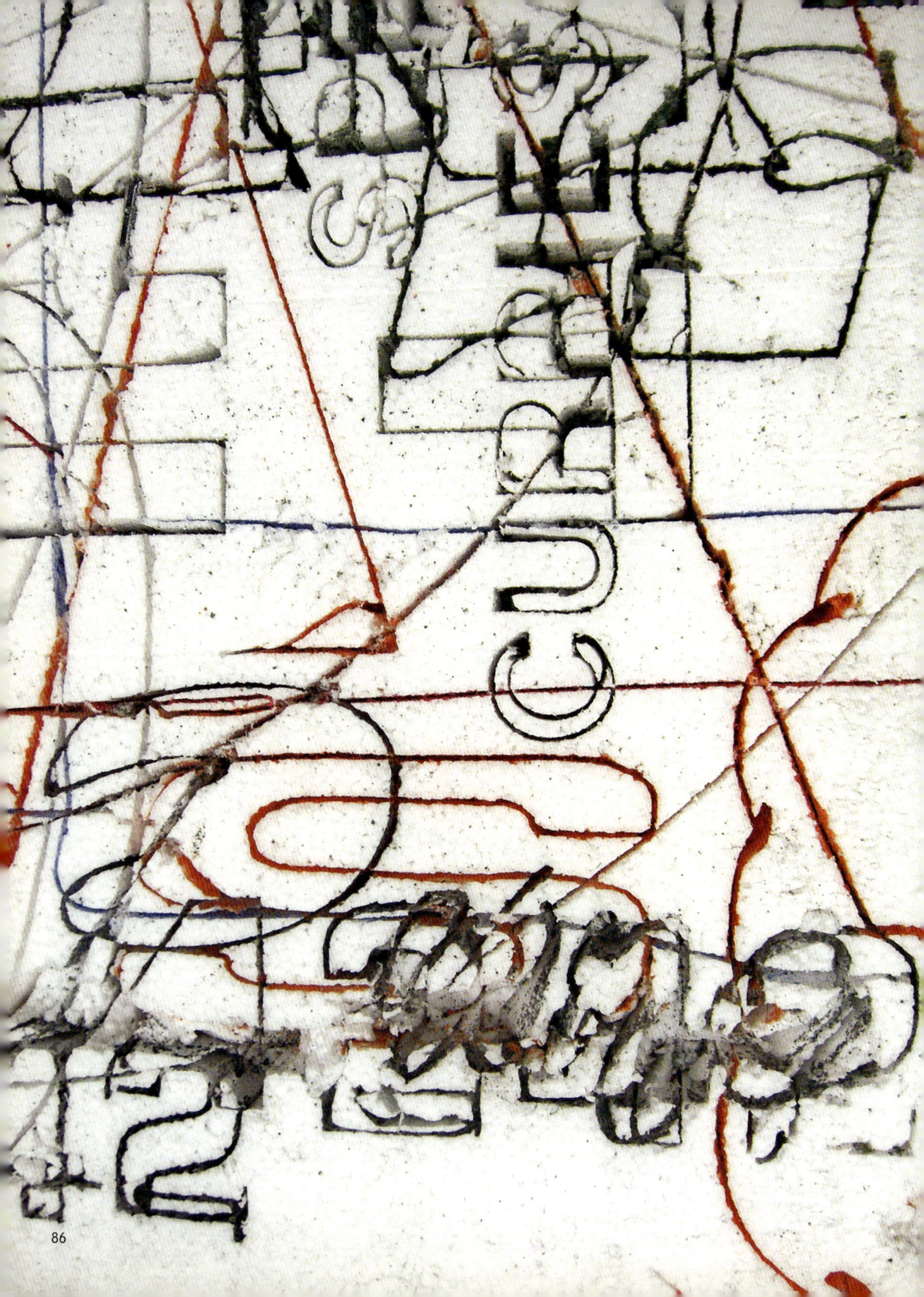

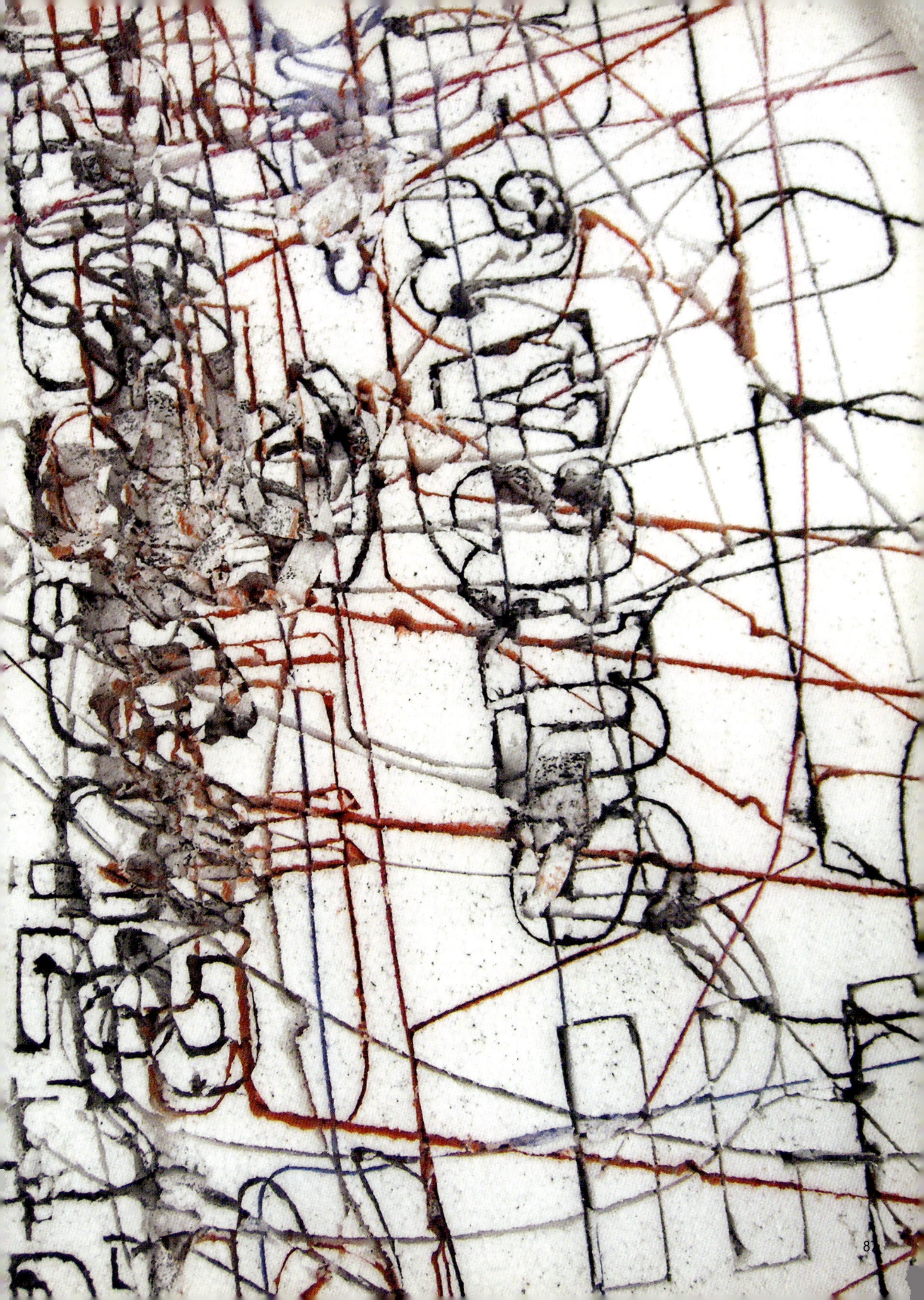

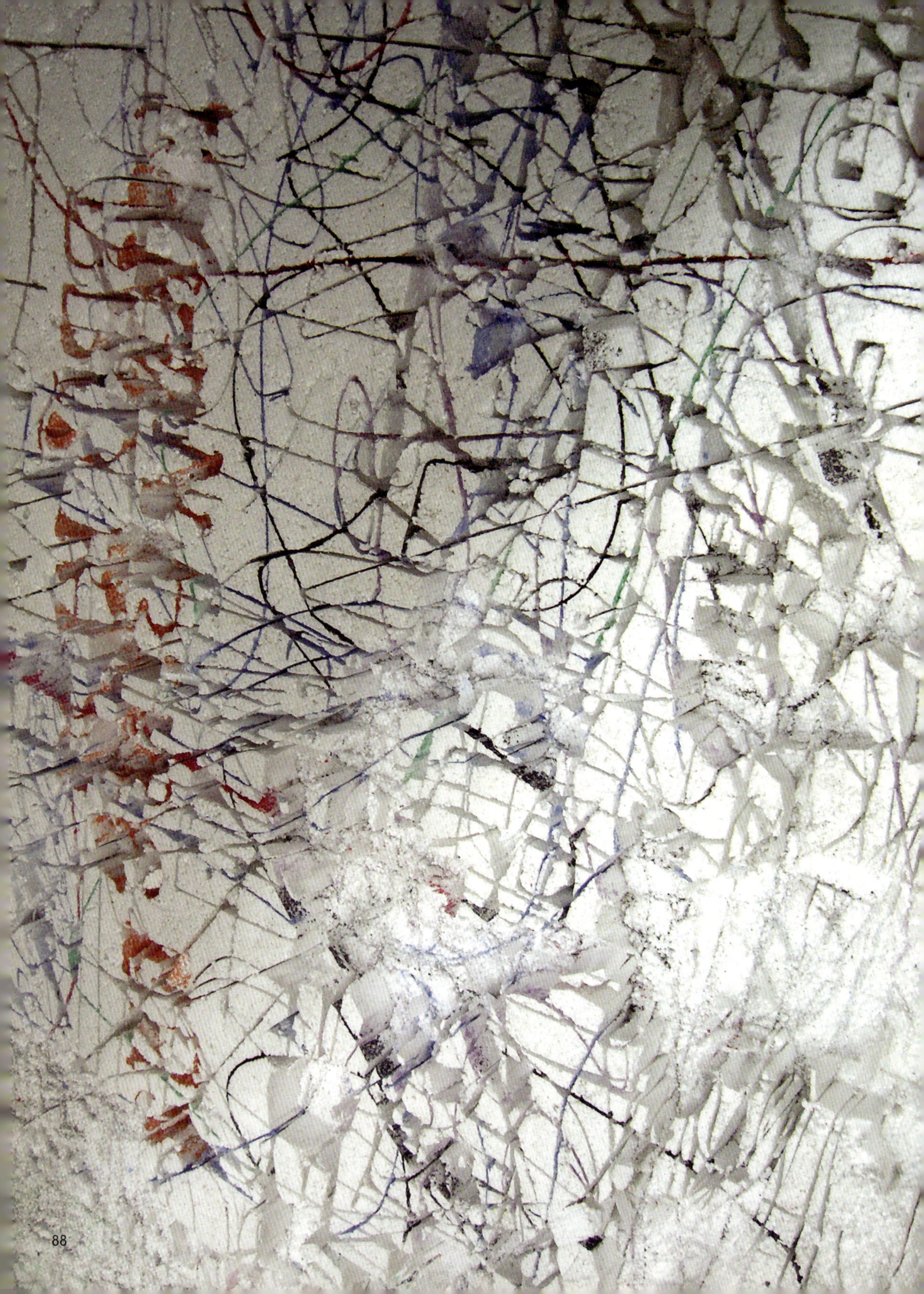

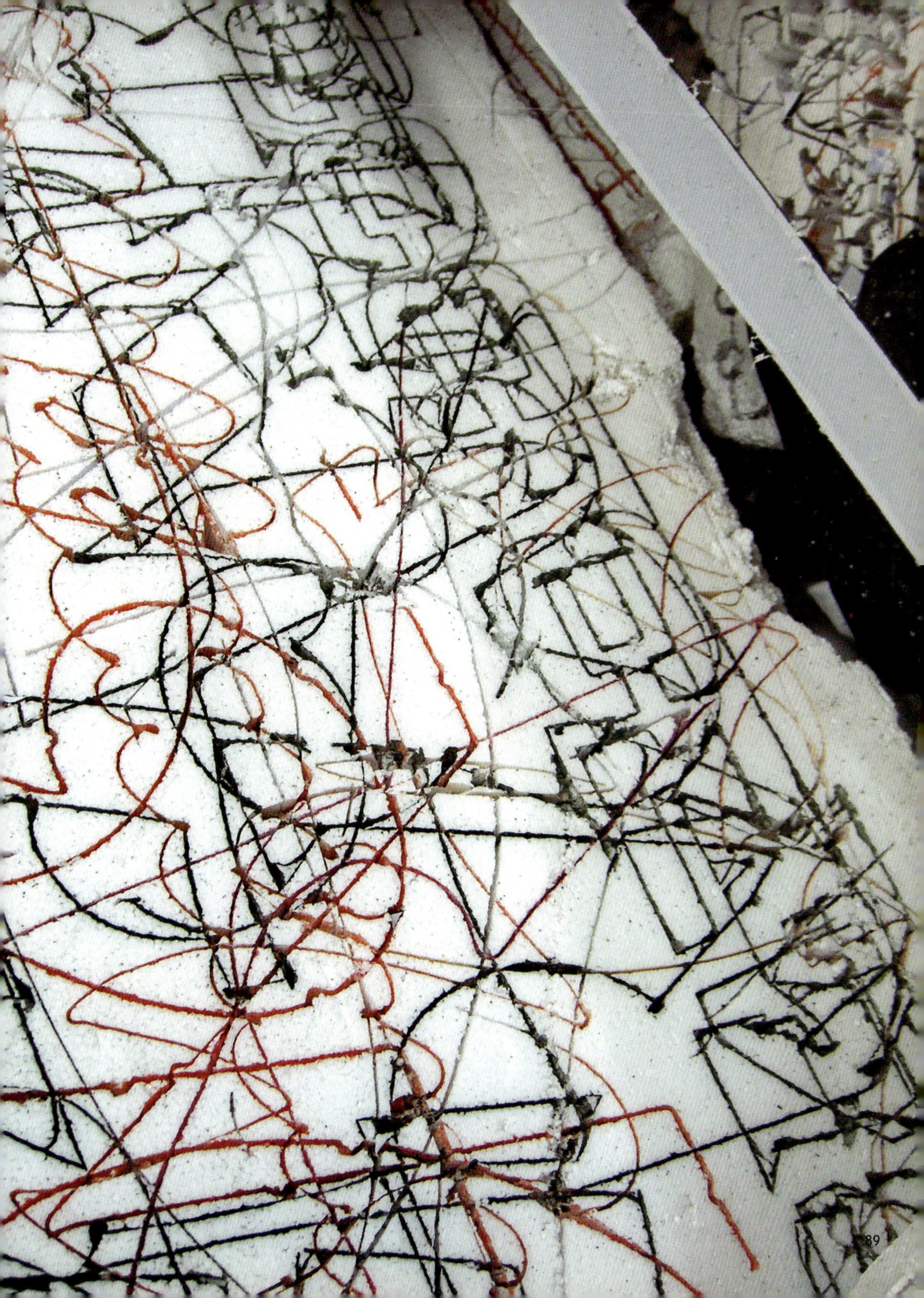

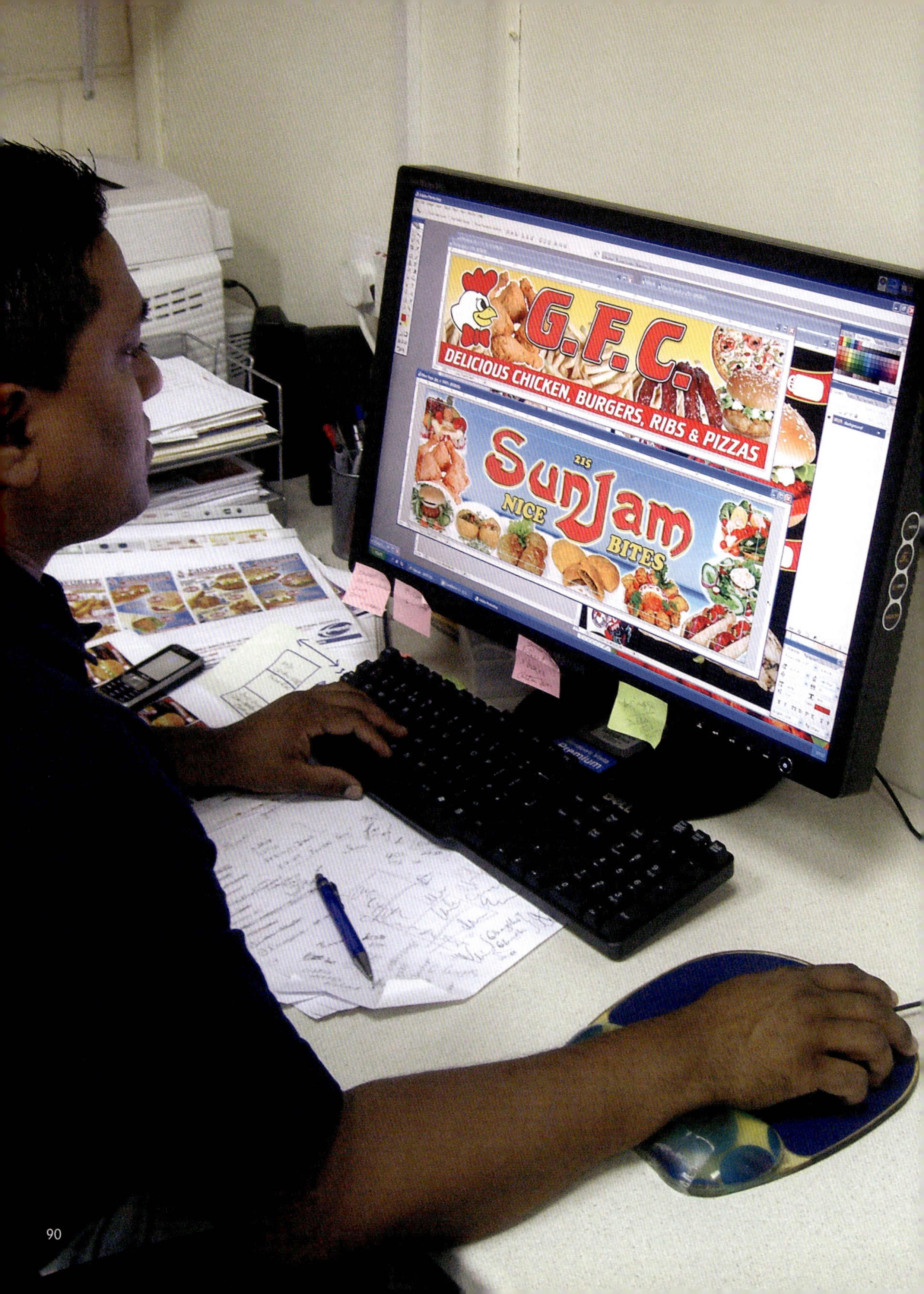
G.F.C.
DELICIOUS CHICKEN, BURGERS, RIBS & PIZZAS
215
SunJam
NICE
BITES
DELL

Richie

Interview with Richie from Compugrafix.

Richie: We do outside and inside, but mainly inside. Mainly the menu displays. I started four years ago. I used to work somewhere else as a graphic designer for another sign-making company.

Siãron: How did you get into it?

Richie: From where I came from in South America, I got into it but we weren't doing nothing like this, just making signs and stuff. Then when I came over here, then I got into it. I knew the basics sort of then when I come over here and started working for this company then it developed from there. Things didn't work out and so I had to leave and then I started up on my own. This thing was owned by Morris and then I bought it out from him, because he doesn't really know much about computers. The guy he had working for him used to make lots of mistakes and cost him a lot of money, so he got fed-up and I used to come here and work on lots of bits and pieces, for additional cash. And then I knew him and he asked me if I wanted to buy it, so I just raised the money and then I bought it.

Siãron: And it's working out?

Richie: Yeah, yeah yeah I've just got to the next level y'know...

Siãron: How does it work?

Richie: The thing is with fried chicken shops they all copy each other. Two-piece chicken fries and drink, three-piece chicken fries and drink, chicken burger fries and drink, y'know they just copy each other mainly, some of them have a few different things also and then designs are different but basically everybody copies everybody. You know the fried chicken world is not a very big one, you don't have to think too much. (laughing) It's just pictures, yeah.

Siãron: But you do change it sometimes don't you, some are on a black background and others are on white...

Richie: Yeah, yeah different designs so they look a bit different.

Siãron: What's the most popular style?

Richie: Nowadays people go for the light coloured background because it's more modern, compared to five or six years ago it was a black background. But black is good I mean, you see the food stand out, y'know? The white gives it a bit more, I dunno... more fresh looking.

Siãron: Do you work with the photographers then?

Richie: I do all the photography myself. Well you don't go into the chicken shop and get a nice burger like the ones we photograph! (laughs) It's all photography tricks. For example, when we do the chicken burger, you don't ever fry the chicken burger like how you would sell it. You like half cook it, then we get a box of buns and you choose the right one the best one, get all the lettuce. We use whole lettuce leaves, we just fold them and stick them in. Normally you just cut bits up and throw some in the bun. And the bun is set back and tilted away so you have sense of it being much bigger! (laughs)

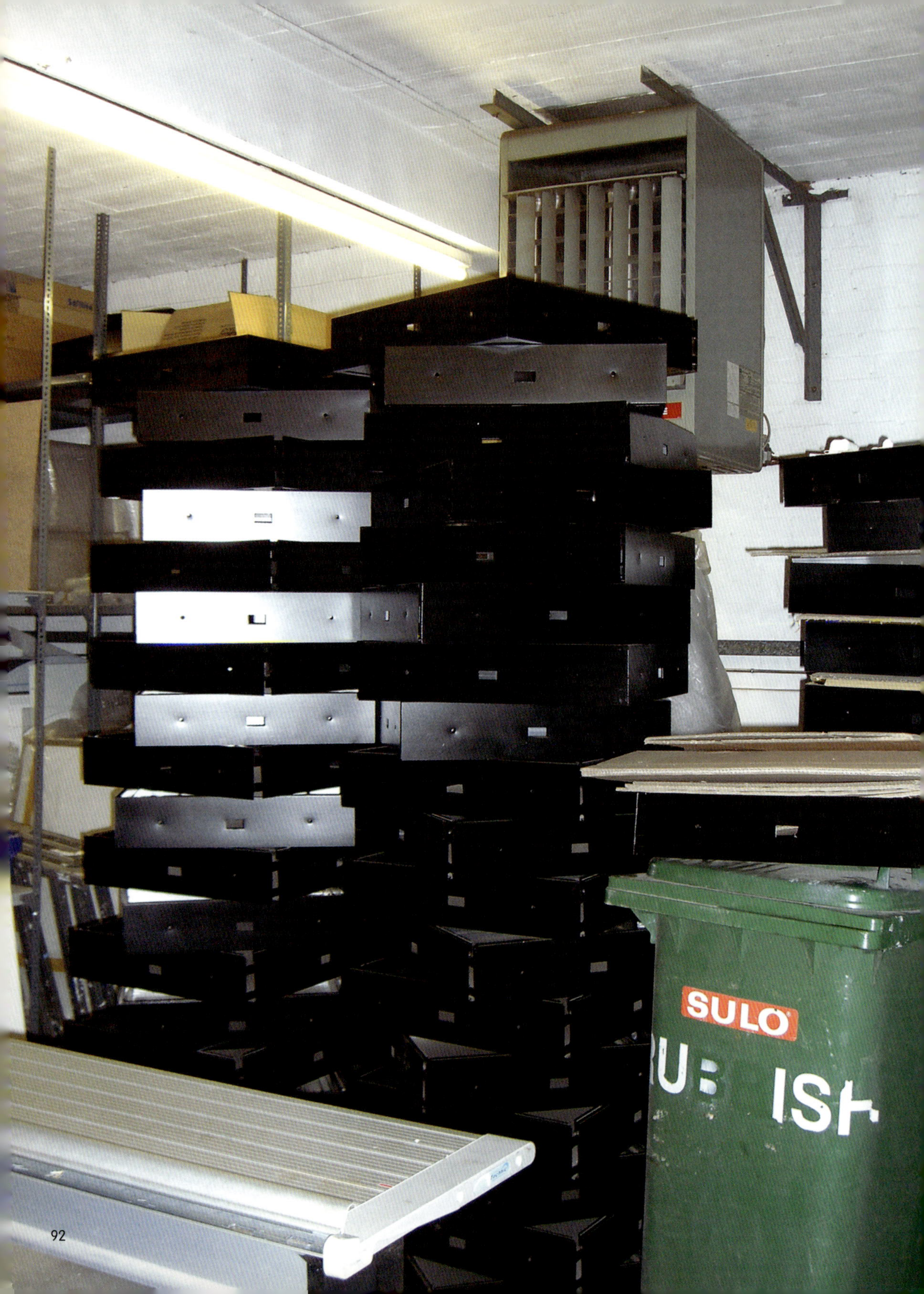
SULO
RU ISH

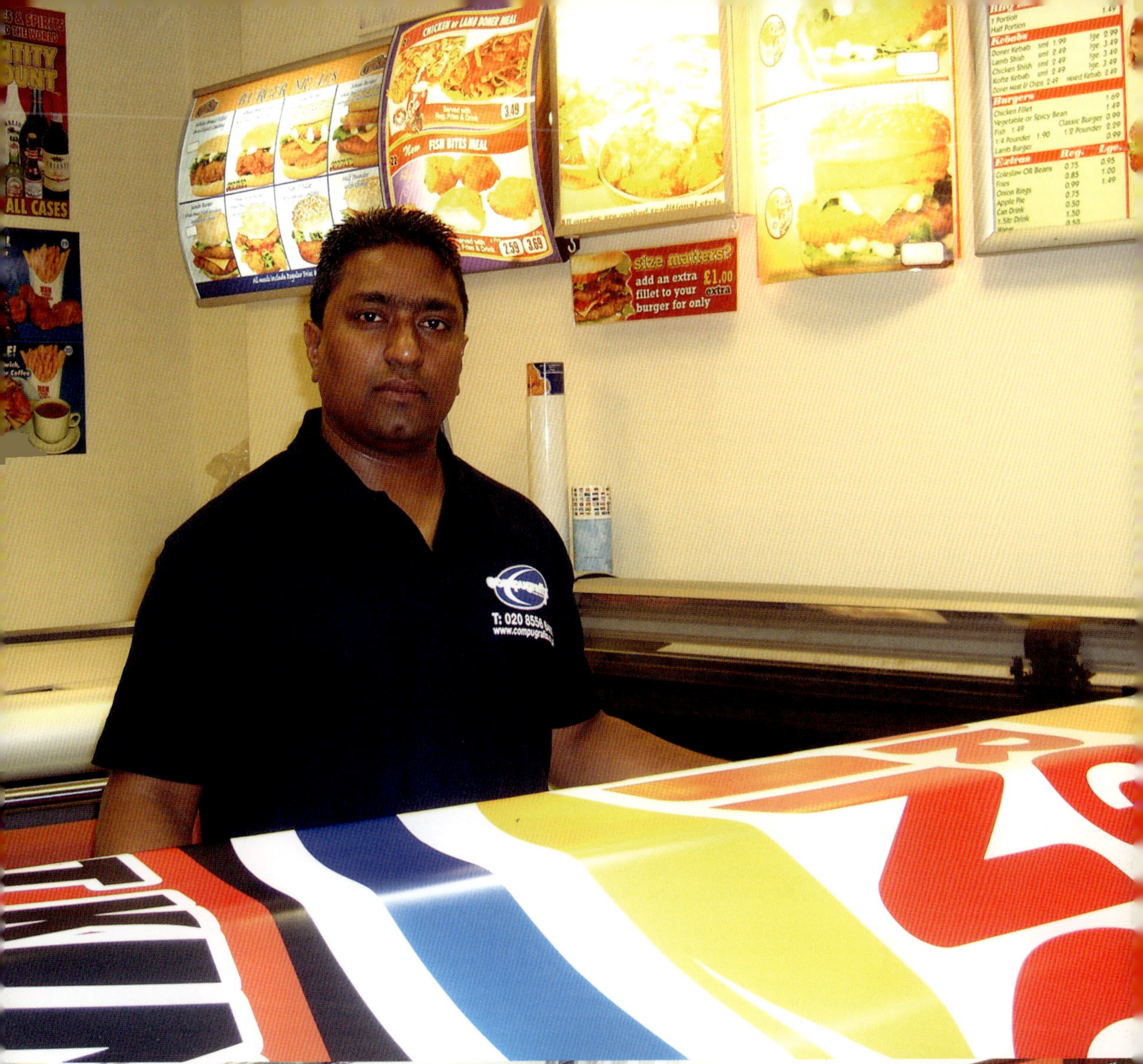
BURGER MEALS
CHICKEN or LAMB DONER MEAL
Served with Reg. Fries & Drink
3.49
New FISH BITES MEAL
2.59 3.69
size matters?
add an extra fillet to your burger for only
£1.00 extra
ALL CASES
Kebabs
Burgers
Extras

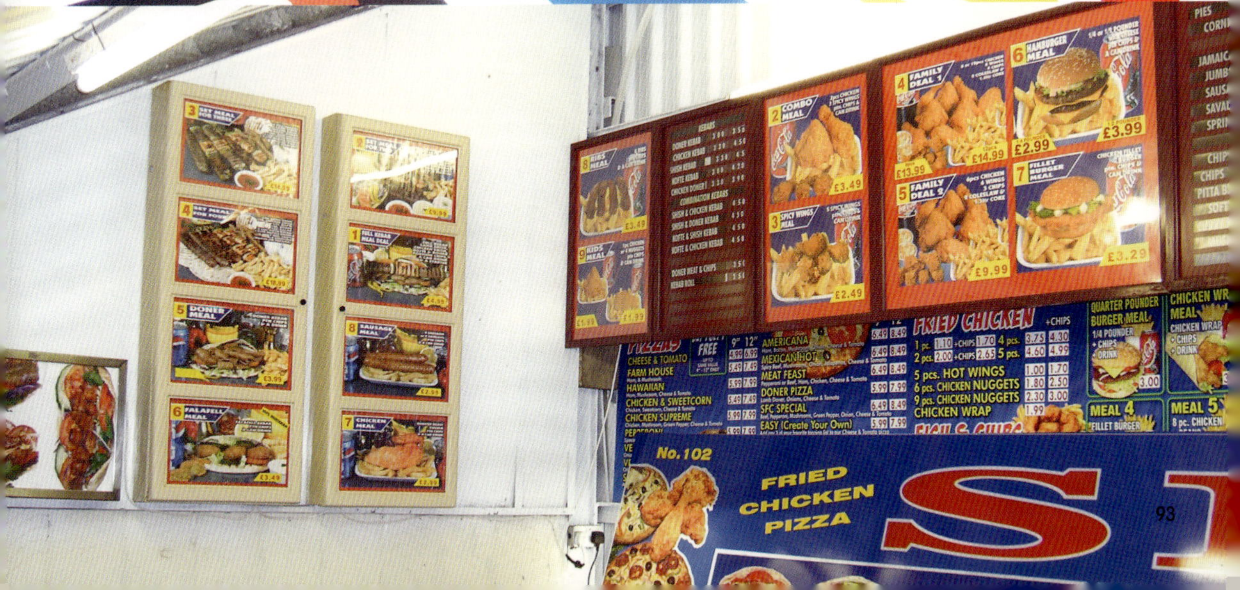
COMBO MEAL
FAMILY DEAL 1
HAMBURGER MEAL
FAMILY DEAL 2
FILLET BURGER MEAL
SPICY WINGS MEAL
KIDS MEAL
£3.99
£2.99
£3.49
£9.99
£3.29
£2.49
FRIED CHICKEN
PIZZAS
CHEESE & TOMATO
FARM HOUSE
HAWAIIAN
CHICKEN & SWEETCORN
CHICKEN SUPREME
AMERICANA
MEXICAN HOT
MEAT FEAST
DONER PIZZA
SFC SPECIAL
EASY (Create Your Own)
5 pcs. HOT WINGS
6 pcs. CHICKEN NUGGETS
9 pcs. CHICKEN NUGGETS
CHICKEN WRAP
QUARTER POUNDER BURGER MEAL
MEAL 4
MEAL 5
No. 102
FRIED CHICKEN PIZZA

USA

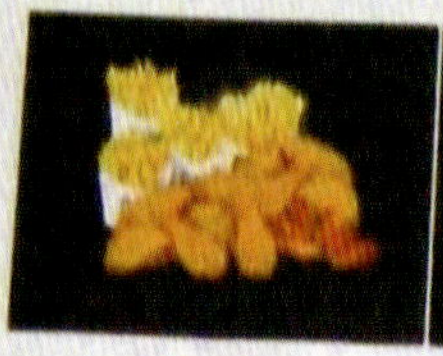
USA001.tif

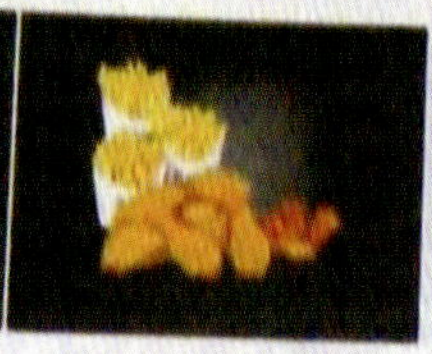
USA002.tif

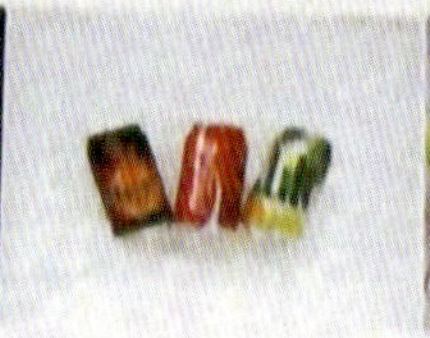
USA003.tif

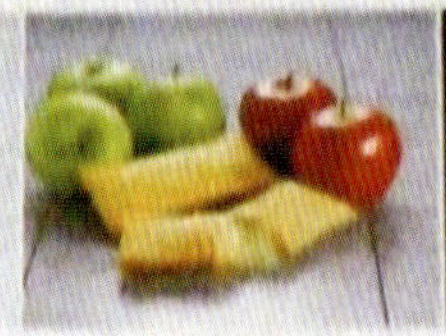
USA004.tif

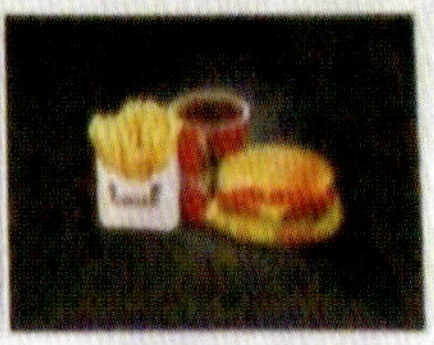
USA005.tif

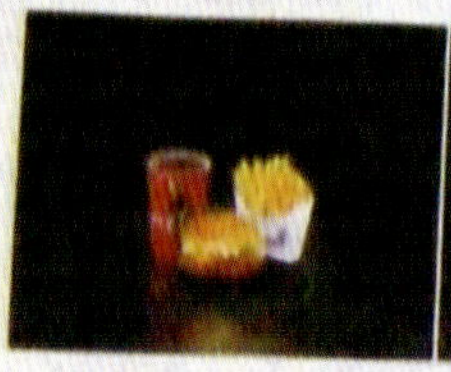
USA006.tif

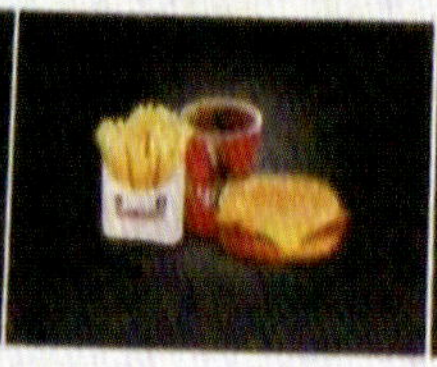
USA007.tif

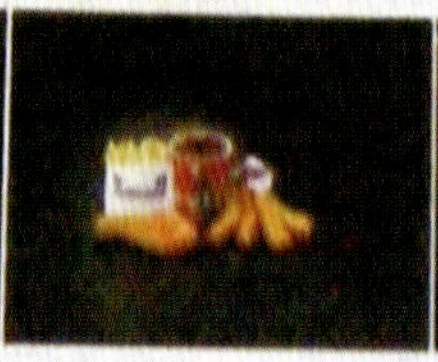
USA008.tif

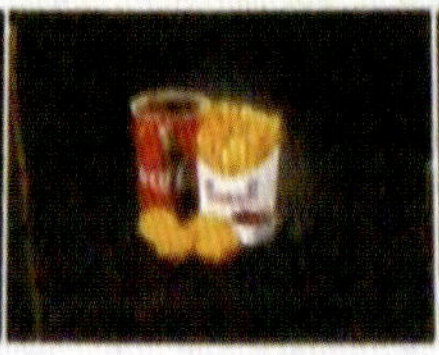
USA009.tif

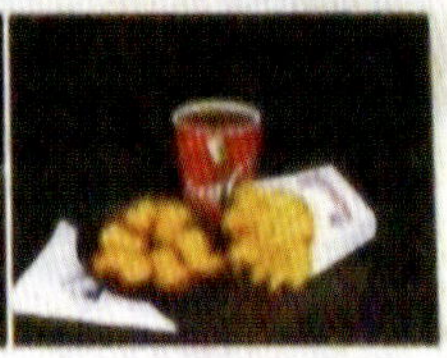
USA010.tif

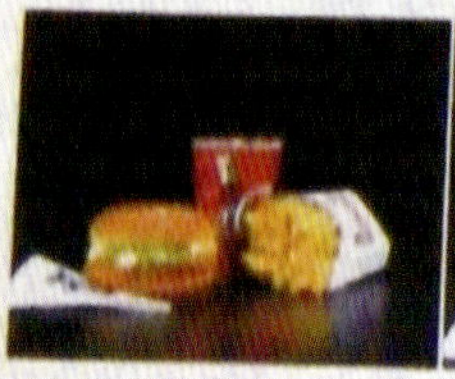
USA011.tif

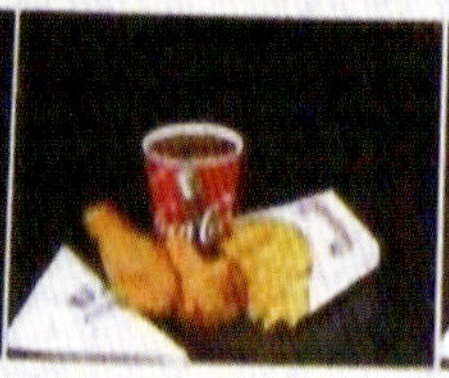
USA012.tif

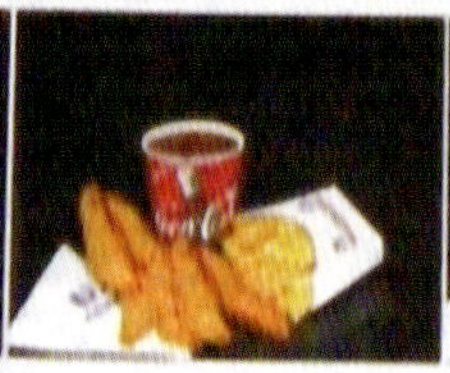
USA013.tif

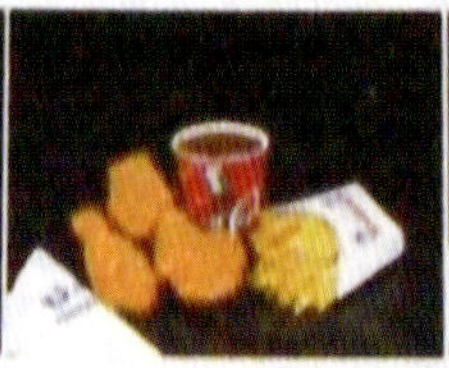
USA014.tif

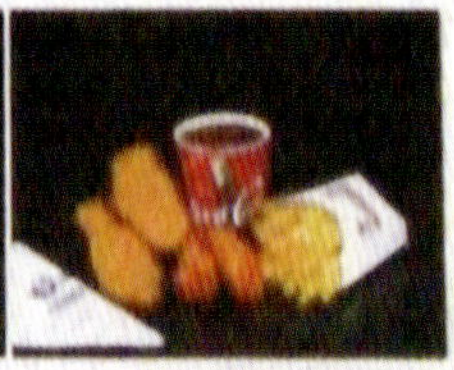
USA015.tif

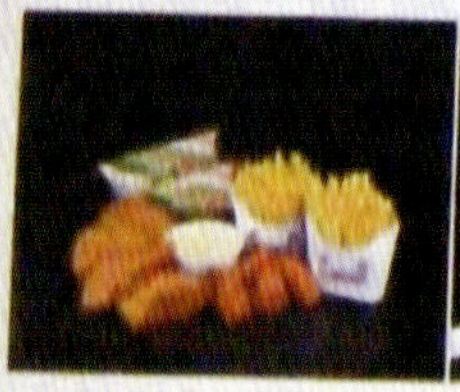
USA016.tif

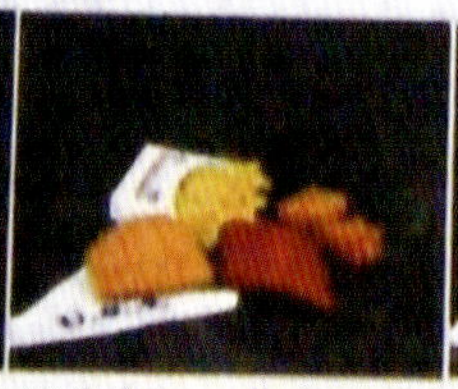
USA017.tif

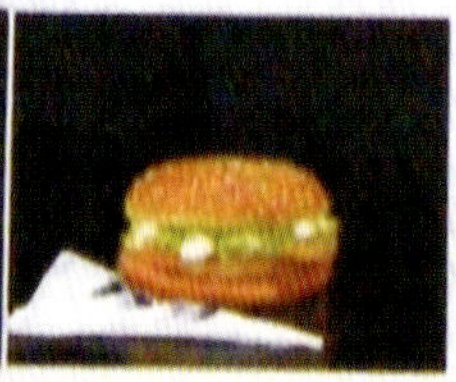
USA018.tif

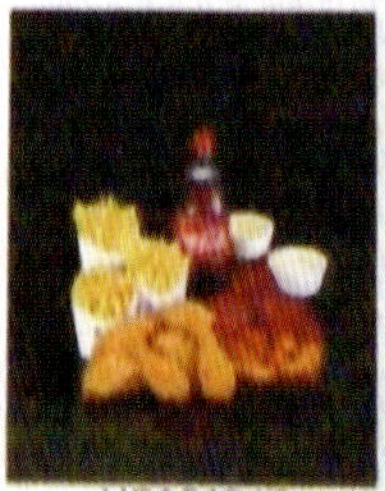
USA019.tif

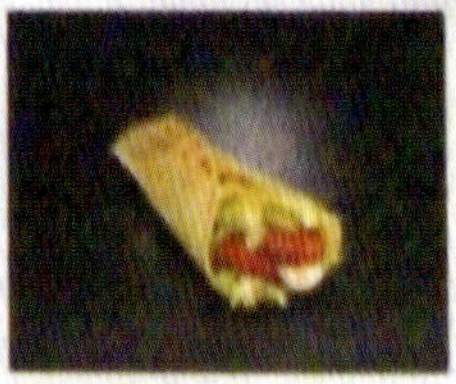
USA020.tif

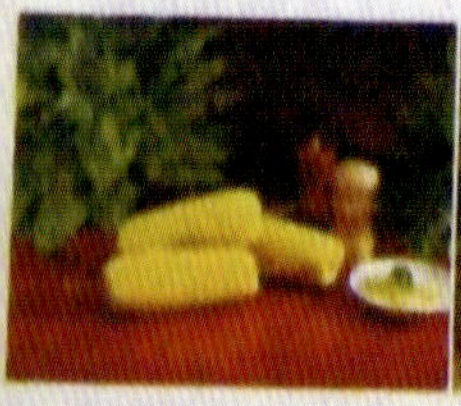
USA021.tif

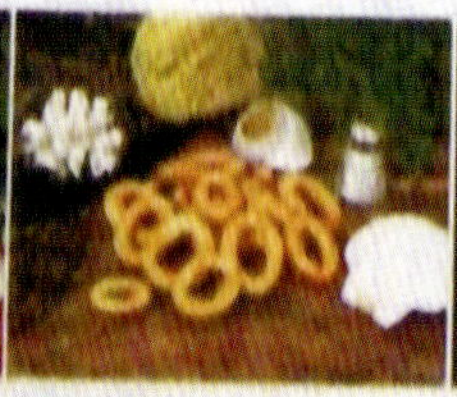
USA022.tif

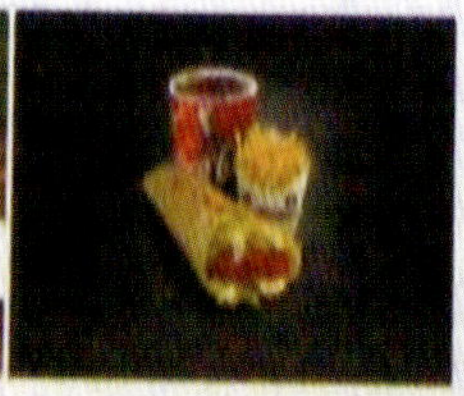
USA023.tif

CHICKEN

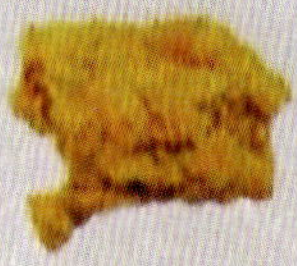
Chicken001.tif

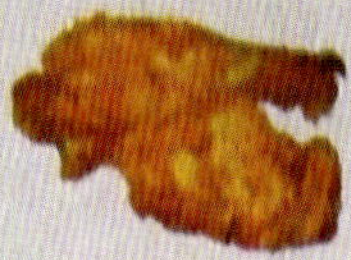
Chicken002.psd

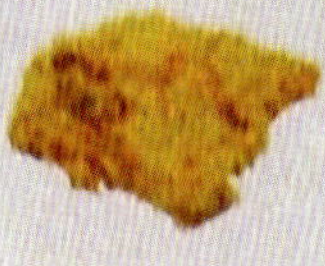
Chicken003.tif

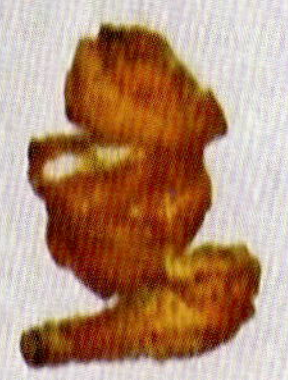
Chicken004.tif

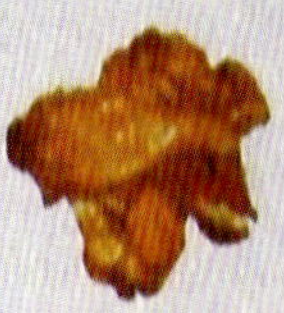
Chicken005.tif

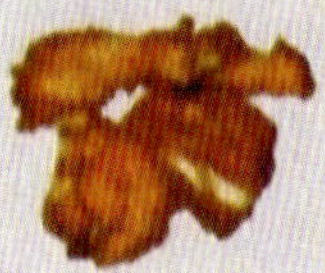
Chicken006.tif

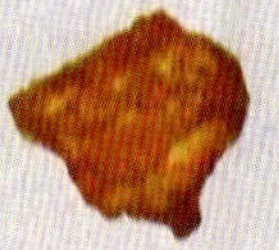
Chicken007.tif

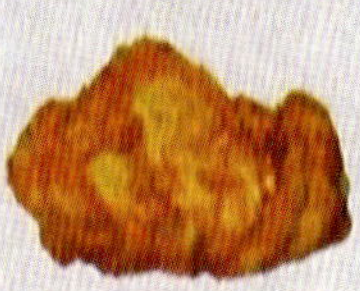
Chicken008.psd

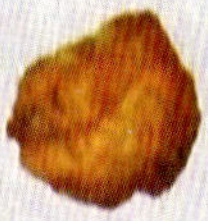
Chicken009.psd

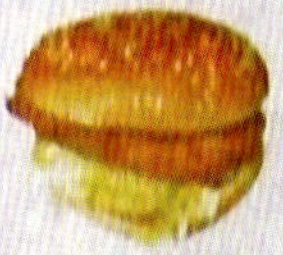
Chicken010.tif

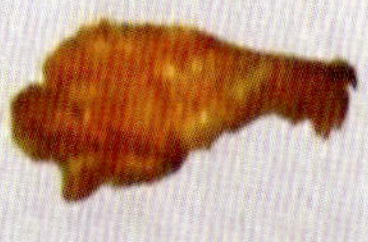
Chicken011.psd

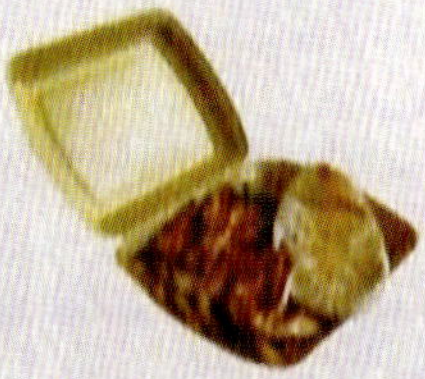
Chicken012.tif

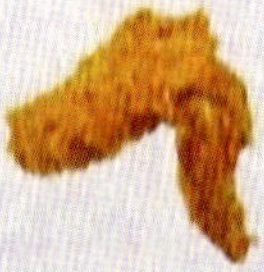
Chicken013.tif

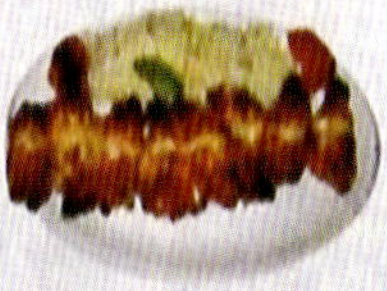
Chicken014.tif

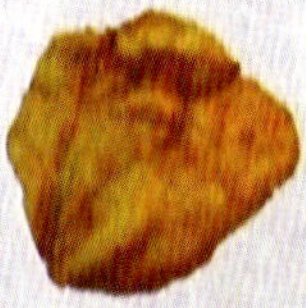
Chicken015.tif

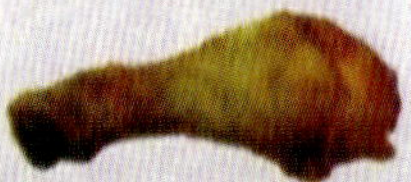
Chicken016.tif

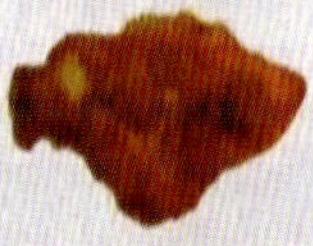
Chicken017.tif

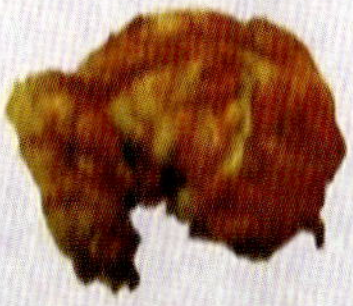
Chicken018.tif

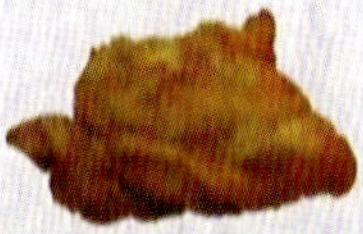
Chicken019.tif

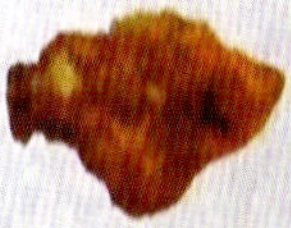
Chicken020.tif

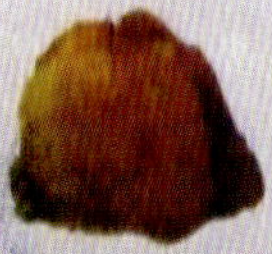
Chicken021.tif

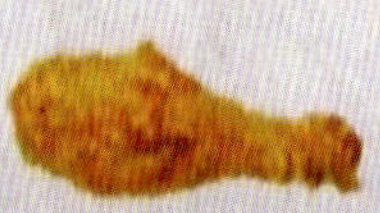
Chicken022.tif

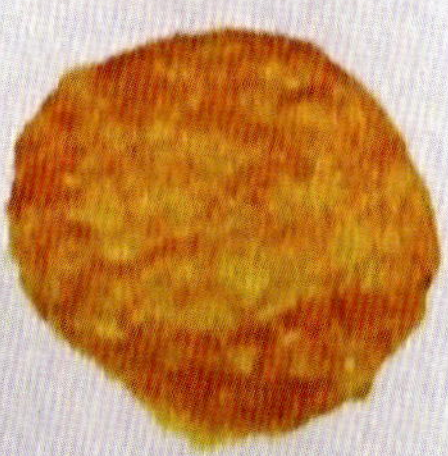
Chicken023.psd

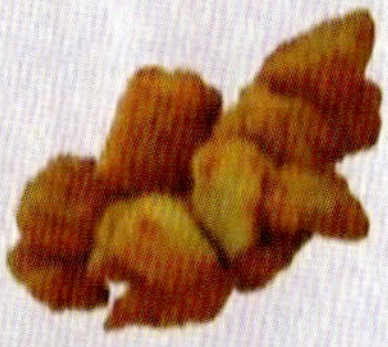
Chicken024.tif

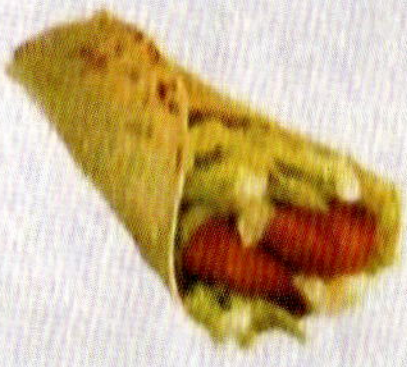
Chicken025.tif

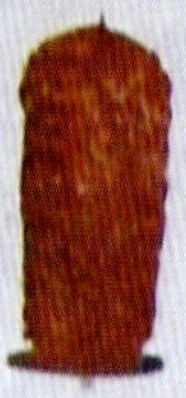
Doner001.tif

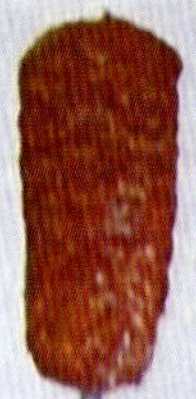
Doner002.tif

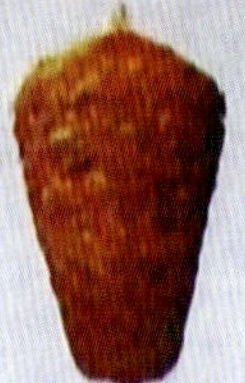
Doner003.psd

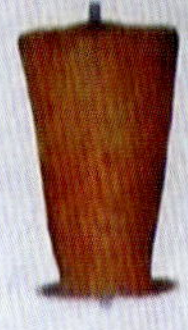
Doner004.psd

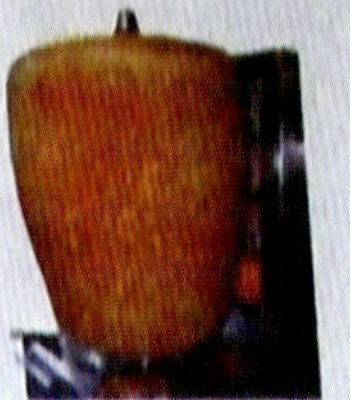
Doner005.tif

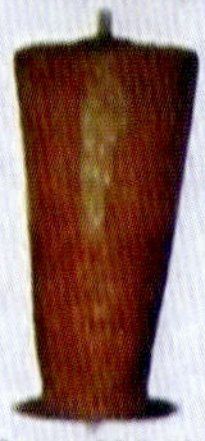
Doner006.tif

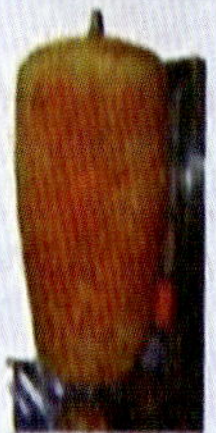
Doner007.tif

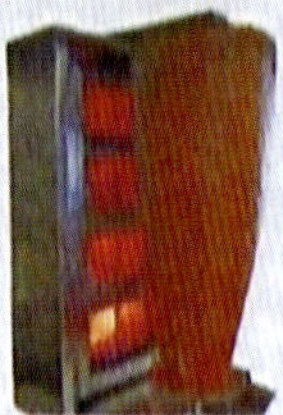
Doner008.psd

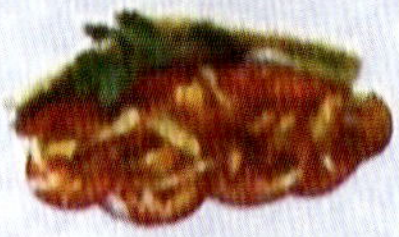
Doner009.psd

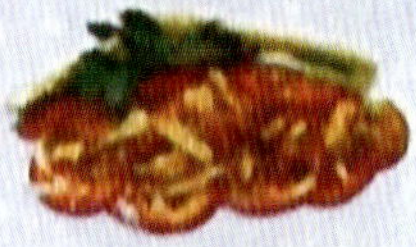
Doner010.tif

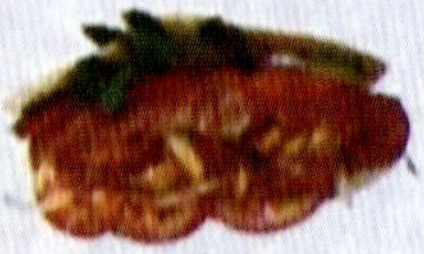
Doner011.psd

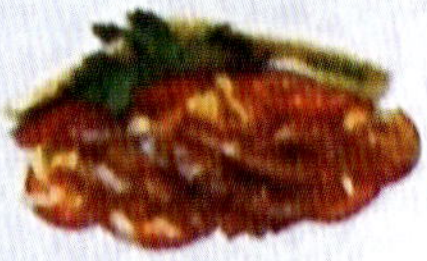
Doner012.tif

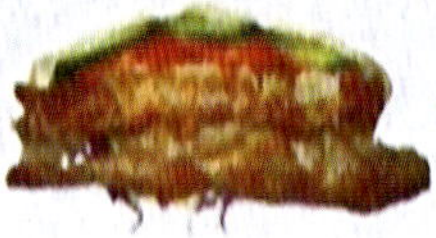
Doner013.psd

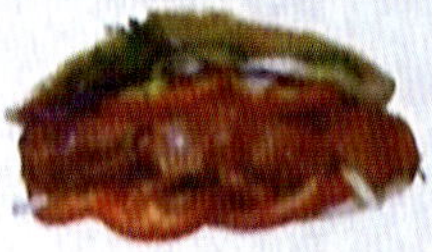
Doner014.psd

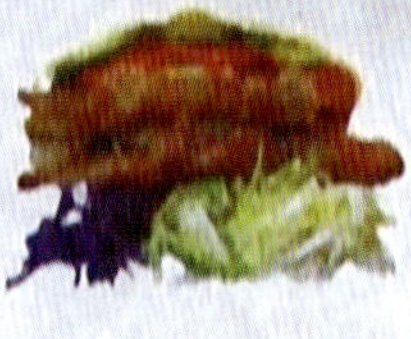
Doner015.tif

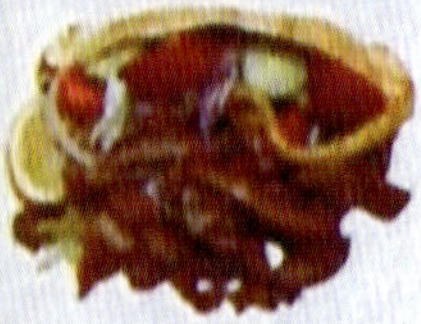
Doner016.tif

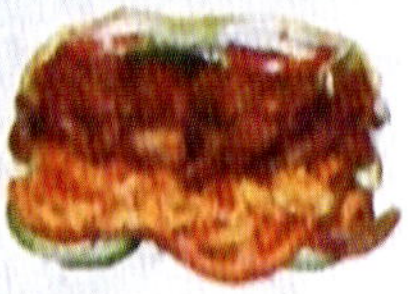
Kebab001.psd

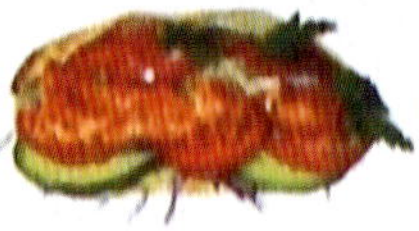
Kebab002.psd

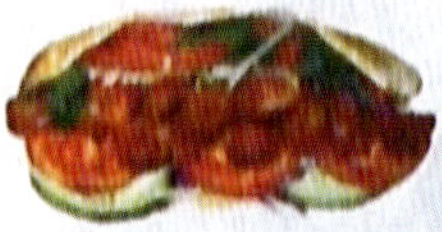
Kebab003.psd

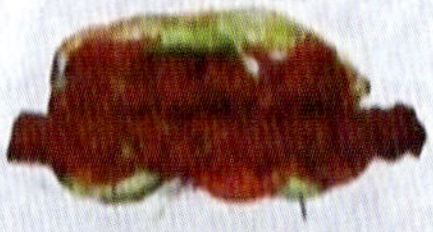
Kebab004.psd

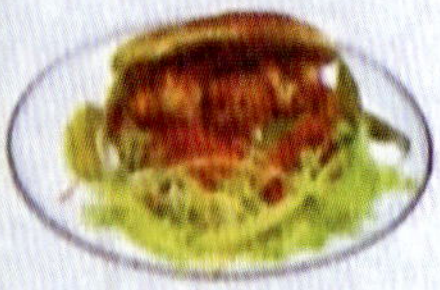
Kebab005.tif

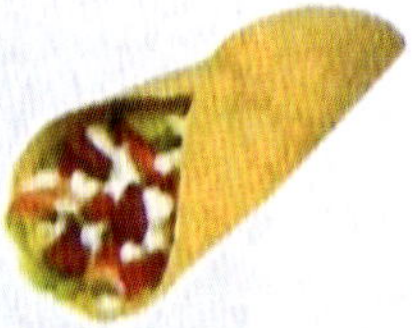
Kebab006.tif

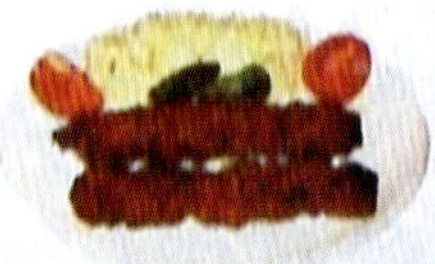
Kebab007.psd

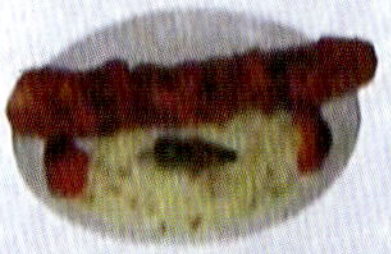
Kebab008.tif

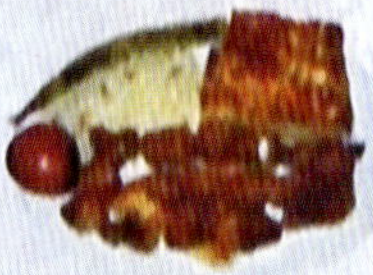
Kebab009.tif

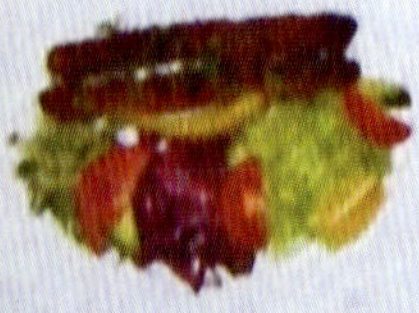
Kebab010.tif

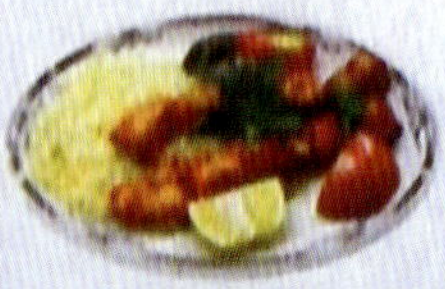
Kebab011.psd

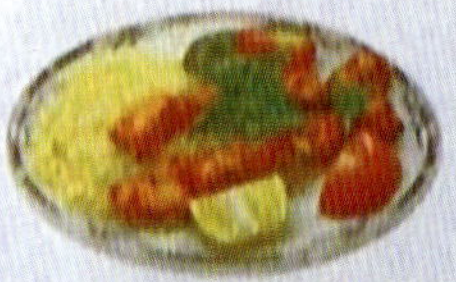
Kebab012.psd

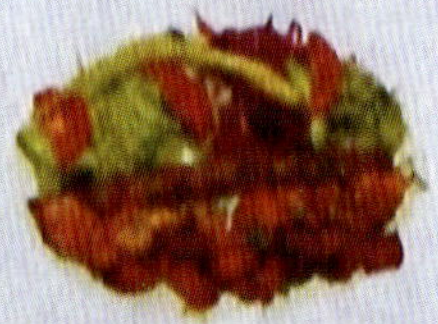
Kebab013.tif

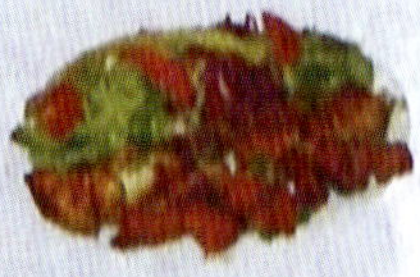
Kebab014.psd

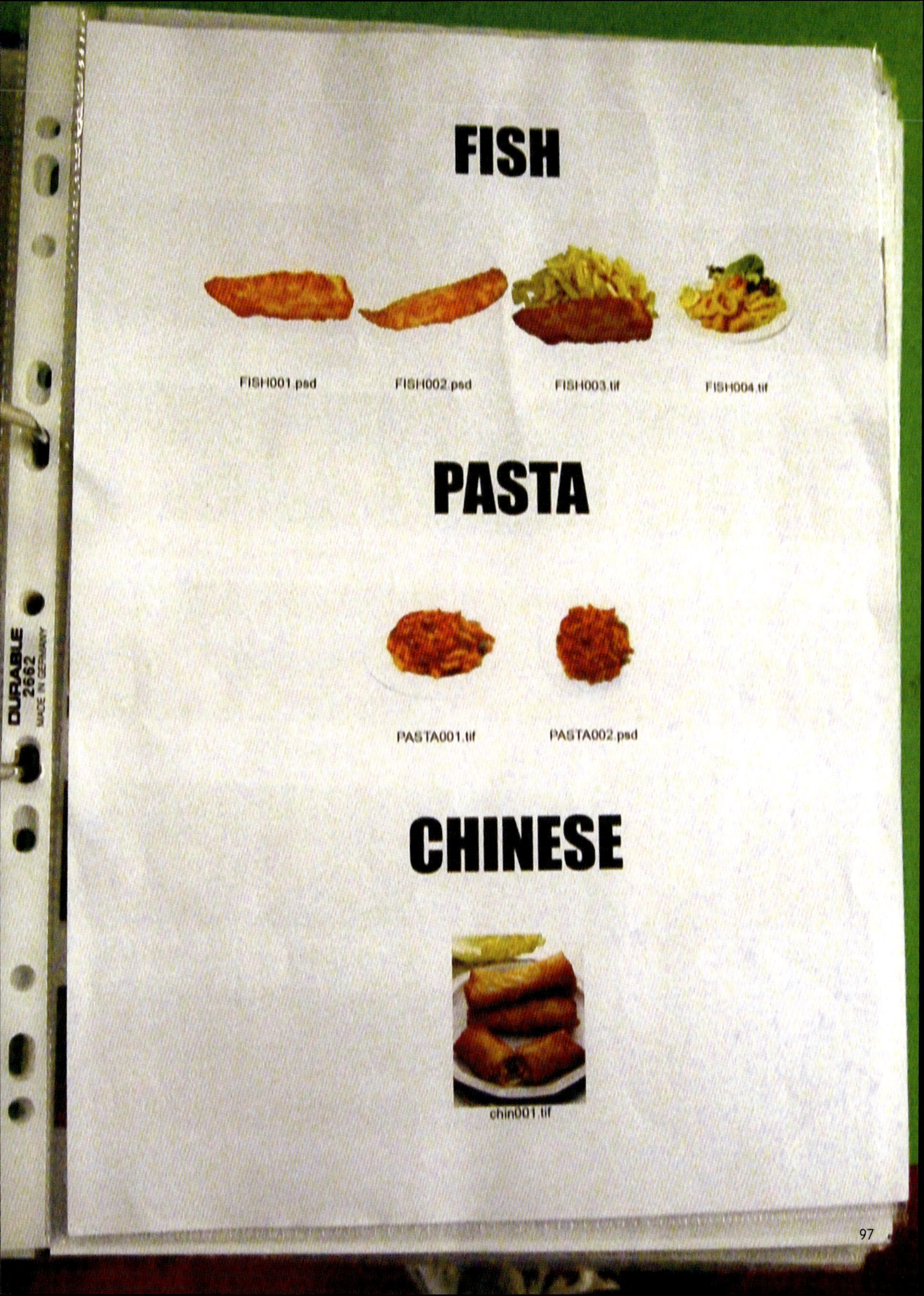
FISH
FISH001.psd
FISH002.psd
FISH003.tif
FISH004.tif
PASTA
PASTA001.tif
PASTA002.psd
CHINESE
chin001.tif
DURABLE
2662
MADE IN GERMANY

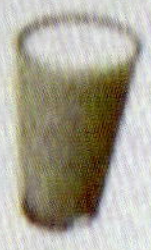
EXTRAS001.psd

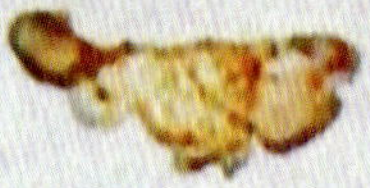
EXTRAS002.psd

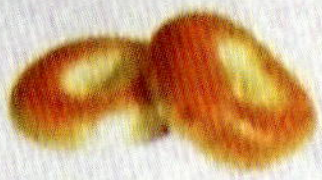
EXTRAS003.psd

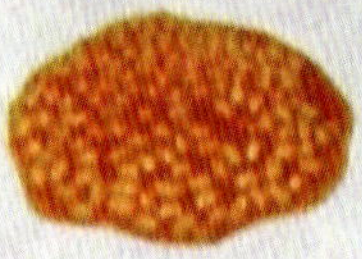
EXTRAS004.psd

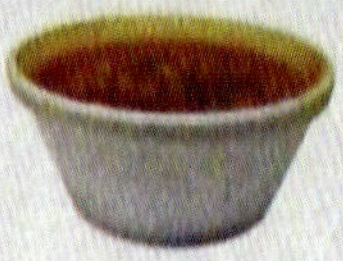
EXTRAS005.psd

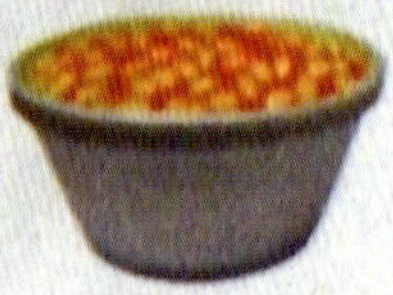
EXTRAS006.tif

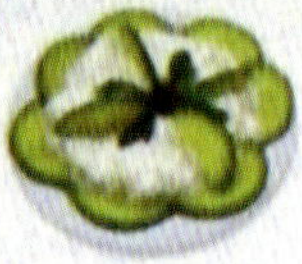
EXTRAS007.psd

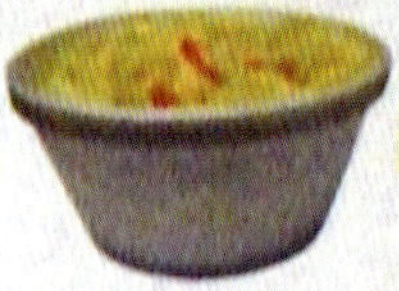
EXTRAS008.tif

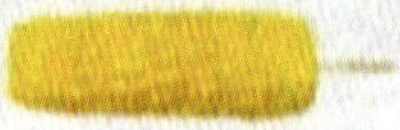
EXTRAS009.psd

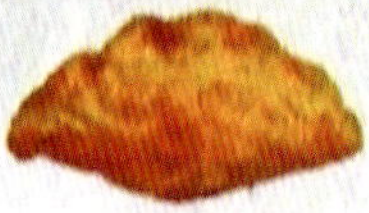
EXTRAS010.psd

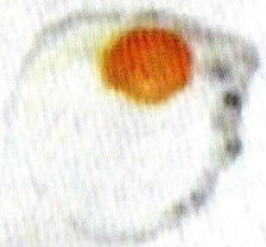
EXTRAS011.psd

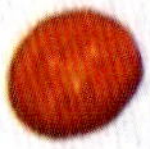
EXTRAS012.psd

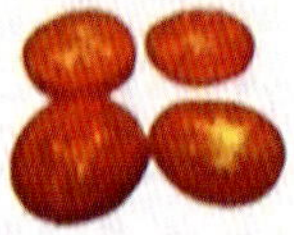
EXTRAS013.psd

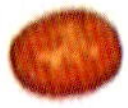
EXTRAS014.psd

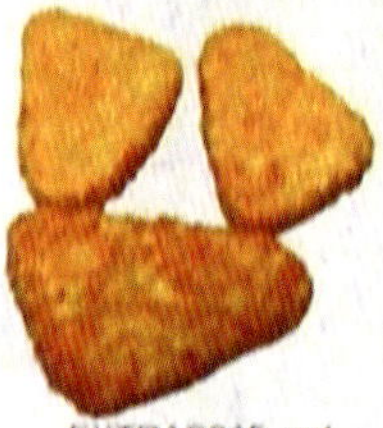
EXTRAS015.psd

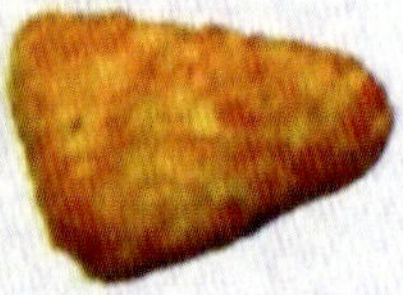
EXTRAS016.psd

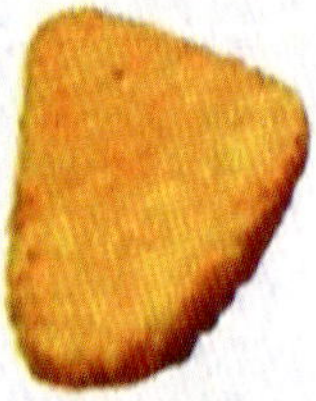
EXTRAS017.psd

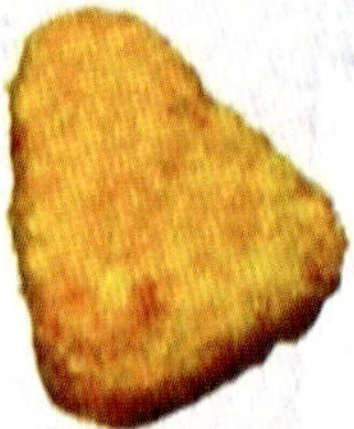
EXTRAS018.psd

EXTRAS019.psd

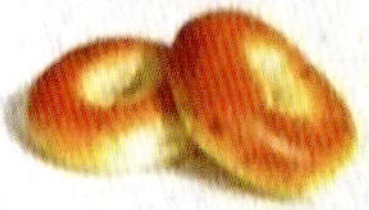
EXTRAS020.jpg

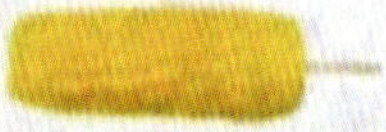
EXTRAS021.jpg

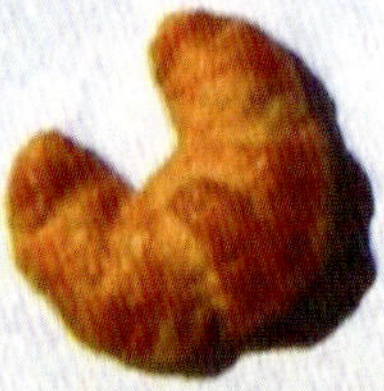
EXTRAS022.jpg

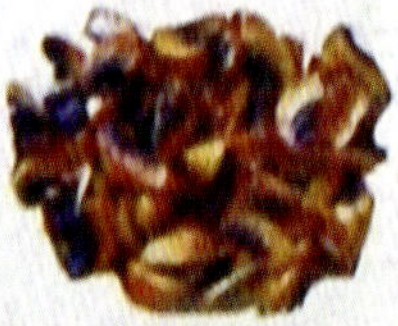
EXTRAS023.psd

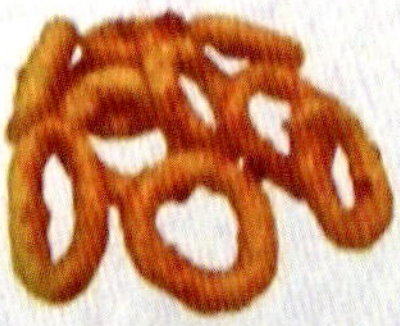
EXTRAS024.psd

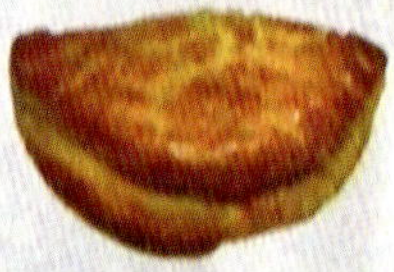
EXTRAS025.psd

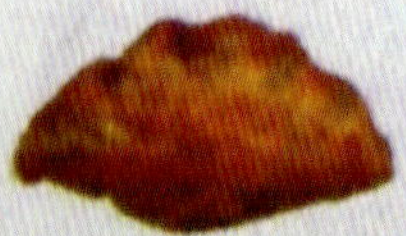
EXTRAS026.tif

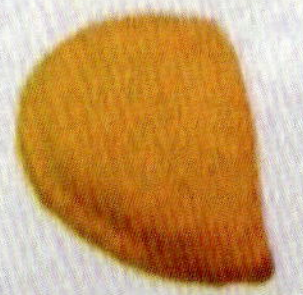
EXTRAS027.tif

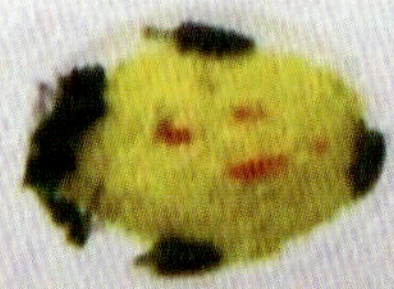
EXTRAS028.psd

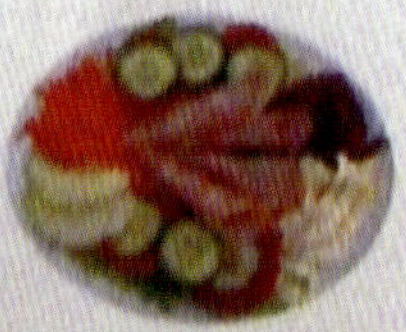
EXTRAS029.tif

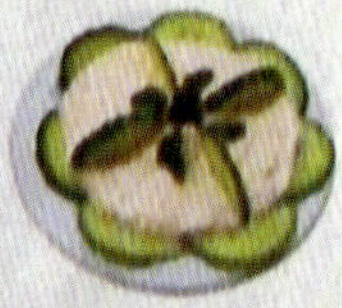
EXTRAS030.psd

FRIES

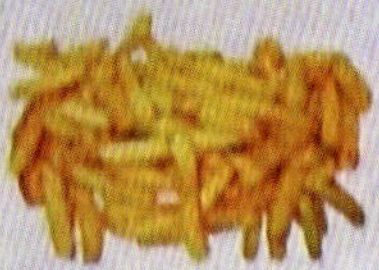

FRIES001.psd

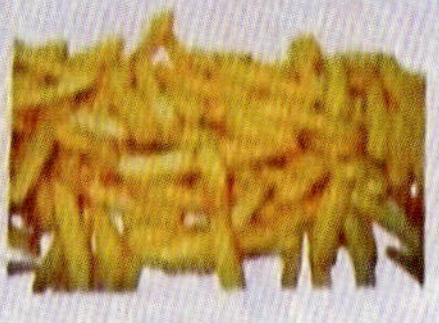

FRIES002.psd

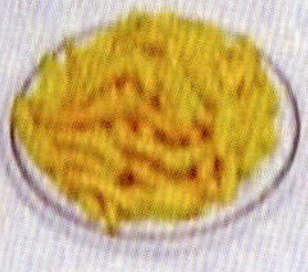

FRIES003.psd

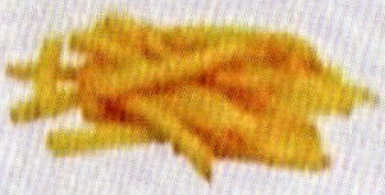

FRIES004.psd

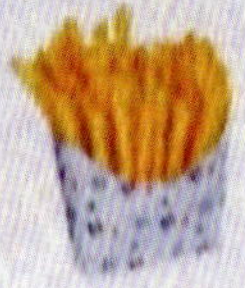

FRIES005.tif

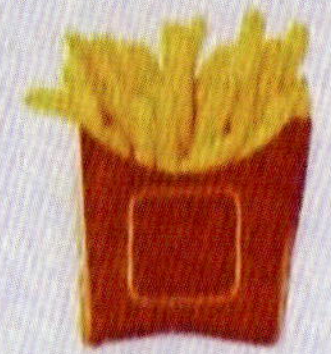

FRIES006.tif

BOX

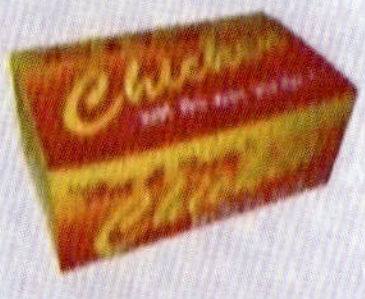

chicken box 001.psd

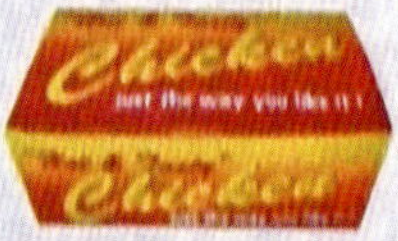

chicken box 002.psd

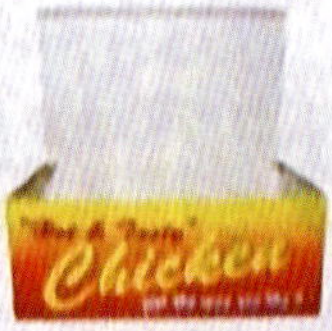

chicken box 003.psd

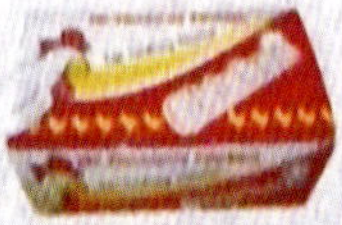

chicken box 004.psd

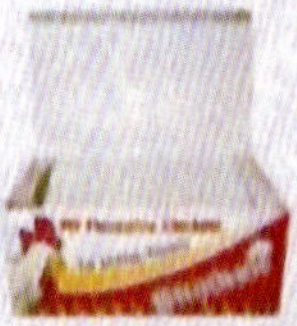

chicken box 005.psd

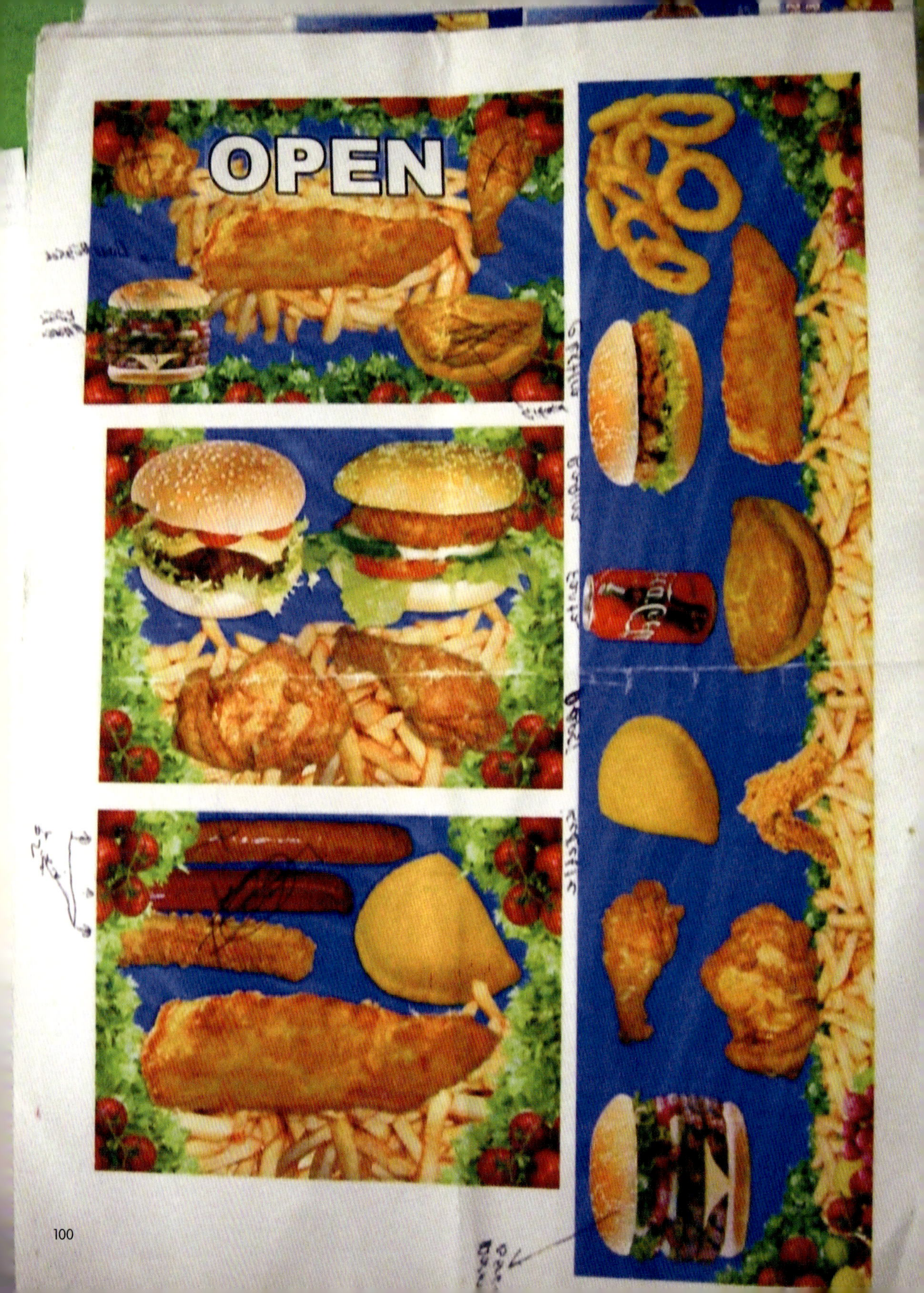
OPEN

DRINKS

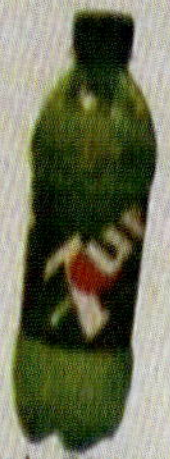
Drinks001.psd

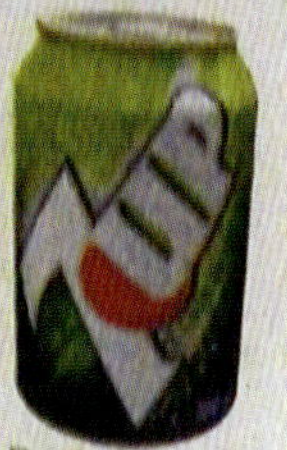

Drinks002.psd

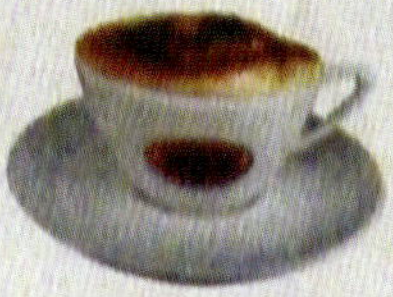
Drinks003.tif

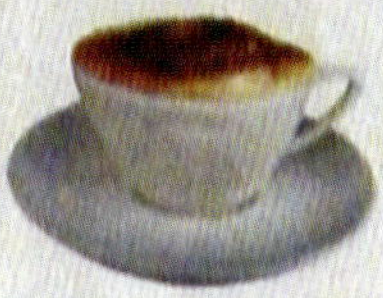
Drinks004.tif

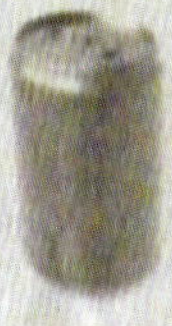
Drinks005.tif

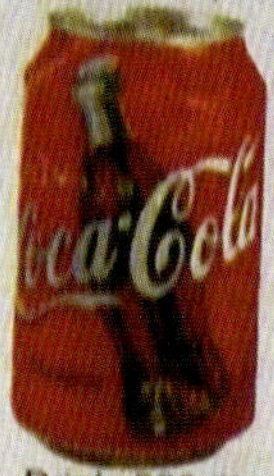
Drinks006.tif

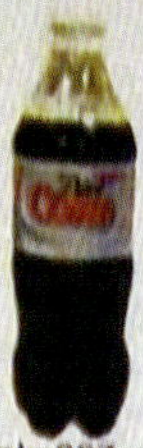
Drinks007.psd

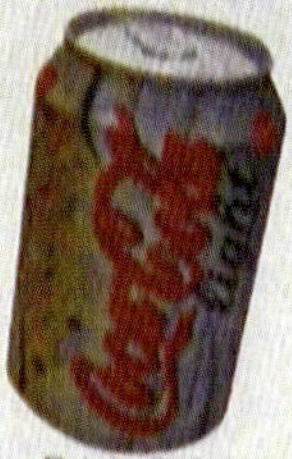
Drinks008.tif

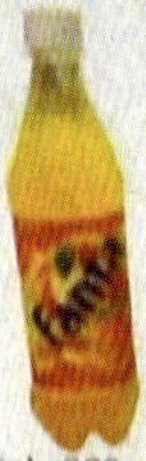
Drinks009.psd

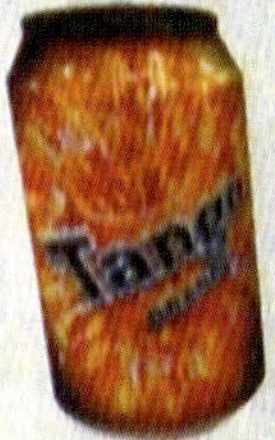
Drinks010.psd

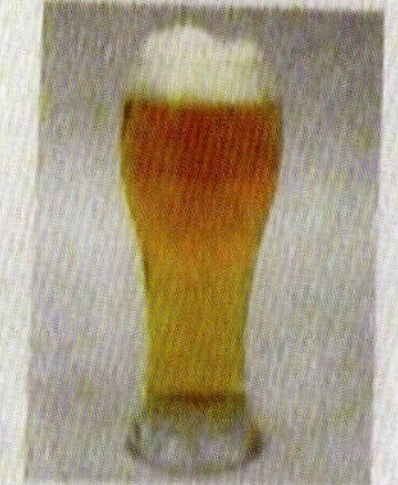
Drinks011.jpg

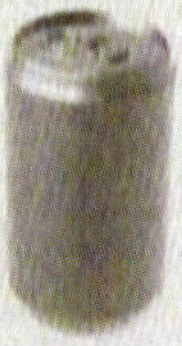
Drinks012.jpg

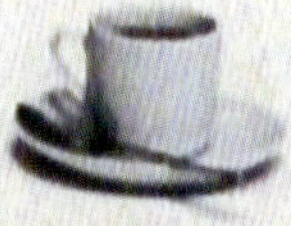
Drinks013.jpg

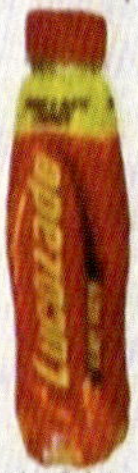
Drinks014.psd

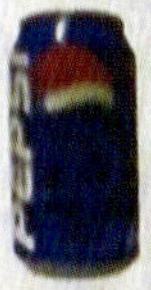
Drinks015.psd

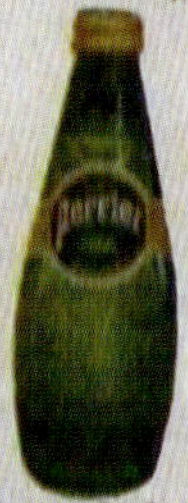
Drinks016.tif

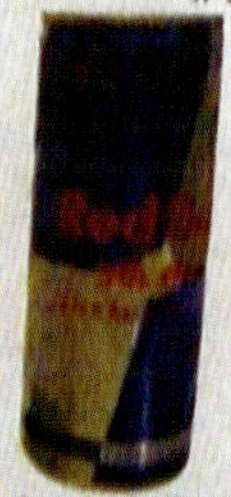
Drinks017.tif

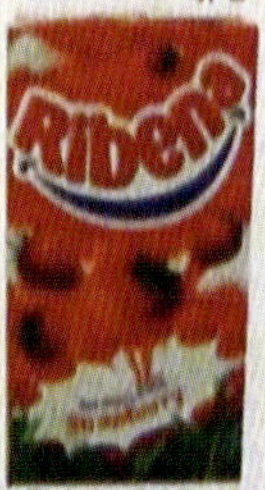

Drinks018.tif

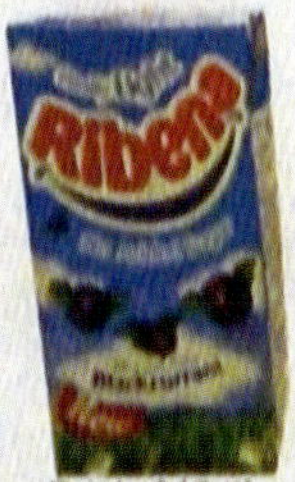

Drinks019.tif

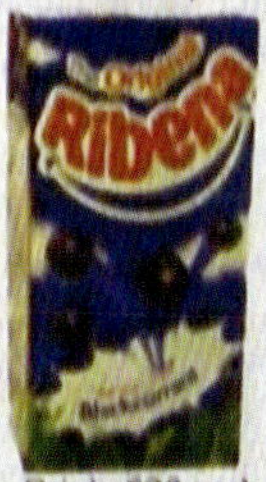

Drinks020.psd

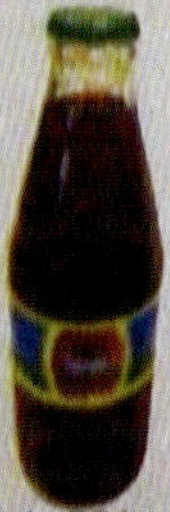
Drinks021.psd

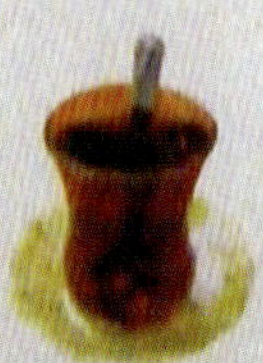
Drinks022.psd

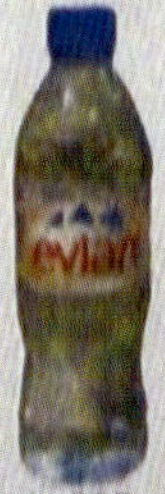

Drinks023.psd

Graphic Language

Carolina
Chicken

CHICKEN LAND

CHICKS CHICKEN & PIZZA

DIXY
حلال Chicken حلال

HALAL

FRIED CHICKEN
KEBAB & FISH

OFC

CHICKEN COTTAGE

CHICKEN COTTAGE

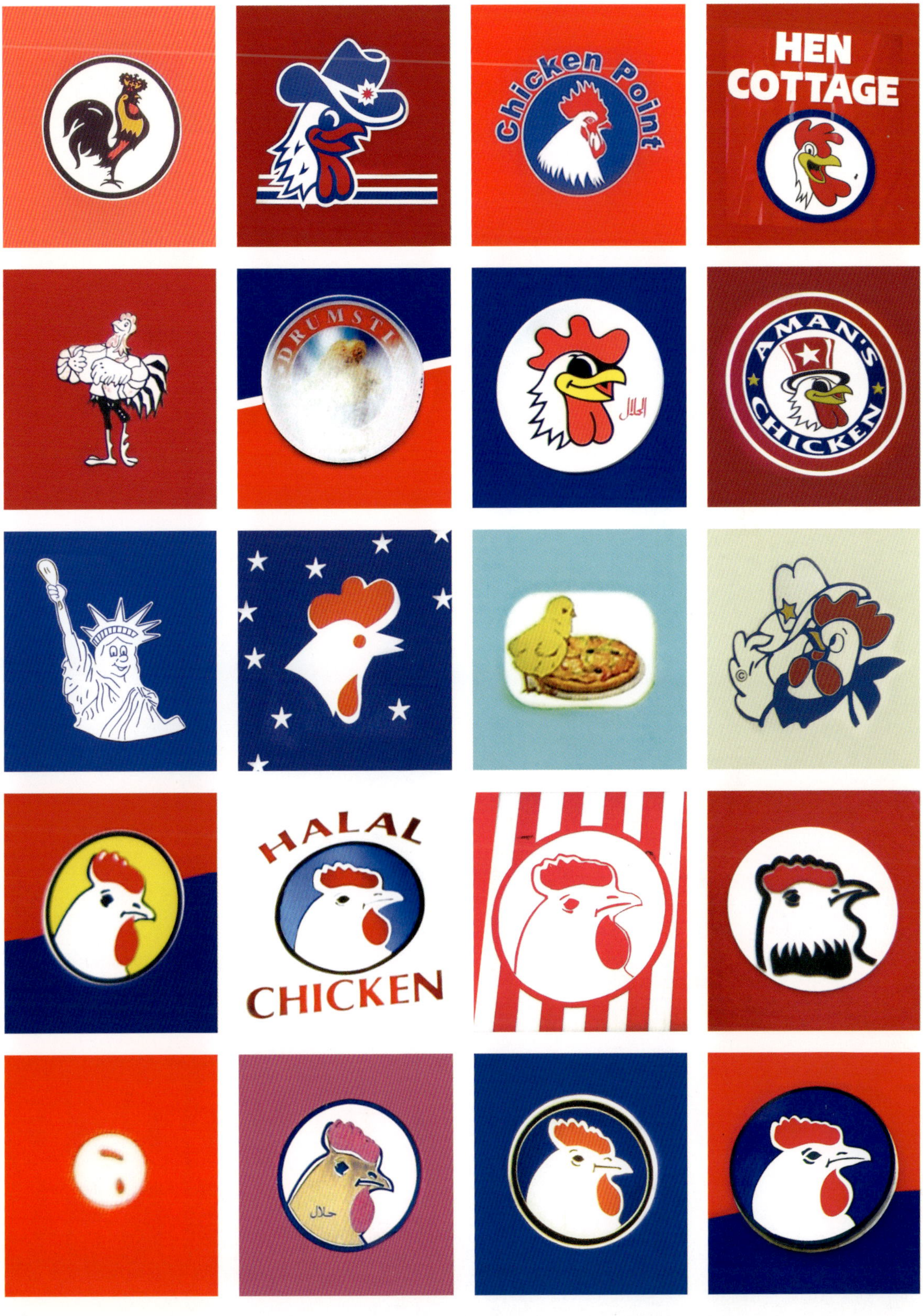
HEN
COTTAGE
Chicken Point
DRUMSTI
AMAN'S
CHICKEN
HALAL
CHICKEN
حلال

DUNK YOUR DIPPER

TASTEME

TENDER LOIN

PARADISE PATTIES!

FRIED CHICKEN A-Z

2 TASTY HALAL MEALS
AL-BADS KEBAB BURGER FRIED CHIKCEN
ALI'S FLORIA FIRST KEBAB IN EAST LONDON 1969
AL-HALAL FRIED CHICKEN 04
AL-HALAL FRIED CHICKEN BURGERS FISH & CHIPS
AL. IKHWAN FRIED CHICKEN
AL PLAICE
ARGOSY TAKE AWAY
BELL A KEBAB
BEST GRILL KEBABS & BURGERS
BEST HALAL TURKISH KEBAB
[illegible]
BEST KEBAB & CAFÉ IN TOWN
BIG BITE
BIG PORTION CHICKEN
BREAKFAST CHIPPY TAKEAWAY
BRITANNIA FISH & CHIPS KEBABS
BRITANNIA FISH BAR
BRITANNIA RESTAURANT
CAROLINA CHICKEN
CAROLINA PIZZA FRIED CHICKEN
CAROUSELS FISH & CHIPS
CHICKEN
CHICKPIZZ
CHICKEN COTTAGE 05
CHICKEN COTTAGE EXPRESS
CHICKEN DELIGHT 02
CHICKEN HUT
CHIP INN
CHICK-KING
CHICKEN LAND 02
CHICKEN POINT ORIGINAL
CHIP INN VILLAGE
CHICKEN SPOT
CHICKEN SPOT BURGERS RIBS PIZZA
CHICKEN VILLAGE
CITY CAFÉ NO2
CINQUE 5 STELLA
CITYKEBABS
CYPRUS KEBAB
DALLAS CHICKEN & PIZZA
DIXIE CHICKEN
DIXY CHICKEN 04
FAMOUS PIZZA
FAVORITE – CHICKEN & RIBS 03
FCKF FRIED CHICKEN KEBAB AND FISH
FIVE STAR FISH BAR
[illegible]
GARY'S FISH HOUSE
GEORGE'S PLAICE
GRAB A BITE
GOLDEN FISH
GOLDEN FRYER
HALAL BITE
HAPPY DAYS
HALAL FRIED CHICKEN HFC
HALAL FAST FOOD
HEN COTTAGE
JACK & LINDA MILLS TRADITIONAL FISH SMOKERS
JOHNS KITCHEN
KEBAB CAGLAR
KEBAB COTTAGE
KENNEDY FRIED CHICKEN
KHAN'S KEBAB HOUSE
[illegible]
[illegible]
KING SOLOMANS
LICK FINGER
LOVELY JUBBLY FISH AND CHIPS
MERMAID RESTAURANT & TAKE AWAY
MIGHTY BITE
MR. COD
NEW CAPITAL KEBAB
NEW CITY KEBAB HOUSE
NEW PERFECT FRIED CHICKEN
ORIGINAL CHICKEN EXPRESS FRIED CHICKEN
ORLANDO FRIED CHICKEN OFC
ORIGINAL TASTE HALAL FOOD
PARADISE COTTAGE
P.C. HOT
PERFECT CHICKEN
PERFECTION CHICKEN
PERFECT FRIED CHICKEN 07
PERFECT FRIED CHICKEN AMERICAN RECIPE
PERFECT FRIED CHICKEN & BURGERS 05
PERFECT FRIED CHICKEN CHICKEN BURGER & DONER
PERFECT FRIED CHICKEN EXPRESS
PERFECT FRIED CHICKEN KEBABS & BURGERS
PERFECT SPICE
PIZZA POINT HALAL CHICKEN & CHIPS
PIZZA RING
PREFERRED PIZZA CHICKEN AND RIBS
RAIS KEBAB FRIED CHICKEN BURGER
REAL FLAVOUR
REAL TASTE HALAL MEALS
ROOSTER EXPRESS
SAM'S CHICKEN
SAUCY KIPPER FISH BAR
SAIF'S FISH & CHIPS
[illegible]
SHOREDITCH KEBAB HOUSE
SIMPLY THE BEST FISH BAR
SOUTHERN FRIED CHICKEN 02
TASTY FISH & CHICKEN
TENNESSEE FRIED CHICKEN TFC 02
TEXAS FRIED CHICKEN 02
THE FISH POND
THE OLYMPIC
THE SAUCY PLAICE
TUBBY ISSACS
US FRIED CHICKEN
USA FRIED CHICKEN
WHITECHAPEL FRIED CHICKEN
WHITE HORSE KEBAB FOOD YOU TRUST

DUNK YOUR DIPPER!

1 100% WHOLE MUSCLE
2 3-PIECE FILLER!
3 AUTHENTIC JAMAICAN PATTIES
4 BEST BREAST IN WALES
5 CHICK KING
6 FAMILY PACK
7 FISHWICH
8 HOT WINGS!
9 HOT & TASTY!
10 HOT & SPICEY WEDGES!
11 HOW DO YOU ENJOY YOURS?
12 LIP-LICKING FLAVOUR
13 MARINATED SPATCHCOCK
14 MOIST DUMPLINGS
15 ONCE TASTED, NEVER FORGOTTEN!

PARADISE PATTIES!

16 PIN N POPPIN PATTIES. POPPED DAILY HERE!
17 REAL KINGSTON CRUSS, NUFF SPICY FILLING
18 SAVA DA FLAVA
19 SEASONED WEDGES SKIN ON!
20 SOFT PATTIES
21 SUCCULENT AND FULL OF FLAVOUR
22 TASTE ME!
23 TASTY DELIGHTS!
24 TENDER LOIN!
25 TRY A BIT ON THE SIDE
26 TRY ONE TODAY IT'S DELICIOUS
27 TRY THE BEST BLING-BLING PATTY TODAY!

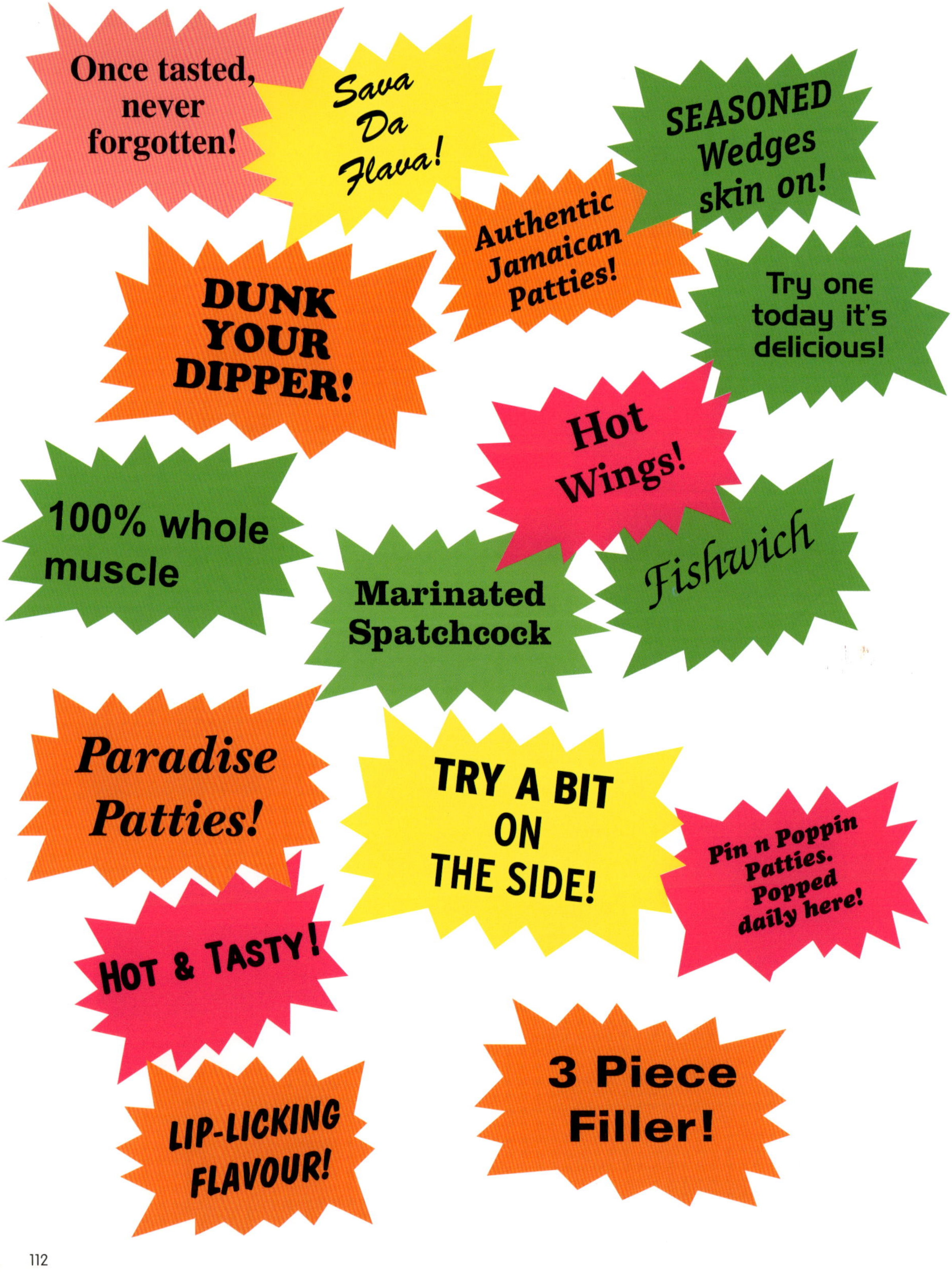
Once tasted, never forgotten!
Sava Da Flava!
SEASONED Wedges skin on!
Authentic Jamaican Patties!
DUNK YOUR DIPPER!
Try one today it's delicious!
Hot Wings!
100% whole muscle
Fishwich
Marinated Spatchcock
Paradise Patties!
TRY A BIT ON THE SIDE!
Pin n Poppin Patties. Popped daily here!
HOT & TASTY!
3 Piece Filler!
LIP-LICKING FLAVOUR!

How do you enjoy yours?

TENDER LOIN!

REAL Kingston cruss, nuff spicy filling!

Best Breast in Wales!

Succulent and full of flavour

Tasty Delights!

Taste Me!

Hot & Tasty!

Try the best bling-bling patty today!

Soft patties

Hot & Spicey Wedges!

Moist Dumplings

Enjoy...

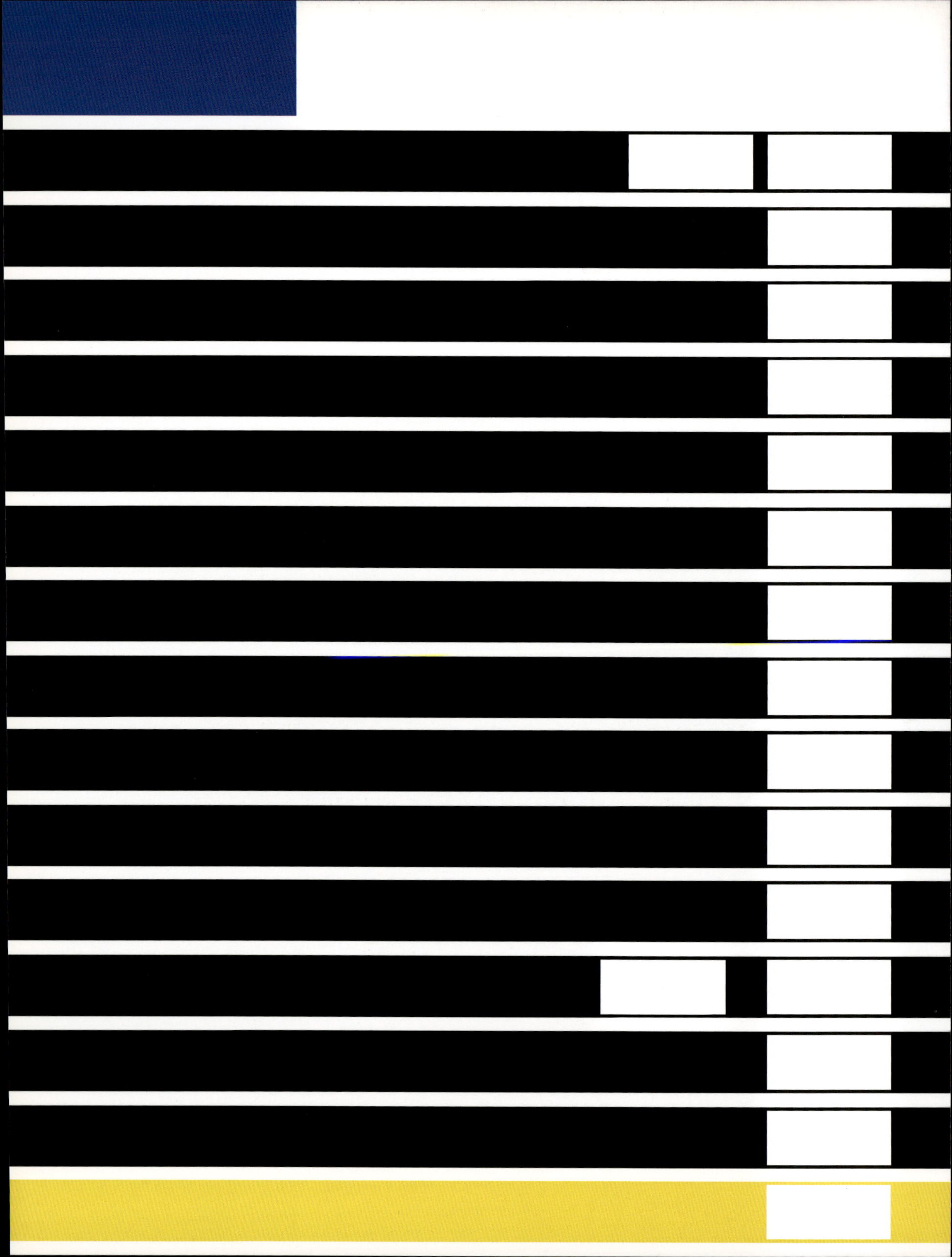

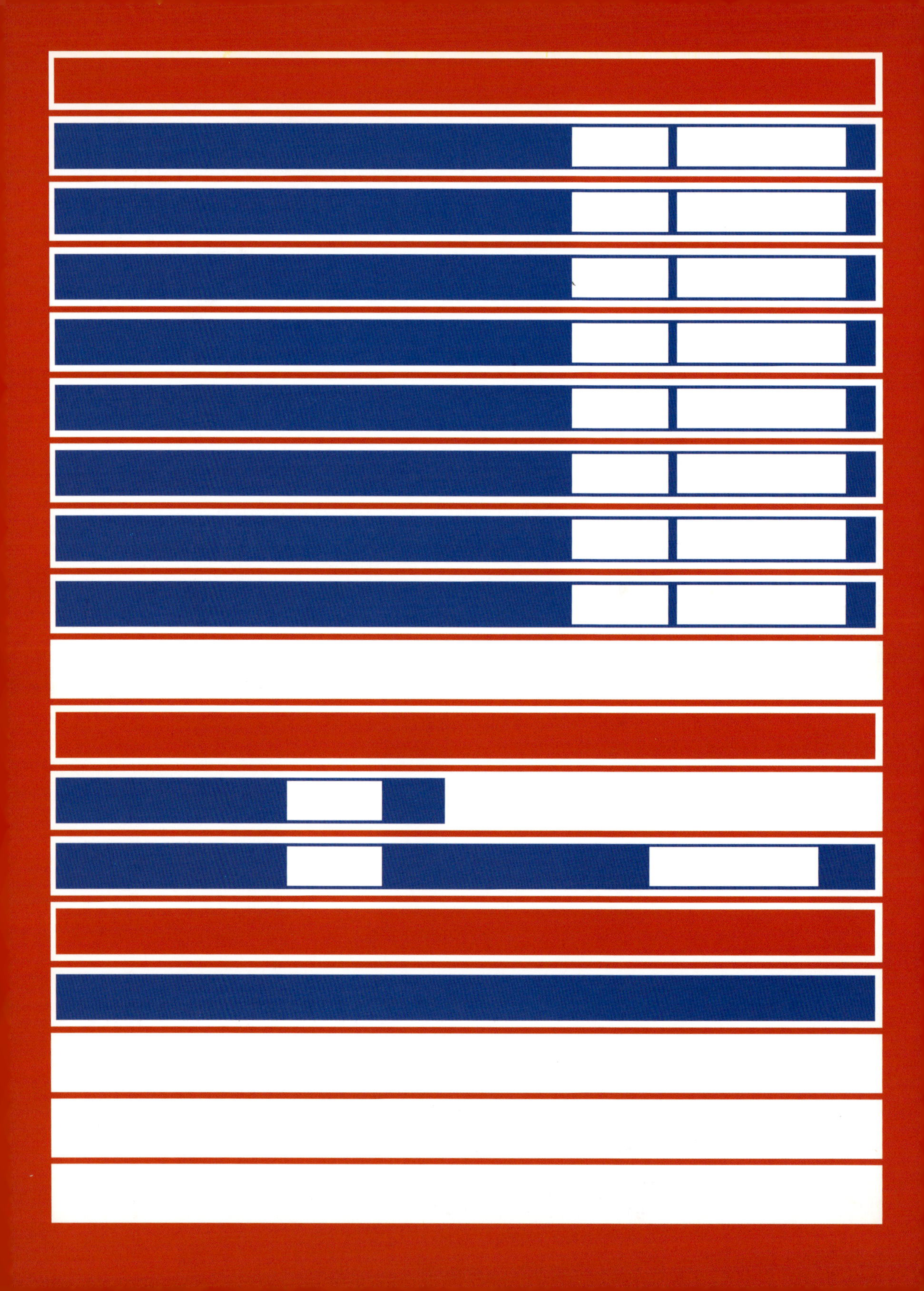

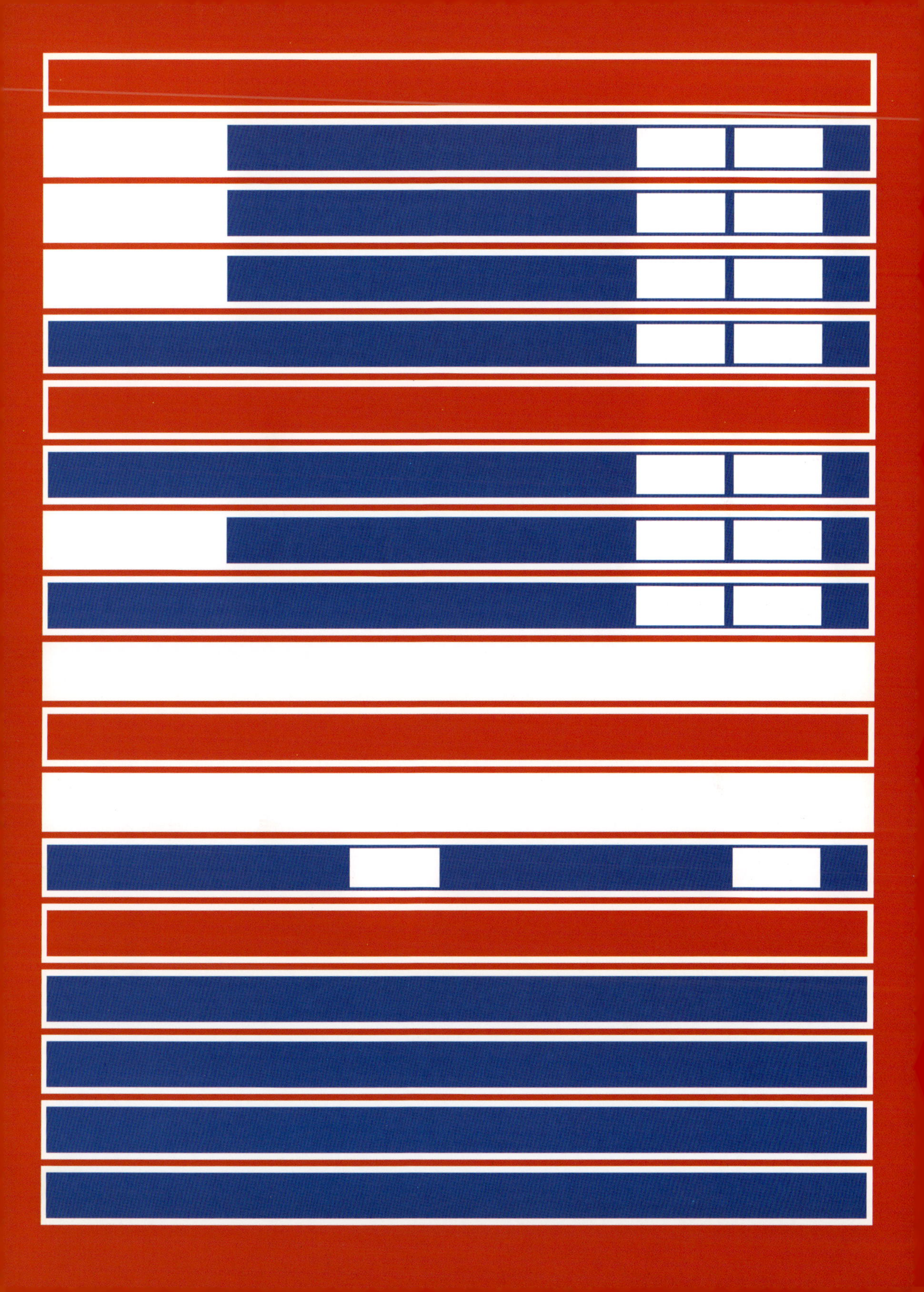

CFC

FCKF

HFC

OFC

PFC

RCP

USFC

S	L
2.90	3.70
3.00	4.00
3.00	4.00
4.00	5.60
4.40	5.80
4.00	5.00
4.40	6.00
3.30	4.60
3.00	4.00
	2.40
	.00

1.00
1.20
3.00
1.50

CFC	CITY FRIED CHICKEN
FCKF	FRIED CHICKEN KEBAB AND FISH
HFC	HALAL FRIED CHICKEN
KFC	KENNEDY FRIED CHICKEN
OFC	ORLANDO FRIED CHICKEN
PFC	PERFECT FRIED CHICKEN
RCP	ROYAL CHICKEN N PIZZA
TFC	TENNESSEE FRIED CHICKEN
TFC	TEXAS FRIED CHICKEN
USFC	US FRIED CHICKEN
USAFC	USA FRIED CHICKEN

Shish

Kofte

Halal

Mixed

Halep

Adana

Bursa

LAMB DONNER
CHICKEN DONNER
LAMB SHISH
CHICKEN SHISH
KOFTE KEBAB
DONNER ROLL
HALEP KEBAB
MIXED DONNER
SHISH & KOFTE MIX
SPECIAL MIX
CHIPS & HUMUS
FALAFEL
KING SIZE DONNER

ADANA KEBAB
BURSA KEBAB

LIP SMACKIN'

VALUE BOX ....

PARTY BOX ....

MINI BUCKET ....

FAMILY PACK ....

COMBO BUCKET ....

KIDDIE BUCKET ....

1/4 POUNDER ....

1/2 POUNDER ....

KINGSIZE ....

MEGA PACKAGE ....

MIXED PACKAGE 1 ....

MIXED PACKAGE 2 ....

PLEASE DONT ASK FOR CREDIT REFUSAL MAY OFFEND.

CAROLINA

CALIFORNIA

DALLAS

DIXIE

TOP DIXY

DIXY

KENNEDY

ORLANDO

TENNESSEE

MISSISSIPPI

NEWYORK

TEXA

TEXAS

SOUTHERN

SMOKY HILLS

USA

1 PCE CKN.	1.75
2 PCE CKN.	2.75
4 PCE CKN.	4.25
6 PCE CKN.	6.50
8 PCE CKN.	8.70
WHOLE CKN.	8.50
2 PCE RIBS	1.95
4 PCE RIBS	3.95

FAMILY PACK

ALL WITH POTS
& 1.5LTR. BOTTLE 9.20

Picture Credits

Alison Davies, (page 36). **Eylem Kaya,** (page 37). **Salim,** (page 41). **Osman** and **Monika,** (page 43). **Mr Shafiulalam,** (page 53). **Husseyin,** (page 53). **Ali Asili,** (page 54). **M. U. Suhei,** (page 55). **Zafer Yildiz,** (page 58). **Ahmet Baysu,** (page 61).

Photographs on pages 22, 23, 26, 27, 39, 42, 47, 66, 67, 68 and 69 © **John Putnam.**

Acknowledgments

With thanks to:
Russ Bestley and **Paul McNeil,** from London College of Communication for their valuable teaching and guidance.

Buzz Poole, my editor, for all his advice and help in revising the text. **Christopher Salyers,** for approving my designs. **Mark Batty** for giving me the opportunity to turn this crazy project into a book! My friends **Marije de Haas** and **Ana Bjezancevic,** for their honest opinions and advise on type and layout.

My interviewees: **Morris Cassanova,** (a.k.a. Mr Chicken), **Richie** at **Compugrafix** and all at **MBC Signs** for being so friendly and helpful. And to the countless fast food workers, all over London who were patient and friendly enough to let me take their portraits, and talk to them at length about their lives.

My family and friends for their never-ending support and enthusiasm throughout the years!

Siâron Hughes is a Welsh Graphic Designer currently working in London. She studied Fashion Design and Promotion at Southampton University and graduated with Honours in 1994. She then worked as a web designer for Lateral.net in London, and also as an illustrator, before enrolling on the MA Graphics course at London College of Communication and graduated in December 2007 with a Distinction.

حلال

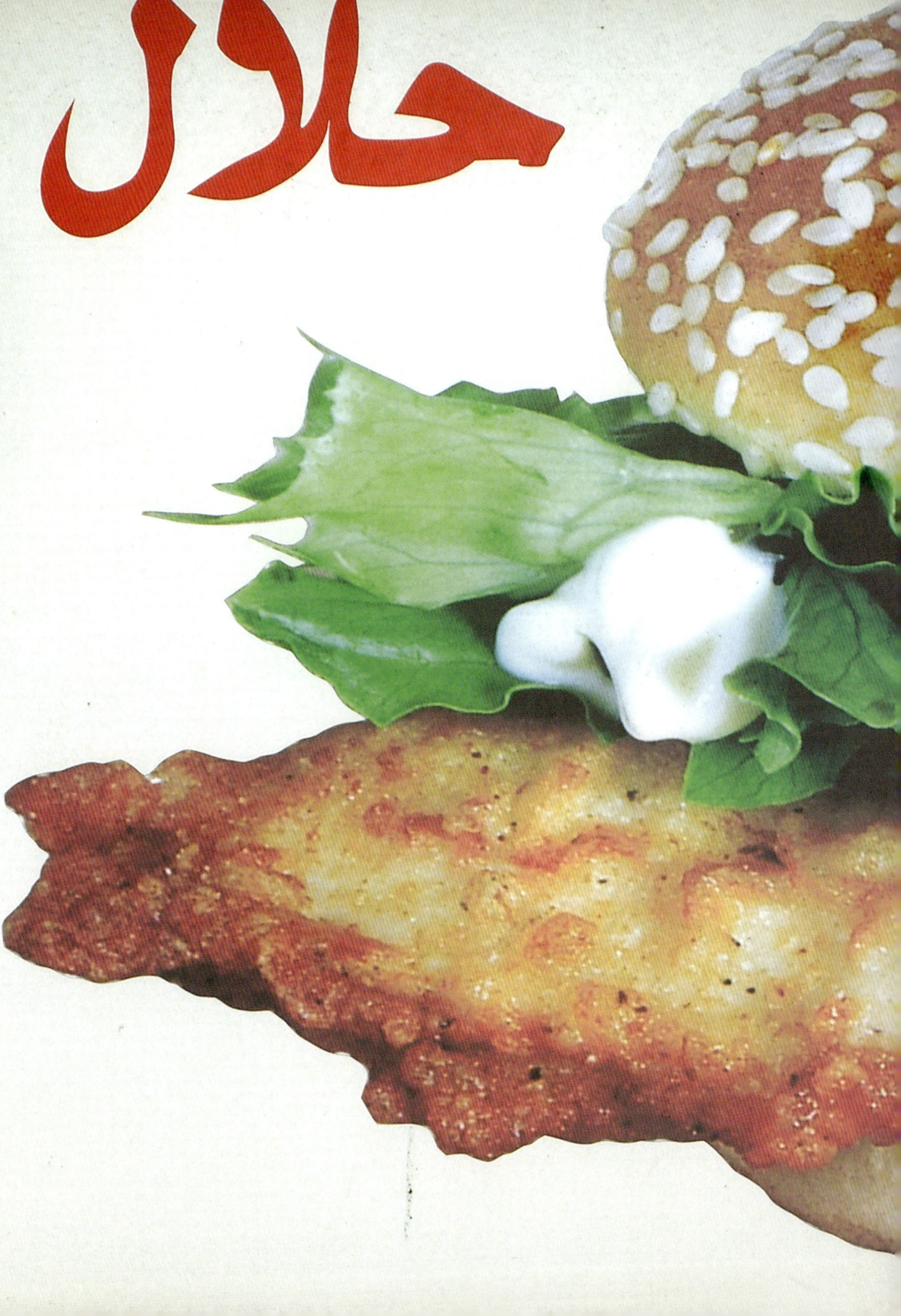